The Die Is Cast

by

Joseph O. McLaughlin

Happy Reading!
I hope that you enjoy reading
my story. May God bless you.
Joe
Joseph O. McLaughlin

D1082544

DORRANCE PUBLISHING CO., INC.
PITTSBURGH, PENNSYLVANIA 15222

ISBN: 978-1-4349-0941-1
eISBN: 978-1-4349-5783-2
Printed in the United States of America

First Printing

For information or to order additional books, please write:
Dorrance Publishing Co., Inc.
701 Smithfield St.
Pittsburgh, Pennsylvania 15222
U.S.A.
1-800-788-7654
www.dorrancebookstore.com

To My Wife, Pat
The Treasure At The End of My Quest
My Life's Reward

1943

1946

CONTENTS

CHAPTER ONE

EARLY YEARS IN FISHTOWN

CHAPTER ONE

EARLY YEARS IN FISHTOWN

Lately, I have been asking myself questions about my parents and my wife's parents. Questions that will forever go unanswered because all of the people involved have passed away. Perhaps it is because I have now reached the point where I am a member of the "older generation," I ask these questions. I never thought about it until after the death of my father-in-law. A friend and co-worker said to me, "Well Joe, do you realize that now you are the older generation?"

Maybe, I can avoid this by jotting down some things that I remember. Some events may or may not be in chronological order but all will be as factual and honest as I can recall them.

Since I have always believed that we are the sum total of all the people, good and bad, that have touched our lives, these writings will necessarily have to include some thoughts, descriptions, and remembrances of many people who have been a part of me and helped to form my personality and make me who I am today.

Knock on any door and you will find a story of depression era kids and their families. We all had one thing in common, although we did not realize it at the time. We were all poor, some more than others. Basically, honest people in the never ending struggle against an economy that they neither created nor understood, just trying to survive. We were kids who respected the neighborhood "cop," admired the local bootlegger, and were in awe of the nuns at school. The nuns demanded respect and obedience in return for a good education. My relationship with the sisters of Holy Name will be told in greater detail later.

Even now, many years later, the odor of exhaust from an old truck can conjure up memories of days long gone. I can picture myself, as a small child, huddled up in the back of a covered Ford pickup truck with my brothers and sisters. The back of the truck was open, allowing the cold air to come in. We were covered with blankets and coats to ward off the cold of the brisk winter night. We were in need of new shoes and Dad was taking us down to South Street to look for some bargains. He was said to have a knack for "Jewing" down the shopkeepers on South Street. Neighbors and relatives, including Uncle Phil Hascher, would ask Dad to go with them to buy new clothing. After haggling over prices with the shopkeeper, interspersed with threats to leave without making a purchase, they would come to a mutually agreeable price. Dad would leave the store with a look of satisfaction on his face of a battle well fought. I still wonder who really was the winner.

In most of my writing, I seem to refer to being cold. Yes! I was cold as a child and as an adult. I just could not seem to shake it. I have been cold indoors, cold outdoors, could in the north, cold in the south, cold in America, cold in Europe; including France, Belgium, and Germany, and at times felt as though I were cold in hell.

The mid 1800's was a time of turmoil and discord throughout Europe. There was a potato famine in Ireland and the British refused to release stores of potatoes in their possession. Many people were forced to immigrate to America. Those who could not afford the trip sold themselves into bondage and servitude for a number of years, usually for seven years and could be extended to an additional seven. They, no doubt, made the voyage in steerage.

John McLaughlin b. 1818 in Ireland and his wife Margaret b. 1827 also in Ireland came to America from County Donegal prior to 1850. John and Margaret had nine children. Their son, Francis b. 1860, was my grandfather. Francis had four children including Daniel Thomas, my father.

Philip Hascher, a tailor, was born in 1804 in Bavaria, Germany. His wife, Sophia was born in 1811 in Wurtenburg, Germany. They had three children; Francis, Marie, and Philip, my maternal grandfather. The Haschers arrived in America in 1844. Both families would eventually settle in Philadelphia, "The City of Brotherly Love."

The Haschers lived west of Front Street on Waterloo Street in the Kensington area. Their home was a couple of houses away from the Duckenfield family whose young son Bill, would, at the age of fourteen, run away from home to join the circus. Young Bill would later become world famous as W.C. Fields. The Haschers had four children; William, Philip, Catherine, and Mary. I often heard Dad refer to Mom as May.

Mary was an extremely shy and very religious young girl. She went to school at Saint Boniface Catholic School and attended mass regularly. "Saint Bonnies" was a mostly German parish at the time. Mary was brought up in a close and strict community by very strict parents. I never knew Mom to ever say a swear word. She never danced, wore a bathing suit, and only on a couple of very rare occasions did she ever become angry with anyone. When she did, it certainly was justified.

The McLaughlins settled east of Front Street in what was known as "Fish Town." I understand that our grandmother had flaming red hair which would account for the red heads in Frank's family. There were three children on Dad's side of the family; Frank, Nell, and Daniel. At some point, these three children were orphaned. They were all placed in a Catholic orphanage where Dad was to get what little education he was to acquire. I remember him telling a story about his stay in the home. It seems that some of the boys had a problem with bedwetting. These boys would sleep on one side of the large dormitory where they could be awakened several times during the night to go to the lavatory. One night when the Brother turned out the lights, one of the boys on the "Piss the Bed" side of the room called out, "Good night Fatso."

The brother immediately put the lights back on, turned, and asked, "Who said that?" The boy who made the remark replied, "Danny McLaughlin said it." The Brother then came up to Danny and gave him a "Cat-o-Nine Tails," a leather strap with nine strands, and said, "Ok Danny, for that remark you can stand all night at the foot of your cot." Then walking away, he turned to Danny and added, "Since you will be up, see to it that the bed-wetters make their trips to the bathroom." Dad told us that numerous times during the night he woke that "Piss the bed" and beat his rear all the way to the lavatory and back.

Danny became very rough and streetwise and yet there was a tenderness and vulnerability about him. He loved to sing, fight, and drink, not necessarily in that order. He would do the "Irish Jig" or play the bones; two bones, about eight inches long, placed between the fingers and clapped together to the beat of an Irish tune, at the slightest suggestion. Always an excuse to attend a party.

At some point in time, these two young people of such diverse personalities were destined to meet, fall in love, marry, and start a family. This marriage would produce nine children, two girls and seven boys, of which I was the sixth.

My birth took place on November 10, 1924 in a "Holy Trinity" or Father, Son, and Holy Ghost House, a three-story house with only one room on each floor. This house was behind a stable in the 2100 block of Arizona Street.

The first home that I can remember was a house on Amber Street near Susquehanna Avenue. I recall it being a nice house with a small lawn in the front surrounded by an iron fence. Just having a lawn in Philly was rare. At that time, Pop was working for Otis Elevator Co. The family must have been doing fairly well at that time. We did not seem to be in want of anything, had nice furniture and nice clothing.

For some reason, unknown to me, Pop lost his job at Otis. We moved into an old three-story house at 2026 Trenton Avenue, near Norris Street. The house only had gas lights, a coal stove in the kitchen for cooking, and an outhouse in the backyard. The heat was from a coal stove in the basement with one register on the first floor, at the foot of the stairs. Needless to say, it was a cold house making it necessary to use not only blankets but every coat in the house piled on top of us to keep warm in bed. We would rush home from school to get a seat on the bottom step to warm up by the heat vent. To this day, I hate to be cold.

Mom made the best of it that she could. She worked hard keeping house, putting meals on the table, and caring for all of us kids. She did wonders with that old coal stove. I remember Mom making doughnuts on "Fastnacht Day." After rolling out the dough, she would cut a piece out with a glass, then use a catsup bottle cap to cut out the hole, which she would deep fry along with the doughnuts. Of course, we would argue as to who would get to eat the "holes." That was always the best part of the doughnuts.

Dad was then working as a driver for "McCauly and Steen Coal Co." At times, if he was in the area, he would stop home for lunch. He would park his wagon, with four beautiful draft horses, outside the house. Dad loved horses and he took care of these animals like members of the family. They were well groomed with a shiny harness and red plumes at the top of their heads like drum majors. The harness was studded with shimmering buttons and rings. Hanging from the back of each horse were numerous strands of various colored knotted ropes to keep away the flies. I thought that they were the most beautiful sight that I had ever seen. Naturally, I wanted a ride and Dad was there to lift me up and sit me on the back of one horse. It seemed to be a hundred feet high and I felt like the "King of the Mountain." Dad delivered coal for quite some time but eventually he lost that job too.

Trenton Avenue was a cobble-stoned street with an elevated railroad running the full length of it. Freight and passenger trains were constantly rumbling past our house on the way to "Berks Street Station." Coal would sometimes drop to the ground, from one of the coal hoppers, which we would pick up and take home for heat. When playing "hide 'n seek," we would climb up the steel uprights that supported the bridge and hide between the wooden railroad ties. Sometimes to get a ride, we would hop a freight car heading north and run the catwalk on the top of the cars. When the train stopped, we would then jump over to a train going south. We would try to pick a flat car filled with hay to ease our fall; however, at times the hay was filled with manure. Many years later, Phil's son would lose a leg doing this same stunt.

During the summer, excursion train trips would go to Atlantic City and other shore points. We knew that they would return home on Sunday night about midnight; therefore, we would not go to bed until late. We would lean out of the window on the third floor front bedroom. When the train would come to a stop, waiting to get into the station, we would yell to the returning passengers who would open the train window and throw "Salt Water Taffy" at us. That was about as close as we would get to the shore at that time.

Frank and I could not understand why Sis would not let us into the house. She kept chasing us away every time we tried to go in. I knew that Mom was not feeling well that day, but when Aunt Jane was sent for, I knew that something was wrong. Aunt Jane was the "Rock" who was depended upon to handle any trouble or emergency, be it an accident, illness, or when Dad had far too much to drink. She was the only one who could handle him. Dad would sober up fast when she came. This time, however, was different. It was the death of Tommy.

I was only four or five years old when Tommy was born, still I remember him as a good, lovable child. It was so easy to get him to laugh and giggle. The poor kid never did get a chance at life. He became ill when he was one-year old and had to be taken to the hospital. He was only there for a few days when he died. Later we were told that the cause of death was "Hospital Pneumonia," meaning that someone had left the window, at his bed, wide open. In those days, the "Viewing" was in the parlor at home. A satin crepe with a bow was usually hung from the front door, black for an adult, white for a child. Mom was devastated when she saw that some kid had gotten chocolate ice cream on the white crepe. Betty and I could not go to the funeral, we were too small. The cost of a stone was prohibitive, so Pop made a wooden form in the shape of a cross and made a concrete cross four inches by four inches thick, five feet high, and three feet wide. He fastened a bronze crucifix where the upright met the cross beam. It took the strength of four men to carry it up from the cellar. No doubt, that cross is still standing today in "Holy Redeemer Cemetery."

As a child, Mom was always trying to fatten me up. I was a frail child. Funds were usually in short supply; still Mom would manage to fill me with "Ovaltine," a chocolate drink that supposedly had the magical qualities to put weight on my bones. It failed miserably. I did, however, acquire quite a collection of "Orphan Annie" cups, mugs, pictures, and games.

Viruses were little heard of; however, I did manage to get every cold, flu, or bug that came around. I would get deathly sick with a very high fever. Mom would meet the challenge with her knowledge and supply of home remedies; a dose of coal oil and sugar (which when administered to Frank, required three adults to hold him down and one to hold his nose), goose grease to relieve congestion of the chest, and last but by no means least, a remedy to bring down the temperature of a high fever. She would cut up onions into small pieces and then wrap the onions into strips of cut up bed sheets. These make-shift bandages would then be tied around my ankles, feet, and wrists. Believe me, the odor was enough to drive any demons from my body. In the morning when the bandages were removed, the onions were thoroughly cooked but the fever was gone.

During one of my fever spells, I became delirious and kept asking for Nick. At the time, Sis was dating Nicky Schilk. Nick was a good-looking young man, with curly blond hair, who always affected the stance and characteristics of James Cagney, a movie tough guy of the period. Nick never seemed to have a job, however, he was always dapper, dressed in an expensive suit and sometimes driving a car. He brought a fountain pen as a gift to me and made a promise that if I would get better, then he would take me to the "Midway Theatre," the newest of the palace-like movie houses. This one was located at K and A Streets. This was a promise never kept and joked about every time that we met over the years. When Nick removed his shirt, it became apparent that he had spent a lot of money and years having his body tattooed. He was covered from wrist to shoulder and waist to neck with flags, serpents, ships, hearts, and names. Nicky Shilk missed his calling because he was a natural musician. Without any formal training, he could play, and quite well, many instruments including the guitar, banjo, drums, and piano accordion.

From what I can recall, one night, Nick had gotten a call to meet someone at the Broad Street Station. He was standing on the sidewalk, waiting for the caller, when a fast moving car suddenly came to a stop. Three men jumped out. Two of the men grabbed and held Nick while the third man beat him with brass knuckles. They came within a fraction of an inch from his left eye. He would have trouble with that eye for the rest of his life. I never did find out what really had provoked the attack. His three assailants were later captured and accused of killing a cop while trying to rob Mr. Levy, manager of the Kent Theatre. They ended up spending the rest of their lives in jail.

Once again it is the Christmas season, my favorite time of the year. A season that conjures up visions, as in Charles Dicken's "A CHRISTMAS CAROL," of Christmas's past, Christmas's sparse, and of deep love and devotion. The earliest yuletide that I can recall was the year that Dad made a small dining table and two chairs for Betty and me. We ate many meals at that little table. I can still remember the pungent odor of the paint that he used to put a finish on the wood. It permeated the whole house for days.

Even in lean years, Mom and Dad did their very best to have a joyous Christmas for us. We always managed to have a tree and a platform (Putz) with little houses, make-believe grass, and little figures placed near the houses. The tree would seem to come alive with brilliance glowing from the multi-colored balls and silver tinsel hanging from the branches. A small angel would be put at the very top of the tree as a beacon to God, in the form of Santa Claus to us kids, to enter into and to bless this house and this family.

I suppose that the trees at that time were not very expensive, however, if it came to a choice between a tree and food on the table for eight kids, the food would of necessity come first. Dad would wait until after midnight on Christmas Eve to try to find a tree. After midnight, the vendor just wanted to get rid of his stock. Dad could then buy a tree for twenty-five or fifty cents.

One year, I received a set of wind-up trains that became a part of the Christmas platform for many years. At times, money was in short supply and Mom and Dad would worry about dinner for the family, but God seemed to provide albeit in strange ways. Many times a basket of food, including a turkey and all of the trimmings would be left on our doorstep. It was all of the food that was required for a holiday feast for the entire family. I suspect the basket was left by a member of the "Holy Name Church." Over the years, we have tried to provide food for a needy family, especially during the holidays.

During prohibition, a holiday meal was hosted by Vic Kenny, the local bootlegger. Mr. Kenny would hold a celebration and meal for all of the kids in the neighborhood. Every child would receive a game and a toy from Santa. Yes, Vic made his living by selling beer and whiskey. I suppose that he did contribute to some of the misery of the depression and prohibition era, but he did give back something to the neighborhood. He bought some empty lots on Trenton Avenue where he built a quoit tossing court. There was a small bleacher area and lights for evening games. This gave entertainment and recreation to all of the adults in the area at no cost. At least this brought a little joy and light into a very hard and difficult time. The kids made a little extra money by finding empty pint whiskey bottles and returning them to Vic Kenny for a couple of cents deposit. Sometimes on our way to school, we would deliver booze to a customer. Even for kids, it was a matter of survival. We made a few cents wherever we could and at times, we just took whatever we needed or wanted.

Just after dark, a truck with unsold baked goods would park behind a bakery on Frankford Avenue. If we were fast enough, we could snatch a few doughnuts before the driver returned. With doughnuts in hand, we would run up Frankford Avenue and enter a mission where we could get a free cup of coffee, rest, and get in out of the cold. They welcomed all sinners, even young ones. Sitting on a bench and enjoying our coffee and ill-gotten doughnuts, we would listen to the preacher and join the drunks in a fervent "AMEN."

My brothers and I would take turns going to the soup kitchen on Front Street. At the soup kitchen, there were three huge vats containing three kinds of soup. Sometimes, we got bean soup or perhaps vegetable or pea soup. Mom would give us a large pot to get filled. This soup and a loaf of bread would feed the whole family for the night. In the morning, before going to school, breakfast would consist of a cup of tea and when we could afford it, a little cereal. If not, then a slice of bread broken up into a bowl and covered with a little milk and sugar. On certain days of the week, one of us boys would have to get up early and go to the police station where the cops would give out bags of stale or day old doughnuts. They were not that bad when dunked into some coffee.

Times were really difficult for Dad trying to provide for a large family but he did not sit around and brood. He was out there every day digging and scraping. He rented a horse and wagon, went down to Delaware Avenue to the docks for some fruit and vegetables, and then huckstered on the streets hoping to make enough money to pay for the stock, horse and wagon, and still make a little profit. He hung wallpaper, painted, stained, painted front doors, and sold flavored ice cones from a cart. He was never ashamed to make an honest living.

Whenever he could, Dad repaired all of our shoes. He had a shoemakers lathe and with leather, provided by Uncle Bill, who worked at the Berks Leather Shop, he would make the much needed repairs. Sometimes it was necessary to insert pieces of cardboard into our shoes to cover the holes. It was not really that bad except when I would step into a puddle of water, as kids of all eras are prone to do in all kinds of weather. Whenever a puddle is in close proximity to a kid, it just has to be stepped into and splashed.

Often in the winter, on our way to school, we would spot a front step where the family had not taken in the milk bottle. The milk would be frozen to the point where the cream would rise to the top of the glass bottle, push the cap up, and a column of fresh frozen cream would stand two to three inches above the top of the container. We would break off the frozen cream and continue on our way to school, contentedly licking the cream like a pop-sicle.

I woke up stretching and yawning, the sunlight coming through the window making it difficult to open my eyes. Even with my eyes closed, I can sense that John and Frank are bickering about whose turn it was to empty the bucket or night pot. The pot was not too full because it was obvious that someone had missed a calling. The sheets were still damp and wet. I got out of bed, got cleaned up, and put on some clothing. I was the youngest; therefore I was spared the bucket chore. Mom was in the kitchen, at the wood burning stove, preparing meals for the day. I sat down to have a cup of tea and a piece of bread and molasses. It was odd that when bread and molasses were dipped into a cup of tea and milk, it would change the taste and color of the tea. The toast was made on a metal wire gadget that was placed on the top of the stove. Frank went through the kitchen and the back shed on his way to the outhouse at the end of the yard. I decided to follow Frank outside so I went into the shed where my eyes caught sight of a rubber-band gun. I was not allowed to play with one, so naturally I picked it up. A rubber-band gun was made with a piece of one inch thick wood, four inches wide and about fifteen inches long, one-half of a wooden clothes pin, one nail, and several strips of inner tube, the nail was used as a trigger. A strip of inner tube, used as a projectile, would be stretched from the front end of the gun to the back, where it was folded and placed between the clothes pin and the end of the board. When it was shot or released, the rubber band would rapidly travel a good distance. Anyone being struck by it would experience a stinging sensation on bare skin. Of course, the closer a person got to the gun, the more dangerous it became.

I propped the gun upright on its end and attempted to load it. The strip of inner tube was stretched to its fullest when the gun slipped and fired with a resounding WHACK as the rubber band struck me full in the right eye. In answer to my screams, Mom came running into the shed.

"Oh my God! Holy Mary, mother of God," she yelled. "Joe, what have you done?"

My eye, covered in a mass of redness and blood, looked like a hollow socket. The look of anguish and terror on my mother's face frightened me to a greater extent than the thought of what I had done, so I cried even harder. As I yelled and screamed, Mom frantically went in search of someone to help. No one in the neighborhood owned a car or even a telephone and most home deliveries were made with a horse and wagon. Someone gathered me up and placed me in a baby carriage and ran the ten blocks to Saint Mary's Hospital. At the hospital, we sat and waited for a nurse to look at my eye. As I sat and waited, I became more scared. The sight of all of those doctors and nurses and the unknown smell of ether certainly did not have a calming effect on a small frightened boy. I could tell Mom, even while trying to comfort me, was very worried. No one, in those days, liked hospitals. People went there to die, didn't they? It was not that long ago that our Tommy had gone to a hospital and I never saw him again. The doctors and the nurses turned out to be very nice and were, after a time, able to calm me down. They treated my eye with salves and drops and assured me that I would be alright and with treatment, I would be able to see. It would require many months of treatment. At first, a cup shaped bandage was placed over my injured eye. Later, I wore a black patch and finally I had to wear black glasses for months. Naturally, I had to endure a certain amount of misguided pity and teasing because some kids thought that I was blind. After numerous visits to the hospital clinic, my eyesight was restored although never perfect but limited for most of my life.

In the hospital, when Mom and the doctors asked me what had happened, I told them that when I ran through the shed, I had not noticed that the shed door was closed and that I ran right into it. I said that my eye was struck by the metal latch on the door. This of course was a complete fabrication because, in reality, the latch was about a foot above my head. I persisted in telling that version of the story because I knew that if the truth came out, Dad would take away all of the rubber-band guns and my brothers would never forgive me.

It was not until I was fully grown and had gone through a war that I finally told Mom the truth. She just sat there silently with her hands gently folded in her lap. She patiently listened and with that "Mona Lisa" like half-smile on her face, she slowly nodded and simply said, "I know, I know." Mom was not fooled for a minute; she knew the truth all along. Mothers are like that, at least our Mom was. As Frank's wife, Jean, would say many years later, "Mom was truly a saint."

The White family had come over from Ireland to find more opportunities in the "States." They settled in a house on Susquehanna Avenue and enrolled their children in "Holy Name School." John White and his younger brother, Tommy, were placed in my class. They were both likeable kids and I soon became friends with both of them. They, like the McLaughlins, did not have much in the way of money or other material things.

The "Depression" was still affecting the lives of many families, the Whites included. There were a few kids in our class whose fathers had steady reliable jobs. Billy Dyer, whose father was a doctor, was the most affluent kid in class. Most of the kids always seemed to have holes in their shoes and holes, usually in the heels and toes, in their socks. An attempt was made to correct or hide this problem by pulling the entire sock forward and folding the front portion over and under the toes, resulting in an uncomfortable bunching at the ball of the foot, especially when the cardboard inside of the shoe began to wear out or became damp due to foot perspiration or rain.

My birthday would soon arrive. I was looking forward to it, not because of gifts because they were rare, if not non-existent, but because Mom would always bake a special cake and we would have a family celebration. The house was illuminated by kerosene lamps. The candles on the cake would add a special glow to the room and sometimes, when she could afford it, Mom would send someone to the store to buy a bowl of ice cream. In those days, ice cream was not purchased in a container or a box. We would take a soup or mixing bowl to the store where the ice cream would then be ladled into the bowl and weighed.

For this birthday, Mom said that I could invite one friend to have cake and ice cream with us. I decided to ask Johnny White since he was a new classmate. When he arrived, he gave me a small package as a gift. It was the very first gift that I had ever gotten form anyone outside of the family and for that reason, was very special. I was delighted and grateful. Upon opening the package, I discovered the newest and the most colorful pair of stockings that I had ever seen. Certainly, I could use them for the ones that I had on did have holes in them and no doubt were handed down from John or Frank before they wore them out. However, I did not get to try them on for size. As we were sitting down and enjoying our cake, Mom noticed that Johnny had large holes in the heels of his socks. Mom took me aside and explained that Johnny needed new socks as much as I did and that although his generosity was appreciated, she felt that it would be very nice of me to return the socks with a sincere "thank you." This of course was Mom, as Mom would always be, looking out for someone else. Although the reasoning for this eluded me at the time, I am sure that I learned an important lesson that night. The story of the socks has lived with me all of my life and certainly, knowingly and unknowingly has been applied to my actions over the years. We may feel sorrow and despair and at the depth of depression but just take a moment to look around and we can and will find someone who is in greater need. May God help the person who cannot see any farther than themselves for then they are truly in need of help themselves.

As I have said before, passenger and freight trains would come over the bridge down Trenton Avenue to the Berks Street Station. Next to the station there was a coal yard where coal cars would unload into holding bins. During this period, coal was still being delivered to homes by horse-drawn wagons. The coal dealer would pick up their supply of coal at this yard. When the trains were arriving at the station, some of the coal would fall off the hoppers down onto the street below, especially during shifting and changing of tracks. The neighborhood kids would scramble to gather up these droppings to take home, providing temporary relief from the bitter cold. Of course, there were periods in between deliveries when there just was not enough coal to scavenge. I was about nine years old and Frank was almost eleven. I recall one exceptionally cold spell when it was almost impossible to get warm without heat in the house. We covered up with every blanket and coat that we had and still we were chilled. I was a little more fortunate because I had to sleep between Frank and John; therefore I had the benefit of their body heat. One evening, Mom gave Frank some money, perhaps a quarter, and told him to take me along with a small wagon, to buy a bag of coal at the yard. It was early in the evening but still after dark. We made our way to the yard and furtively entered through an opening in the iron fence on the Norris Street side. We held our breath in the cold stillness of the night. Even our shivering appeared to make unwanted noise. Was our shivering and chattering of teeth due to the cold or were we just plain scared? The dark eerie shadows that were cast by the moonlight shining through the fence and the bushes seemed to move with each gust of wind as we tried to hide in the shadows, until we saw the night watchman go into the shed, either to get warm or to get something to eat. Pulling the wagon behind us, we made a dash for the pile of burlap bags filled with coal. Together, we both struggled to put a bag onto our wagon and just as fast made an exit through the fence. When we got home, we gave the money back to Mom and told her that the watchman would not take the money. The little bag of coal provided not only much needed warmth for a bunch of cold kids, but also fuel for Mom to cook on her coal-burning kitchen stove. Our ill-gotten coin could then be used to buy bread and perhaps a dozen eggs. Had we been found out, we would have had to do some fast explaining to Dad. The night watchman had performed a good deed and an act of kindness that night, for I have no doubt that he had heard or seen us lurking in the darkness.

"BANG, POP, BANG, BANG!"

I awoke with a start, climbed over Frank and jumped out of bed. Finally, I realized that it was the Fourth of July, "Independence Day" and my friends got out before me. Getting dressed as fast as I could, I ran down the stairs. As usual, Mom was in the kitchen preparing meals for the day, a task that she never seemed to finish. Rushing outside without breakfast and anticipating a day of fun and celebration, I was stopped by the heat of the day. It was early, however already you could see vapors of heat rising from the sidewalk. It was somewhat cooler under the bridge that ran above and parallel to Trenton Avenue for its entire length and beyond. Under the bridge, down at Norris Street, the alki gang, a group of drunks, or to use a kinder word, alcoholics, was well into its celebration. They must have begun the night before because some of them could barely stand.

It seemed to me that every home on the block was decorated in red, white, and blue. Flags were hanging straight down from poles without a hint of a wave, due to a lack of any breeze. There never is much of a breeze in the city on a hot summer day. Red, white, and blue material was draped from windows. Even the horses pulling milk wagons were adorned with plumes and knotted ropes, to chase the flies away, made with the colors of the flag. People in the neighborhood did not have much of any-thing; still they shared what little they did have. The one thing that they did have in abundance was love of country and patriotism.

Some kids were firing cap guns. Others had a little metal device which, after inserting caps into, was thrown into the air. When it came down and hit the ground, it would make a loud bang.

I had no caps, so I thought that I would go to "Reds" Lewis's house, a few doors up the street. I knew that Reds and his brother, David would have noise makers. David was there with a pair of crutches. He had broken his leg the previous week. The three of us had rigged up a parachute by using an umbrella, pieces of rope, and a belt. The rope was strung from the belt, which was worn around the waist, to the cloth of the umbrella. We were quite sure that this contraption would support one of us, after jumping from a high place. Everyone wanted to be first, so we had to draw straws. David was the dubious winner. Reds and I watched as he climbed onto the roof of a garage across the street. Without any hesitation, David donned the "parachute" and stood on the edge of the roof. Just for a moment, I thought that he was going to back off. He went into a crouch with bended knees and with a mighty push, he became airborne. At the exact moment that he left the roof, I experienced a sharp pain in my left leg. The umbrella did not billow out as intended, but just laid flat and wrapped itself around David's head as he came crashing to the ground. Yes, he did break his left leg. I still felt that the parachute would have worked if the garage had been a little higher. Maybe we should have tried a two-story building.

We could hear music, in the distance, coming from the Fourth of July parade on Frankford Avenue, so we all started to run as fast as we could, we headed toward the sound. Most of the parade had already passed, so we had to hurry to Palmer Street Cemetery for the ceremony. The parade was led by a couple of cars which were decorated with red, white, and blue ribbons and banners. An American flag was draped over the hood of each car. Each vehicle carried several arm waving local politicians or dignitaries. Following the cars was a group of young men wearing World War I Army and Navy uniforms. Next in line, there were horse drawn cannons and behind that, the American Legion Band, a contingent of older men in their Civil War uniforms, more cannons, the Penn Treaty Jr. High School Drum and Bugle Corps., smartly dressed in grey uniforms and high plumed hats. The sound of the music provided the cadence for the marchers and a spirit of joy and patriotism to all of the bystanders, including myself. I experienced a feeling of envy as I watched the bands go by. Someday, I swore that I would be a part of such a group. Eventually, I did play the bugle, for a short time, with the American Legion Drum and Bugle Corp. By no means or imagination was I ever a "Bugler." The parade was then followed by anyone on foot, roller skates, or bicycles carrying flags of all sizes. Most of the people were trying to march to the beat of the drums, without much success. I am sure that the majority of them did, at a later time during World War II, learn as I did, to march to a different, perhaps more militaristic, drummer. What did I know of the future? We were enjoying the moment.

At the cemetery, the local bigwigs made their patriotic speeches and prayed for the soldiers who gave their lives in past conflicts. Even then, these political speeches left me with a strange feeling of hollow words spoken by someone who had no idea of the sacrifices made by the soldiers, both living and dead, who struggled and yes died, in sometimes unnecessary conflict, against a reluctant enemy. The bands played more Sousa marches while the cannons boomed. The ceremony ended with a squad firing a salute into the air as the soulful sound of "TAPS" was played.

The crowd silently dispersed and in quiet respect, walked back to their homes. The sounds of the bands faded into the distance. My thoughts slowly drifted to Uncle Bill Hascher, the only war veteran I knew. Mom always had an oval, colored picture of her brother hanging in a prominent place in the living room. The photograph was of a rather good looking, uniformed young man with an aquiline nose, looking into the camera with a serious but not stern expression; the epitome of a confident and able officer. I was ten years old so the Great War was ancient history to me. The World War had ended sixteen years ago, but in just seven more years we would enter into another "War to end all Wars." When I reached eighteen years of age, I enlisted in the Army. Uncle Bill, along with his picture, was always treated with respect. He and Aunt Jane had two daughters, Dorothy and Phylis. The Haschers were not rich but lived comfortably. Whenever our family would be short of funds, I would be sent to suffer the humiliation of asking for a dollar to provide supper for the family. I hated that task.

The backyard outhouse was a duplex, connected to the toilet next door and sharing a common wood wall, that separated the two holes.

One day, Dad was in the process of using the outhouse and was enjoying a cigarette and a newspaper, which served a dual purpose of reading material and toilet paper. As he sat there, he heard the squeak of the rusty hinges on the door next to ours, as the neighbor lady, a huge woman of about 300 lbs. entered in to make use of the facilities. Dad purposely sat quietly until the silence was broken by the strained suffering sound of someone in deep pain.

"Oh God! Help me."

"Ooooo my God, please help me."

With that, Dad knocked on the wall and called out.

"Mrs. Fleckinstien, God helps those who help themselves."

He left the shed and headed towards the house, laughing as he could hear the muffled voice of Mrs. Fleckinstien, as she called out to him.

"Danny McLaughlin, I'll get you for that."

I am sure that she did play a trick on him at some time but not too long after.

Dad loved to play baseball; in fact, he was a good first baseman. All of his kids would go to Newton's lot to watch him play. Newt's was a neighborhood playground with a ball field, a pool, swings, and playground equipment. The playground was near the Palm Theatre, a local movie house that we could seldom afford. Some of us would pool our money together until we reached ten cents. The money would be given to one kid who would pay his way into the theatre. When inside, he would open a side door to let the rest of us in, where we would immediately scramble to find seats in the dark building. After the ushers tired of looking for us, we would gather together again.

Mom's only entertainment was going to the movies once a week on dish night. That was usually on a Wednesday night when a dish or a cup and saucer were given to every person who attended the movie. In time, a family could acquire a full set of dishes. Invariably, during a quiet moment in the story of the movie, someone would accidentally drop a dish on the floor. The smashing of the plate was met with a roar from the crowd. While enjoying a night out, Mom eventually had a complete set of new dishes.

CHAPTER TWO

PRE WORLD WAR II

CHAPTER TWO

PRE-WORLD WAR II

When Dad was sure that his job at Harbison's Dairy was safe and secure, we could finally move. Boy, what a change! The house on Arizona Street had electricity, large rooms, and a back bedroom that had been converted into a bathroom with a tub and a toilet but no wash basin. Mom and Dad had the second floor front bedroom, Betty had the middle room, Phil and Dan shared the third floor front. John, Frank, and I slept in the back room, in one bed. Dad was able to get some new second-hand furniture. We now had a living room and a dining room. The kitchen was big enough to have a table and chairs where we spent many hours, after supper, harmonizing with Dad. He encouraged us to sing many Irish songs, such as "Galway Bay," "When Irish Eyes are Smiling," and "Danny Boy." We also sang "Molly Malone" and many more. Pop loved to sing but after a few drinks, he would become very critical. I think that Mom enjoyed these times but she never gave any indication. She would just continue washing dishes or, being Mom, reserved and shy, she would sit with folded hands and that half-smile, without ever joining in, just enjoying her family enjoying themselves.

Did I say that Phil and Dan shared a room? I do not recall those two ever getting along, except for brief moments during the war. More than once, we were awakened in the middle of the night by their fighting. Sleeping in the same bed, it was inevitable that one would put an arm or a leg over the other or perhaps infringe on the side of the bed belonging to the other. They would start a fight at the slightest provocation. The door, being locked, would have to be broken into, for us to stop the fight. They did not get along but woe be it to any outsider with the audacity to take advantage of either brother.

Often, the bathroom became a haven of piece and quiet. In a household of nine or ten people, depending on who was living with us, at any given time, the bathroom was a place to retreat to after an argument or just to get away, for a moment, to be alone. I spent a considerable amount of time on that hopper, just thinking of better times, of the future, or fantasizing and making up some stories, where I was the central character. Frequently, my reverie was interrupted by a loud knock on the door and a pleading cry.

"Joe! Will you hurry up? I have to go."

"C'mon, unlock the door before I break it down."

Oh well! Nature calls and dreams will of necessity just have to wait, to be continued anther day, another time.

In the house on Arizona Street, as I said before, John, Frank, and I shared a bed in the third floor back bedroom, and I being the youngest, was placed in the middle, which was not all that bad in the winter because the room was cold. Besides the blankets, we covered with every topcoat and jacket that we had.

During this period, toys were scarce. The best toy that we had was our own imagination. Our bed was one of those old metal beds, painted white. Occasionally, on a Saturday morning, when we did not have to rush off to school, Frank and I would change the headboard and the footboard into two beautiful horses, with our pillows as saddles and a tie as the reins. In no time at all, we would be riding over the Western Plains and across the hills, either being chased by blood thirsty Indians or chasing after outlaws such as the Daltons or Frank and Jesse James. Suddenly, we could change the whole scene by using a sheet as a turban and robe. The room became hot and humid as we raced across the burning sands of the Sahara on a pure-white stallion, in search of an oasis where surely, in addition to water, we would find a buried treasure. Ah! Imagination, how it could take us to the far corners of the Earth much faster than the swiftest supersonic jet of a later era. The sound of Mom's voice could bring us back just as fast.

In this small bedroom, the bed was tucked back against the corner allowing space, just barely, for a little table, the top of which was only about 1 ½' by 1 ½'. Placing a white doily, that I had obtained from Mom, on the table, I would add a statue of the

Blessed Virgin, thus creating a makeshift altar. In the Spring, when the Lilacs were in full bloom, I would break some flowers from the over-hanging branches at the Palmer Street Cemetery. They were hanging over the sidewalk; therefore, I assumed that they were free for the taking. Lilacs were Mom's favorite flowers; at least she told me that they were her favorite. I gave Mom a small bouquet of Lilacs but I kept a few to put into a drinking glass that served as a vase, for the Holy Mother. The whole house was filled with the sweet scent of the freshly cut blooms. Before retiring to our bed, at night, I would stop to say my evening prayers. Kneeling in front of my little altar with my arms stretched out to the side, I would pray to the Virgin Mary to intercede for me and ask God's forgiveness for any sins that my innocent mind could manage to conjure up. With each prayer, my arms would get heavier with my small muscles straining to support them. I would pray until I could no longer hold up my aching arms.

What unspeakable sins could really warrant such self-inflicted physical torture? I took a piece of penny candy from the counter of Hymie Goldberg's store when he was not looking. Had I disobeyed or cursed? Did I fight with my brothers or sister? Did I or did I not steal those Lilacs? Could this possibly ease the opening of the gates of understanding of an all-merciful God? In my young and impressionable mind, it certainly could and I felt as one with my maker and could sleep as restful as a newborn babe.

God! It was cold and wet. It had started to pour as I walked to school. I was in the fourth grade at the time. My shoes had holes in the soles so my feet and stockings were soaked by the time that I reached school. My jacket and pants were drenched and I was shivering with cold, when I entered the classroom. Sister Marie Fidalious immediately took me into the cloakroom, where she had me remove my wet clothing. She put chairs together to form a place for me to lie down. She covered me with a dry blanket and left me there to get warm and to sleep while she conducted the class. My wet clothing, she had placed on a radiator to dry.

When the Nuns became aware of my ability to draw and that I was attending art classes at the Graphic Sketch Club, they did encourage me to make use of my talent. Just before an upcoming holiday, I would be assigned a couple sections of blackboard and told to draw a scene or mural depicting that particular holiday. I would spend hours and sometimes days at the task. Still, I was expected to keep up with the class on my school work. This task was passed onto me from class to class and nun to nun for several years. Did I receive special treatment from the sisters? I am sure that I did.

As a child, nuns were always special to me. They seemed so spiritual and untouchable to the world. They were not only spiritually clean but physically clean. When held close by a nun, as a way to show encouragement or love, you could always detect an odor of cleanliness. The Sisters at Holy Name gave me knowledge, warmth, and love. For this, I will always be eternally grateful.

One day, Dad was driving a team of horses up the cobblestone paved Frankford Avenue, attempting to break a horse into pulling a wagon. He would pair a green or untrained horse with an experienced animal. The huge draft horses responded to his gentle commands and directions as they maneuvered the narrow streets. At some point, the horses broke the traces and pulling Dad off of the wagon, they bolted up the street, dragging him along behind them as he held onto the reins. After bouncing on the cobblestones, he was forced to release his grip on the reins. Dad lay in the middle of the street almost in front of Aunt Nell's house. Upon hearing the commotion outside, she looked out of her front window and seeing her brother lying prostrate on the ground exclaimed, "Oh God! Danny is drunk again."

I remember that day vividly. When Dad arrived home that afternoon, he stood at the dining room table. His knuckles and face were cut and bruised with traces of blood darkening his usual ruddy complexion. He slowly put his sore hands into the torn pockets of his jacket and pulled out two fists full of marbles. When he released the hard glass balls, they rolled across the dining room table reflecting a variety of colors as I stood wide-eyed in momentary joy. He had promised me that morning that he would get some marbles for me. Although sore and hurting, he did not forget a promise made to his son now looking up, into his bruised face with sadness and tear-filled eyes and yet gratefulness for a promise fulfilled.

As on many occasions, Frank, Billy Molter, and I were walking down Susquehanna Avenue on our way home from school. It was one of those nice warm spring days and we were out of school so we were feeling great. The smell of spring was in the air and as we approached the blacksmith shop, the familiar smell of horse manure also filled the air. This particular blacksmith took care of all of the Harbison horses. A group of horses came stomping out of the shop. From ground level, these animals were monstrous. They were white, roan, sorrel, and pinto. Seated high upon the lead horse with about ten other animals attached to a lead rope was my Dad. When he spotted us, he called out, "Hey kids, do you want a ride home?" We jumped at the chance. Dad reached down and one by one, he grabbed us by the arm and hoisted us up and sat us down on our own horse. With our legs spread about as far as they could spread apart on these massive creatures, we rode all of the way home feeling like the king of the mountain. Many envious eyes were upon us as we held on to the hairy manes for dear life, fearful of falling off and not only losing our seating but also our ego.

Attending "Holy Name School" did present some problems. Having five family members precede me created some family name recognition. Phil was tall and despite his worrying nature, could handle himself quite well when forced into a fight. Dan, of course, did not have to be forced into anything. He had a reputation for fighting and was known to belong to the "Onion Gang" a group of toughs who, as the name implies, could bring tears to one's eyes. John, although a comic, did command respect and was known never to back away from a fight and could fight with the best. Frank was, without a doubt, the best fighter in the neighborhood, although he never looked for or started a fight. Most of his encounters were in defense of someone else. One fellow student, Bernard McAnany, according to him, would practice boxing during the summer months just to take on 'Mick," as Frank was known. At the start of the school year in September,

Berny would pick a fight with Frank. He always lost but they would be good friends for the rest of the school year.

The reputation of the "McLaughlins" did not bode well for me. While some were scared off by and respected the ability of my brothers, others were determined to beat a McLaughlin and it did not matter which one. I being the youngest and the smallest became the target for anyone harboring such animosity. Certainly, I knew how to box, to some degree. At one time, Dad had put up a punching bag and a small boxing ring down in our cellar. Any argument between brothers was settled in the ring. Again, being the smallest and prone to nose bleeds, I always lost, even when just fooling around, I did learn, from my father and my brothers, all of the right moves; how to stand, how to feign, and a variety of punches. They could not, however, instill in me the "killer instinct."

One older and larger student decided to pick on me, in pursuit of a sure conquest. We met outside of the school and squared off in the middle of the street. We were surrounded by screaming and yelling kids, mostly on the side of the bigger boy. Frank was holding my jacket and calling encouragement. In spite of doing everything that I knew and what Frank was telling me to do, my opponent, with his height advantage, was getting the best of me. I could fend off head shots but I was taking a lot of body punches, which began to take their toll. It hurt like hell but I did not dare to cry. I could go home and tell Dad that I lost a fight but I would not dare tell him that I cried or quit.

Frank then called "time" and we stopped throwing punches. Frank pulled me aside and whispered in my ear. When we began to fight again, according to my brother's instructions, I kept backing away until I was backed up against the curb. I stepped up onto the curb and with the added height, I swung a solid right cross directly to the nose of my opponent. His blood gushed from his nose and splattered both of our white shirts. End of fight! I could now go home with honor. It was a good day for me, my brother, and my father.

We heard a lot of noise coming from the other street corner and assuming that is was another fight, we hurried toward the commotion. A large crowd had gathered at the corner of the school building. In the center, of the group, a small dark man was demonstrating the use of a "Duncan Yo-Yo." Wow! What a sight. He was spinning and twirling that yo-yo in ways that I had never seen before. He had come to visit schools in order to teach kids how to play with a Duncan and, of course, to sell some of these inexpensive toys. Someone said that he was a Filipino, whatever that is. We had no idea where he came from. To most of us, our world did not extend beyond our own "Fishtown," surely not outside of "Philly." Originally, the toy was brought to the United States by a young man from the Philippines named Pedro Flores. He began to manufacture the toy in Southern California under the trademark name "Flores Yo-Yo." Donald Duncan, a business man from Chicago bought the Flores Company for $25,000.00 and started to market the yo-yo on a national scale. Duncan hired Filipino demonstrators to tour the country and put on demonstrations and contests. Most kids in the 1930's had a yo-yo and became quite proficient in its use. I did learn how to "Rock the Baby," "Around the World," "Over the Waterfalls," and "Walk the Dog." This skill, like riding a bike, you never forget. Even later in life, children and I might add, many adults would look on in amazement at the ease in which I controlled this ancient plaything.

At times, during the summer, when I wanted to make some extra money besides what I made running errands for neighbors. Mom would line a basket with clean, white dish towels, attach a jar of mustard to the inside of the basket and give me a dime. With the ten cents and the basket, I would head for the pretzel bakery where I could buy twenty pretzels at two for a penny. I would then walk the streets of the neighborhood, calling out "Preeeeet-zels, Preeeet-zels." "Anybody want to buy a pretzel?" After selling the twenty pretzels, I would hurry back to the bakery and purchase forty more pretzels. If business was good and I didn't eat any of the profits, I could make out quite well. Before going to a matinee at the movies, a small group of us kids would go to the bakery where for a nickel, we could buy a large brown paper bag full of broken up pretzels. Some of which, no doubt, where on the floor but no matter, we had enough to last us for the whole show. A show that included a short comedy, news, a serial, a couple of cartoons, and a double feature. The Kent Theatre usually would have one feature film accompanied by a live vaudeville show. We could be in the movies from twelve noon until six o'clock at night. We had little time to be running the streets and getting into trouble.

Bill Molter and I were to be confirmed. On the day of confirmation, we would be accepted into the family of the Holy Roman Catholic Church. Preparations had been going on for days, perhaps even for weeks. As we stood in the rear of the nave, I was taken aback by the beauty of this old church. Certainly, I had attended mass every Sunday since I had started school at Holy name and probably going to church, in a carriage, every day with Mom. She attended mass and prayed daily in spite of her hardships in attempting to raise a family of nine children on meager finances. The church and her family were always her only reasons for existence. Dad had long since given up on the burden of devotion and attending church after years of unanswered prayers and the constant search for steady employment, working at all kinds of odd jobs to feed and sustain us for yet another week. Mom and Dad were, I was sure, seated among this mass of people, waiting to catch a glimpse of one more of their children going through this age-old ceremony. Holy Name Church, as I have said earlier, looked beautiful bathed in brilliant light, the profusion of flowers decorating the altar were illuminated by rays of sunlight coming through the stained glass windows. The priests were robed in their finest vestments and attended by neat and cleanly scrubbed altar boys and awaiting the appearance of the bishop. This was about as close as I would ever come to being an altar boy like my brother, Phil. The stark whiteness of the marble altar, scrubbed, I am sure, by the same women who could be seen every Saturday morning scrubbing the front steps of their modest row homes, contrasted with the cerulean blue of the vaulted ceiling. I too had been scrubbed to unwanted cleanliness, nails and hair trimmed, hair searched for cooties and slicked down upon my head before being permitted to don my blue serge suit.

An eighth grade altar boy, carrying a crucifix on high, led the procession up the center aisle. Sister gently but surely prodded us along and cautioned us to use short slow sissified steps. The procession, with the ever present and vigilant Sister close behind, was endless. Bill and I were seated near the end of the second pew. We sat, side by side, in apparent piety with our hands clasped in silent prayer we surely must have exuded pious innocence, I with my cherubic red complexion and Bill with the overhead lights causing his bright red hair to glow in a halo like fashion. Was it the lights or the sunlight through the stained glass windows that seemed to cast a heavenly aura upon these two angelic young boys? Never before had Bill and I looked so angelic and heavenly, a scene that would be perfect for the brush of Norman Rockwell. We, along with the rest of our class, were dressed in blue serge suits with knickers, a high, white starched "Buster Brown" collar and a flowing white bow at the neck. "When would this service end?" I thought. It seemed to go on forever. Unlike Sunday mass, when one priest gave a sermon, at this service several priests took to the pulpit to lecture these errant children on just what was expected of us in the future as accepted members of the Holy Roman Catholic Church. Bishop John O'Hara; later Cardinal O'Hara of Philadelphia, was to officiate at this religious rite. When the bishop finally appeared in his rich colorful robes and high pointed miter, I thought that we were in the presence of the Pope or at the very least a saint. Surely, after this day, we would enter into the Kingdom of Heaven with no problem from Saint Peter. Our minor transgressions, which were many, would be erased, gone and forgotten. I could feel the stare of Sister's look upon the back of my neck. I began to pray. Pray, that when it was my turn, the bishop would ask me only one question from the catechism. I had studied my catechism thoroughly therefore I felt rather confident. I began to wonder if he knew about some of my transgressions, maybe only some little sins. He did appear to be all-knowing. Maybe he will ask me about the doughnuts that I had stolen from the bakery truck while the driver was in the store or the lilac flowers that I took from a bush hanging over the fence at the Palmer Cemetery and used to make a small altar for the Virgin Mary, in our bedroom. Was it a sacrilege to use stolen flowers to honor the Blessed Mother?

The service continued on, and on, and on. The flow of words began to drone as each word would mesh into the next in a jumbled fashion. I suddenly felt a twinge of nature calling, starting at my groin and traveling inward to my bladder. I crossed my legs and squeezed my thighs together in a futile effort to stem the flow. The priest continued to talk and talk, now in an unidentifiable kind of gibberish. My eyes started to tear and the scene before me then blurred into a mass of color. No longer able to contain my natural urge, I felt a warm moist sensation traveling down my legs to the bottom of my knickers, stopping only when it reached the tight elastic bands located below my knees. The darkness of the blue serge material did help to mask the evidence of my anxiety and embarrassment but could not disguise the unmistakable odor that accompanied it. I looked around in a furtive glance hoping to pass the blame onto someone else. Sister did not miss my movement, quietly calling out "JOSEPH." Finally, it was our turn to approach the marble communion rail. I did not even want to tell Bill about my problem. Fortunately, we did not have very far to walk because now I had to walk with my legs slightly apart to avoid getting my legs wetter than they were. Going up with my back to the congregation, which included my Mom and Dad, was no problem except that I was walking funny, but I prayed that the bishop would not ask me any questions that would require a long answer thus prolonging my suffering. When I was blessed by the bishop, with his hand on my head, I had difficulty in displaying an air of pious holiness because my mind was filled with visions of discovery and untold embarrassment. What do you know, he did not ask any questions. He passed over me and went to Bill. Returning to my seat in the pew and now facing the congregation, I felt that every eye was centered on just me and me alone.

Before the service, we had met in our classroom where Sister was to review us on the questions and answers in our Catechism. I raised my hand to ask for permission to go to the boys' room. Sister ignored me. I use the term boys' room carefully and freely because in no way could this be compared to a lavatory of later days. It was a separate out-building containing a row of wooden boxes with a series of holes in the top. The urinal was one long metal trough, the odor of which was just as unbearable as the army latrines that I would encounter later in life. Sister continued to ask questions. I raised my hand again. Sister asked in a voice that was definitely irritated, "What is it Joseph?" I asked to leave the room. Sister refused to give me permission because catechism was more important and she did not want to suffer the humiliations of one of her pupils failing to answer correctly a question asked by the bishop. I had to tighten my legs and cheeks together as we formed a line and proceeded across the street to the church. The outcome, of course, was inevitable.

When I was growing up in Philly, there were no school lunches or buses. We walked to school and even walked home for lunch. Mom fed us with whatever she had available, sometimes a sandwich or perhaps leftovers from the night before. One day, on our way back to school, Frank and I stopped on the corner of Frankford Avenue and Susquehanna Avenue where we got into an argument about something that has been deposited into the recesses of my mind and long forgotten, however, the incident remains with me still. I became angry enough to foolishly take a swing at my older brother. I brought back my right arm in anticipation of settling our disagreement and misplaced anger by force. Before I could release my cocked arm and fist, I experienced an excruciating pain in my neck, a pain that laid me up, for a week, with a stiff neck. Never again did I attempt to strike my beloved brother again.

Frank was easy going, caring, and sentimental. I can still remember Mom sitting in a chair and crying from physical or mental pain, I know not which, but Frank sat on the arm of the chair, reached out, lovingly placed his arm around her shoulder and cried along with her. Being younger, I had no idea what had brought on this burst of tears, yet I felt that I must do likewise so I sat on the opposite arm and joined in their sorrow with tears running down my cheeks. No one could ever say that Frank was soft, he could be tough and able to defend himself. He could also be angered to the point of fighting in defense of someone else. Frank could easily be brought to tears when angered within the family especially when we called him "Reds" in reference to the slight tinge of red in his hair.

Young men, during this period, tried to emulate real life gangsters, such as "Scarface" Al Capone, "Machine Gun" Kelly, the infamous John Dillinger or motion picture hoods; Paul Muni, George Raft, James Cagney, Edward G, Robinson, and Humphrey Bogart. Young people with nothing had a tendency to look up to and idolize others who attempted to get a share of the good life by whatever means and regardless of the cost. Favorite movies were "They Gave Him a Gun," "They Made Me a Criminal," "Fugitive From a Chain Gang," and "Public Enemy." Heroes of good standing? Perhaps Babe Ruth or "Luck Lindy" Charles Lindburgh but who could bat a baseball like the Babe or fly across the Atlantic Ocean? A faster and more lucrative path to fame and yes fortune seemed to be outside the law. In order to counteract this influence, by the criminals, Colonel Swartzkoph, (the father of General Swartzkoph of "Desert Storm" war fame) of the New Jersey State Police, narrated a weekly radio show called "Gang Busters" that portrayed the law enforcement agencies in a better light and winning the war against crime. FBI agent Melvin Purvis, who led the group of agents who were finally able to locate and kill John Dillinger, started "The Junior G-man Club" for kids. Each member would receive a badge, certificate of membership, and a book containing rules of behavior that would help children to attain an honest and honorable life. Cards, similar to baseball cards, bearing pictures of police officers and an account of their participation in the capture of criminals or in an act of heroism, were sent out to kids all over the country.

Clyde Dillon, sometimes known as Clyde Cannon, had a younger brother named Herbert Sibley. Their mother, Laura, was married to Lou "The Indian" Cannon. Clyde and I were to become very good friends, in spite of the fact that Clyde could, at times become very weird. I felt then, as I do now, that he could and might well have been a rebel, a revolutionary or a subversive. I never did meet Herby's father because he was always away in the Marine Corp.

Clyde and I were playing catch with a "pimple ball," a soft, hollow, white ball with pimples on the surface, which when hit with closed fist could soar an unbelievable distance. We used this type of ball to play street baseball, using the street corners as the bases. Whenever my brothers and the older boys were playing ball, there were occasions when the ball would roll down the storm sewer. These balls cost five cents; therefore, no one could afford to lose a ball. When this would happen, Dad would call out, "Don't worry, someone go find Joe, he can get the ball." Dad and one of my older siblings would take hold of my ankles, turn me up-side-down and lower me into the culvert. This was fatherly trust at its best. I would then fish the ball out of the water and call to Dad to bring me back up.

"Clyde, let Herby play with you and Joe," his mother called from the front steps.

"Aw Mom, we are busy," Clyde answered.

'Clyde Dillon, you and Joe just play with Herby."

"Ok Herb, what do you want to play?" asked Clyde.

"Cowboys," replied Herby.

"Ok Herb, you can be the cowboy and me and Joe will be the horses."

We took a long piece of clothes line, tied one end of it around my left arm and the other end around Clyde's right arm. We then joined my right arm and his left together. Herby picked up the center of the rope and began to drive us, running down the street like a team of horses. When he pulled the rope on my left arm, we would turn left, and to go right, he would pull the rope on Clyde's right arm. Everything was going fine until we came to a telephone pole. As our arms unclasped, I went to one side of the pole and Clyde ran on the other side. Herby, being pulled along with us, ran right into the pole. He was thrown, stunned, to the ground. Fortunately, for all of us, he was not seriously hurt. It was, however, a long time before Herby would join us at play. Not too many years later, Herbert Sibley, would lie about his age and like his father, join the Marine Corp. At the age of seventeen, during the invasion of the Island of Tarawa, in the South Pacific, Herbert Sibley lost his life. He was killed, along with over one thousand other young marines fighting to capture the islands of the Tarawa Atoll.

I could feel the burning sensation as Mrs. Stevenson applied iodine to the cut on my left arm. The Stevensons had taken me with their family to a park. While climbing on a "Monkey Bar,"

I had slipped and tore my arm on a rusty bolt. I did not want to tell Mom because she would only worry; therefore, even though it was summer, I wore a long sleeve shirt to cover the bandage. Every morning, I would go over to Mrs. Stevenson to have the cut redressed.

George and Katherine Stevenson and their two sons, Howard and Kenny, lived across the street. Mr. Stevenson had a steady job in the office of the Pennsylvania Railroad. They were not rich but by neighborhood standards, they were well off and in want of nothing. They always had nice clothing, good food, and the means to enjoy life. The boys always had spending money and toys. As Howard's friend, he shared his toys and bikes with me.

Howard and I were the same age, so we did become very close friends and the family welcomed me into their home and family life. I spent many hours in their home as Howard and I studied our homework together. Mrs. Stevenson would conduct spelling bees with a group of neighborhood kids. A penny would be given to the one who spelled a word correctly. At that time, I was quite good at spelling, so I did win consistently. As we sat around the dining room table, it soon became apparent that the game was becoming somewhat unfair. She did, however, continue these sessions because they did help us to improve our spelling skills.

The Stevensons took me along with the family when they went on a picnic at a park and, at least one night a week, they had me accompany them to a movie at a nearby theatre. Wednesday, Friday and Saturday there was vaudeville at the Kent Theatre and I was usually asked to go along with the family. The program began with the news, followed by a couple of cartoons, a short comedy, perhaps a serial, a live vaudeville show, and then the main feature. Many well known entertainers and motion picture stars got their start and training at these small local theatres.

Howard and Kenny had all kinds of toys, including skates and bicycles. Dad felt that skates and bikes were unsafe along with the fact that we could not afford them. Through the generosity of Howard in sharing with me, I was able to learn to skate and ride. During the winter months, we would play, in the evening, in Howard's basement which unlike ours, had a concrete floor.

One time, when we were younger, a small metal truck caught my eye. It was quite simple to slip it into my pocket. I hid the truck at home for several days. When I, in my youthful mind, felt it was safe took it out of hiding and began playing with it. It did not take my father long to notice something out of place.

"Joe," he asked, "Where did that truck come from?"

My fear of telling Dad a lie far exceeded my reluctance to admit that I had indeed taken the truck, so I told him the truth. Dad got his jacket and mine and walked along with me over to the Stevenson's house where he stood by my side, on the front step, as I returned the toy, along with an apology to Mr. Stevenson and Howard. The incident did no harm to my relationship with the family. In fact, I believe that we became closer and I certainly did learn an important lesson.

One day, Howard and I were standing at the curb with our Hi-Li bats, a small wooden paddle that had a rubber ball attached to it by a rubber band. The purpose was to hit the ball, stretching the rubber band to its full length, causing the ball to be brought back to the bat, to be struck again. We became quite proficient at it. We could hit the ball over one thousand times without missing. We were practicing for a contest sponsored by Mr. Levy, the manager of the Kent Theatre. The contest was usually held on a Saturday, before a matinee. A couple of hundred kids would line the curb side, displaying their talent with the Hi-Li. Win or lose, each child would get a block of ice cream. The winner was presented with a new two-wheeler bike. Howard and I never did win because there was always someone better.

"Joe!" I heard Mom call, "Come here."

I stopped playing and ran across the street to Mom. She told me to go around the corner and tell Dad that supper was ready. I ran to the bar at Emerald and York Streets, where Dad spent most of his free time. He went to this saloon, where he cleaned up and swept the floor. Of course, he got a couple of shots before work. He would go there after work, go home to eat, and then go back to the bar for the evening. When television became a mainstay in the bars, the habitués just had another reason to stay longer in the bar.

I looked under the swinging doors and saw Dad standing at the bar. I did not dare enter the bar but called out to my father.

"Dad," I said, "Mom said that supper is ready."

"I'll be right there," he said.

I knew that he would not, so I sat down on the step below the doors and waited a couple of minutes before I tried again.

"Dad," I called, "Mom said to come right home"

"JOE," he yelled, "Go home, I'll be right there." Still sitting on the step, I waited again for a short time. Again I called.

"Dad, Mom said that supper is getting cold."

Dad, now getting irritated, almost screamed, "JOE, I TOLD YOU TO GO HOME, NOT TO WAIT, NOW GIT."

I realized that now was the time to leave. I did not want to stretch my luck. I returned home and Dad did follow shortly after I did. When he entered the house, Dad told Mom to make up a plate of food for a man in the bar who needed something to eat. Mom, uncomplaining, gathered together what food that she could and made up a dish for Dad to take back to the bar. We may not have had much, but there was always enough to share with someone who needed it more. Mom could stretch ground meat farther than anyone else. Mom could make potato cakes take the place of meat and you would enjoy it. It was amazing how mothers in those days could feed a family of ten or eleven on very little meat and potatoes. Thank God for those moms. What would we children have ever done without them? They nurtured us, fed us, taught us, comforted us, and above all, gave us their complete and undying love, never asking for anything in return. Of course we all, at one time or another, gave our mothers moments of deep distress, worry, and grief but hopefully we also did give them moments of peace, pride, and love. Thank you Mom wherever you may be and may God bless you for all eternity.

Kids of the 1920's and 1930's did not have the privilege of a weekly allowance. We did not even know what the word meant. If we wanted to have money for an occasional movie or some candy at recess, we had to engage in various enterprises to earn a little change. At recess time, Sister would bring out a box of candy, for sale at a penny or two each. Most of the kids would have a cent and walk to the front of the room to make a purchase, while others would suffer the indignity of remaining in their seat. Occasionally, on a Wednesday afternoon, a movie would be shown in the undercroft of the church. Those children without a dime would remain in the classroom. I must add that there were times when Sister would give us some free candy or let us join the others at the movies.

Certainly, there were ways to make some honest money. Some ways, of course, were difficult to define in terms of honesty while others were just on the borderline. I used to run errands for elderly neighbors for a few cents. Delivering a pint bottle of booze to a bootlegger's customer on the way to school was profitable and we got two cents apiece for every empty pint bottle that we could return to the bootlegger. At Christmas time, Clyde and I got some saw dust from a local sawmill. We would dye some of the saw dust green and some brown. When it dried, we would take it up to Front Street in a wagon where we sold it at so much a quart. We had to measure it into a paper bag with a quart can. Many people used the dyed sawdust for artificial grass and roads on a platform or "Putz." This, of course, was not a very safe, practice.

Frank and John collected old newspapers and cardboard from stores on Front Street. The papers and cardboard would then be tied into bundles and sold by the pound to a junk dealer. The dealer was well aware of the practice of inserting a brick into the center of the bundle to increase the weight. Once in a while you could get away with putting wet papers into the middle of the pile.

One day, Dad presented me with a shoeshine box that he had made for me so that I could join Frank on a shoeshine route. Our route included most of the bar rooms along Kensington Avenue, up to Allegheny Avenue, over to Frankford Avenue, and then down Frankford to home. The best time to shine shoes was on a Friday or Saturday night, which were paydays and usually date nights. The men who frequented the bars were, on these nights, free-spending and more inclined to pay better to impress their dates or buddies. We were not above taking advantage of their over zealous generosity by singing a song while giving a spit shine. At times, we could get as much as a quarter and a soda for a shine. We could bring home as much as five dollars on a Friday night. Sometimes we could catch some dudes outside of the "Cambria Athletic Club" before the "Friday Night Fights." The Cambria AC was later used in the "Rocky" movies where Rocky would get his start in the boxing game. A part of our earnings we would give to Mom and we were allowed to keep some for ourselves.

"Hey! Mister, you want a shine? You can use one."

Looking down at his shoes, the young man replied, "Yeh kid, I guess I can. How much?"

"Ten cents," I answered.

"Ok, go ahead."

As I took polish and rags from the box, he put his right foot on the footrest at the top of the shoeshine box. I began to daub polish on the shoe, as the men turned their attention back to the drinks on the bar. I worked this bar room as Frank worked the one up the street. The long mahogany bar was the focal point of the room. It had a brass foot rest going the full length of the bar, with strategically located spittoons placed on the floor. The bar was almost chest high, just high enough to minimize the distance from bar to mouth without being forced to straighten the elbow. Leaning against the bar were young, old men, some still in work clothes who, obviously, had not been home since leaving work, some far on their way to drinking up all of their pay. The sights, sounds, and smell of stale beer were all too familiar to me, since Dad spent most of his leisure time in a similar bar.

John had gotten a full time job at "Father and Son" shoe store. I guess that Dad felt that this was a good time for me to join Frank on a shoe shine route. Working on the young guy's other shoe, I looked up and asked, "You want a spit shine?"

"Yeh, kid," he answered, "but take a break first."

"Bartender, give the kid a soda."

"What kind do you want, kid?"

"Do you have cream soda?" I asked.

"Ok, here it is."

As I drank the soda, the odor of beer and booze filled the room. The sound of chatter and laughter, talk of sports and politics, talk of utter nonsense, and minor arguments came from the bar.

I wet three fingers with spit and applied it to the tips of both shoes. A few more rhythmic snaps brought forth a hard brilliant shine that would last a long time.

"Harry, make it another round."

"You should see this chick. She has the best body in the world."

"Oh ye, you say so."

"Did you hear that Babe Ruth and Ty Cobb are going into the "Hall of Fame"?"

"Shit, I could have told you that."

"What do you mean the Giants are the best team?" "The Yankees beat the hell out of them four games to two in the series. You don't know what the fuck you are talking about."

"Hey! Watch your language, there is a kid in here."

"So what, he has heard it before."

"Not in my bar. You watch your mouth."

A group of young guys are shooting darts in the back corner. This was before television, so most of the bars had dart boards for entertainment. Later, some of the larger bars would install shuffle boards. Some of the customers could and did spend the entire evening in the saloon until closing time at 2:00 a.m.

The snapping sound of my cloth grew louder as a hush seemed to fall over the room. "All talk and activity came to a sudden halt. When I looked over my shoulder, I saw two young black men come through the swinging doors. No blacks lived in the neighborhood. The nearest black families were down on Hope Street. None would ever venture this far. I automatically looked for an escape route in case of trouble. The two blacks walked up to the bar and asked for a beer. The big Irish and Polish laborers eyed them with suspicion and hatred. Any little thing could spark instant and intense violence. Heads began to appear in the doorway to the back room. I heard the bartender say, "I'll give you each one beer and then you get th'hell out of here."

It seemed like an eternity for the black men to finish one glass of beer. They were obviously taking their good old time. They were either looking for trouble or were just plain crazy. They finally finished, turned, and walked out the door.

Nothing was said, as all eyes were focused on the man behind the bar. Without a word, the bartender raised both glasses above his head and smashed them against the edge of the bar. Had he not done so in full view of everyone, he might just have to close his establishment because no one would ever drink in his bar again. The news would travel fast into the surrounding neighborhood. Everything including conversation went back to normal.

"Good job kid. Here is a quarter, Why don't you try the back room? Maybe you can give someone a shine back there."

"Wow! A quarter, thanks a lot mister."

Occasionally, we had a generous customer but most would only pay a nickel or a dime. We learned fast how to spot a potential customer. Usually it was a well dressed guy with an air of pride and neatness. A guy with a good looking girl on his arm was a sure bet and probably a good tipper because he would not warn to look cheap in front of the young lady. Sometimes, the girl would prompt the man into giving a better tip, with a sweet admonition.

"Come on Honey, the kid looks like he can use it. Give him a little more."

He then, sometimes very reluctantly, would dig a little deeper into his pocket, looking for change.

The back or side room was furnished with tables and chairs and was frequented by couples or unescorted ladies. Women were not encouraged to sit in the bar. These rooms served the best fried oysters and sandwiches. Dad often woke me up, even after midnight, to share with me fried oysters that he had brought home from the bar. We were the only two in the family who enjoyed oysters.

"Hey! Joe, when is your dad coming home?"

"Don't worry, he will be here soon."

"It is getting damn hot. We want to get under the plug."

Dad, no doubt, had stopped off at the bar for a couple of cold beers. His usual stop was at the saloon at Emerald and York Streets. The sun, beating down on the asphalt streets, created heat vapors that rose from the hot asphalt, sometimes even causing a mirage. There was little or no breeze. There were no public pools within about eight blocks but they were always overcrowded and not very sanitary. Trying to swim was impossible with people jumping into the pool. Going to the pool would be the last resort. By mid-afternoon, most people were getting irritable. Mothers had to remain indoors doing housework and preparing the evening meal. The lucky families perhaps had a fan. Television was still but a dream, so all of our Moms relied on the radio to escape momentarily into a land of make believe. They listened to midday shows such as "Ma Perkins," "Our Gal Sal," and even the rantings of Father Charles E. Coughlin, a Catholic priest who at first supported the "new Deal" policy of President Roosevelt, then later blamed him for everything from the Depression to war mongering. None of our homes or public buildings had air conditioning. A few movie houses had just began to display banners that advertised an air-conditioned theatre. That alone was worth the price of admission, just to get a few hours of relief from the stifling heat. On Trenton Avenue, we had no indoor plumbing or electricity. All evening activities were done by candlelight or kerosene lamp. The overhead railroad bridge spanning the length of Trenton Avenue did provide day long shade where we could play in relative comfort. Arizona Street, on the other hand, was open with absolutely no trees or shade. It was just hot, unbearably hot. On many nights, it was cooler to sleep on the floor or on a chair in the back yard. All windows and doors were left open to take advantage of even the slightest breeze. At other times, everyone in the neighborhood sat on their front step until the last possible moment before going into the hot house. On the night of an important heavy-weight boxing match like the Joe Louis-Max Schmeling bout or any fight featuring the flamboyant Max Baer, the entire neighborhood would be outside with the booming voice of the announcer, coming through the open windows, giving a round-by-round blow-by-blow description of the fight. This was the big city version of community socializing.

All of the kids were anxious for Dad to come home because he had obtained from his Irish friends in the Fire and Police Department permission and a special wrench to turn on the fire hydrant on exceptionally hot days. He also had a special device made from 2" diameter pipe that was shaped into a double "T" and could be fastened to the opening of a fire plug. Holes were drilled into the front of the device in such a way that it created a shower-like spray, thereby saving a lot of water. Ordinarily, neighborhood kids would illegally open the plugs, allowing the water to come out full force and thousands of gallons of water to run down the gutters and go down into the storm sewers. Large groups of kids would romp around under the cooling spray of water. No one owned a bathing suit, so we just used old cut-off pants. Dad supplied a welcome relief from the blistering hot sun, if only for a short period of time.

During the Prohibition years, people who could not afford to frequent the speak-easies resorted to making their own beer. Pop was no exception. He would buy some hops and yeast and whatever else it took to complete the recipe. I have no idea just how much beer was made in a batch, but I do recall watching Dad bottle the brew and then cap each bottle with a hand-capping device. By the time we moved to Arizona Street, Prohibition had been repealed, so Dad put his beer making talents into making root beer. We were now allowed to assist him with his bottling chores. Dad was by no means a bootlegger. He brewed just enough for his own consumption and to quench the thirst of his friends, who were many.

Also while living on Arizona Street, Dad organized a group of neighbors into a committee to run a "Block Party." A banner was hung at each end of the street announcing the date and time of a party to be held in our block. The affair usually would be held on Thursday, Friday, and Saturday nights, never on Sunday. Sunday was a day of rest and devotion. No businesses were opened, all stores were closed, bars and saloons were also closed, and even movie theatres were not permitted to be open on Sunday until many years later. On the nights of the party, a platform was erected to hold a small musical group, an area of the block, in front of the band stand, was roped off for dancing, and stands were put up for games of chance and skill. Food and drink stalls also lined the sidewalks. People came from all over to enjoy the entertainment. Everyone had good wholesome fun.

Troublemakers were hastily and unceremoniously ejected from the area. I think that my favorite part of the whole affair was after the closing night. The street had to be cleaned up and all of the neighbors pitched in to help. When the cups, bottles, and trash had been cleared away, everyone brought out their garden hoses to clean the street and pavements. Naturally, when the final cleaning was accomplished, someone had to squirt anyone within the distance of the spray. One fast squirt led to another until the entire block was involved and everyone was soaked to the skin. Pity the poor soul who ventured near and was perhaps returning from a date and was dressed in a suit and tie. He would immediately be drenched. It was all done in good fun and everyone took it as such, besides it was a perfect way to cool off on a hot night. Three nights of a carnival-like atmosphere were over. The light bulbs that were strung from the electric poles were removed and the neighborhood settled into a temporary unfamiliar quiet.

The proceeds from the block party were used to hire two buses. The buses were loaded with all of the neighborhood kids and some adults and headed for an all day outing to an amusement park, usually "Woodside Park" or "Penn Valley Park" which was on the outskirts of Philly. It was like a day in the country. Hot dogs, chips, and sodas were served all day long. It was a day that city kids only dreamed about, thanks to my Dad.

Trenton Avenue in Fishtown was in the Holy Name Parish. Every family living on our block was Irish-Catholic and poor. Wasn't everyone? At Holy Name School, some of my classmates were "Frog" Hamilton, Joe Conway, "Fish" Herron, Jim Cassiday, the White brothers, just over from Ireland, and Joe Riley. There were Flynns, O'Brians, McAnanys, and of course the McLaughlins. Holy Name was all Irish. As kids, we knew that we were Irish but we did not know that we were poor. Everyone lived that way except maybe Billy Dyer, the son of a doctor. He was a nice kid but as the son of a benefactor of the church, he was pampered. Billy and I were often the last two kids left standing when Sister held a Spelling Bee. Sometimes he won and at other times I would win. Billy was always well-mannered, well-dressed, and well-off. No one in the class could do better than I in drawing and art, thanks to Oscar for sending me to the

Graphic Sketch Club. I continued to create holiday scenes on the blackboards.

Moving to Arizona Street was a culture shock. Dad now had a steady job taking care of the horses at Harbison's Dairy. With a steady pay coming in every week, Dad now could afford to rent a house at 1932 Arizona Street. It was only about five blocks away from Trenton Avenue, however, it was a big step. The house belonged to Mr. Nestle, a German baker who ran a bake shop on Dauphin Street. I often went, early in the morning, to ask Mr. Nestle if he had any stale buns or cakes that we could have for breakfast. Since we were his tenants, he would give me a bag of day-old sticky buns or doughnuts. They usually were a little hard but never-the-less, they were great when dipped in milk or tea. The people on Arizona Street were different. All of the fathers had jobs to go to every morning. The mothers were clean, wore nice dresses, and appeared to be happy. The Browns, who lived next door to us, were not Irish; I do not know what they were. Mr. Brown worked for the PTC (Philadelphia Transit Company) and played on their baseball team. He often took me along with their son, Frankie, to see the ballgames. Mrs. Brown had a job at Sears and Roebuck. Young Frankie was somewhat spoiled, a little sissified, and a Mama's boy. Someone said that the people on the other side were Polish or Hungarian, whatever that was. The Stevensons were English. Mr. Stevenson had a good job in the office of the Pennsylvania Railroad. I would become very good friends with their son, Howard, and spend many enjoyable hours in their home. The Millers and the Grassbergers were German. The McLaughlins and the Joe Green family were the only Irish on the block, although the block was in St. Boniface Parish, a German Parish. Mom told me that she was German and had gone to school at St. Bonnies. Hey! That made me part German. When you mix German and Irish together, what do you get? Some of our neighbors were Catholic, some, God bless us, Lutherans, Presbyterians, and "Holy Mother of God," Baptists.

I soon became friends with Joe Green, Frankie Brown, Hooch Miller, Howard Stevenson, Charlie Grassberger, Herby Sibley, and Clyde Cannon-Dillon. We were a mixed bag of nationalities and religions. One morning, Howard and I were sitting on the curb discussing God only knows what. The talk got around to sex. He tried to tell me how babies were made. I was sure that he had it all wrong and tried to get a mental picture in my head. It just did not make any sense. As thoughts bounced around in my head, I told Howard that I did not believe what he was saying and that he did not know what the hell he was talking about.

"You are making it up," I said.

"Didn't you ever see dogs do it?" he asked.

"Yeh, but they get stuck and somebody has to throw a bucket of water on them."

"Well, men and women have to do the same thing."

"Not my Mother," I said indignantly.

"Yeh, yeh, everybody does it."

"Not my Mom."

"Oh yeh?"

"What do you know? You're a Baptist and your mother and father weren't married by a priest, so they're not really married."

In spite of my young, innocent stupidity, we remained friends for many years. I even attended some Baptist services with the Stevensons, especially on Easter Sunday when they gave each child a hardboiled egg and a chocolate covered coconut cream egg. After church, Howard and I went around the neighborhood yelling, "Epper, Epper," a challenge to anyone and all to match eggs with us. Any kid accepting the dare would hold his egg in his hand with the small tip of his egg surrounded by the bent forefinger and thumb. The challenger would then forcefully come down with the tip of his egg against the other causing one of the eggs to crack. The owner of the strongest egg would get to keep both eggs. Occasionally, you could meet a cheat who would fill his egg with "Plaster of Paris" and go home with a basket full of eggs, which is providing he was not caught. Oh well! I would have to go to confession next Sunday and tell the priest that I had gone into a protestant church. I should be forgiven because I shared the chocolate egg at home.

It was a cold brisk morning. I could hear the wind whistling down the narrow street. Even the cold air could not hide the smell of horses, hay, and manure. On the one side of Dreer Street, were the row homes. The opposite side of the street contained nothing but stables. Harbison's had over one hundred horses housed in that building. They were very well kept and well-groomed animals that were used to deliver milk to customers on a specific route. These well-trained horses would go ahead of the driver and then wait for him at the next stop. Young and old, everyone liked the milk wagon horses. Dad worked at Harbison's as a trainer and hostler. His favorite was a black and white pinto named Nora. Mom told us that, more than once, in the middle of the night, while Dad was still sleeping, he would smack her on the fanny and call out, "Back Nora, mover over Nora." Fortunately, Mom knew Nora was a horse.

A two by four beam with a pulley attached protruded above a small opening in the second floor hayloft. It was my turn to take Dad's lunch to him on the way to school. He went to work very early, therefore Mom would make a lunch for one of us to deliver to him. At the sound of my whistle, Dad appeared at the window. He lowered a wooden box tied to a rope that was fed through the pulley. I placed the lunch bag into the box and Dad pulled it back up. After a few remarks and a "goodbye," I was again on my way to school.

Knowing that I was late, I made a feeble attempt to sneak into class. Even then, I knew that it was futile. Sister Marie Alphonse, seemed to have eyes in the back of her head. I realized, later, that they could use their glasses and a blackboard to reflect a mirror-like image. "Midge" as she was commonly called, could stretch herself to a full four feet two inches. She was a good teacher, very fair, and sincere, albeit a very strict disciplinarian, as Phil could attest. He carried a lump on his forehead for the rest of his life after she bounced his head off of the blackboard. No need complaining, Dad would have said that Phil must have done something to provoke Sister. We all must obey and do as we were told or suffer the consequences, either at school or at home.

As I tiptoed down the aisle, I was stopped in my tracks.

"Joseph!" she yelled, without even turning from the blackboard.

"Yes, Sister?" I meekly answered.

"Where have you been? Why are you late for school?" She asked.

I answered, "I had to take my Dad's lunch to him on the way to school."

"How could you?" She asked. "Your brother, Francis, said that he delivered your father's lunch."

I looked over at Frank. He was sitting at his desk with a pious look on his face, and I swear a halo hovering above his head. I did not dare say another word.

"I want to see you after school." Sister said.

After school, I reported to the convent for a reprimand and punishment. Sister put me to work cleaning up the small garden behind the convent. When I was finished, she came out with a full plate of food and some milk. I still feel to this day that her keeping me after school was a pretext to see that I got something to eat. I must have been very puny because everyone was always trying to fatten me up.

I remember a warm, sunny day in June. I was taking my good old time walking up Norris Street on my way to nine o' clock Mass. I felt great. I was filled with a sense of pride in my new scout uniform. The scent of the newness filled my nostrils. The wool high stockings, breeches, shirt, and neckerchief added to the heat of the day. This didn't bother me at all. The only thing that I felt was a feeling of belonging. I was not alone as I marched up the street to the beat of the music in my head. Did I march to a different drummer? Probably, because I was always a dreamer. I did not make the choir, although I had a pretty good voice. I was not an altar boy. I was, however, on the safety patrol. Now I was a scout.

Holy Name had started a Boy Scout troop. After completing the tests that were required by the "Boy Scout Handbook," we were issued a uniform by the school. Uniforms were to be worn to Sunday Mass. Each grade was assigned a section of pews. Sister would sit at the end of the last pew where she could see, at a glance, anyone who misbehaved or did not pay attention. She could also see which pupils attended Mass; but, more importantly, who did not attend Mass. The absentees had better have a good excuse on Monday morning. Nuns not only had eyes in the back of their heads, but they knew every pupil by the back of this or her head. How did they do that?

It appeared as though an army of police had invaded the neighborhood. There were police cars all over the area. Everyone was being subjected to questioning. Apparently there had been an escape from Eastern State Penitentiary or Holmesburg Prison. "One-arm Joe" Tonuto owned a small coffee shop and restaurant on Front Street. Joe was a huge, tough but amiable Italian man. H always wore a white shirt, a white apron, and a broad smile. The young people would gather in his shop to buy a soda or just to play the pinball machine. We would spend a lot of time there talking to Joe or just passing time. "One-arm Joe" was liked by all of the young people of the neighborhood. He could be trusted.

One of the escapees was an armed robber, Fred "The Angel" Tonuto, a brother of "One-arm Joe." The police knew that "The Angel" and another man had jumped on a milk wagon and forced the driver to take them down Kensington Avenue. It was assumed that they would try to contact "One-arm Joe." The second escapee was "Slick Willie" Sutton, a notorious bank robber, who would become nationally famous for his reply when asked why he robbed banks. He answered plainly and seriously, "Because that is where the money is."

The search that day was fruitless. There was no sign of "The Angel" or "Slick Willie" A search of Joe's restaurant yielded not a single clue as to their whereabouts. Sometime later, however, a young man in New York City spotted Willie and notified the authorities. Shortly thereafter, "Slick Willie" was taken into custody and returned to prison. A couple of weeks later, the young informer was found shot to death. There was well founded speculation that "The Angel" was behind the execution. To my knowledge, Fred "The Angel" Tonuto had never been found.

In saying that other people become a part of us, we all seem to have one acquaintance that had the most influence in forming our personality. For me, that person would have been Stanton (Oscar) Haines. He was definitely a friend and a guide during my formative years.

The early 1930's were "Depression years." At that time, Stan Haines was an engineer at the RCA plant in Camden, New Jersey; therefore, he was doing quite well, career wise and financially. He rented a room from Mrs. Stella Glenn on Norris Street Stan also rented a garage that was across the street from our house on Trenton Avenue. When he would be working on his car, some neighborhood kids would help him or more accurately, get in his way. He did not mind because he loved kids and he would help them in any way that he could. We gave him the nickname of "Oscar." Keep in mind that this was a poor neighborhood in poor and distressing times. Pop was struggling to keep the family afloat by huckstering (selling fruit and vegetables from a hired horse and wagon), by selling flavored ice cones from a push cart and by hanging wallpaper, a skill that he passed on to all of us, and one that I would be called on to use throughout my lifetime. I thank Dad for that.

Saturday morning, I was to meet Oscar for the first of many times to come. It was a nice spring morning and I could have been running the streets or getting into some kind of trouble. I walked down Norris Street to the house where Oscar lived. I knocked on the door which was answered by Mrs. Stella Glenn, the landlady. She was a pleasant and lovely woman with gray hair and eye glasses that were held by a chain, draped around her neck. She was the picture of a well-educated dowager. She invited me into the house and I stepped into a foyer that led to a large living room. I stood wide-eyed looking at the room. Never before had I seen a room such as this. Practically everyone that I knew lived in a rented house with second-hand or very little furniture. This room had floors covered with oriental carpets, fine Victorian furniture, a fireplace topped with a huge mirror. The mirror was framed with, what I believed to be, a real gold frame. Beyond the parlor was a dining room that had a complete dining room set. Believe me, I was amazed. An open staircase led up to the second floor.

Mrs. Glenn sat for some time and chatted with me, as she would over the years. Even as a child, she never talked down to me but listened to whatever I had to say and respected my opinion. I was to learn much during these chats. She wanted to start breakfast, so she told me to go up to Stan's room. His bedroom was a large room in the rear of the house. It was obviously a bedroom of a man of very diversified interests. A very large desk was at the foot of the bed. Its top was barely visible, as it was covered with engineering and sports books, magazines, and papers. Every available wall space contained shelves of books. There were numerous trophies, medals, and awards that he had won in marathon races. Certainly, the room was indicative of the man who occupied it. There were signs of a gamut of interests; science, history, opera, engineering, stamps; and as I said before, a myriad of trophies and medals.

Oscar introduced me to good books. He had given me the first two books that I read in their entirety. The first one was "The Count of Monte Cristo" and the second was "Les Miserables." When I would meet him on a Saturday, he would quiz me on what I had read during the week. What other child began serious reading with two such classics?

A typical Saturday began with a walk to Mrs. Glenn's house and a visit with her after which she would serve breakfast to Oscar and me, usually consisting of orange juice, eggs, and toast. After breakfast, we would drive to the Malta Boat Club on Boathouse Row, along the East River Drive. If a race was not scheduled, Oscar, along with the other members of the Passon Athletic Club, would have a practice run, which began at the Malta Clubhouse, went down the East River Drive, across the Spring Garden Street bridge, down the West River Drive to the Girard Avenue bridge, then cross over to the East River Drive, and then continue back to the Malta Boat Club. I think that the distance was about twelve miles.

While the men were running, I would occupy myself in various ways. At times, I would walk through the park and look at some of the statues; Lincoln on the East River Drive, a statue of a group of Pilgrims, sitting at a large table for a meal (this statue has since been removed from the park), and the most memorable, Frederic Remington's "The Cowboy." I can remember climbing on the back of the horse behind the cowboy. At other times, I would stay at the clubhouse, where I would sit, either on the dock or on the porch. There I would spend hours reading "Esquire" magazine or doing some sketches of scenes along the Schuylkill River. A small group of us, mostly children of athletes, would sit on the dock and watch the scullers glide through the water. John

B. Kelly Sr. was an Olympic champion sculler; he was barred from the regatta because he was a commoner and worked with his hands as a bricklayer. After he became a millionaire contractor, his son, John Jr. (Jack), raced in the Henley Regatta in 1947 and 1949 and became the winner. John B. Kelly was also the father of Grace Kelly, and international beauty, movie star, and Princess Grace of Monaco.

I loved the time that I spent at the Malta. It was an entirely different world than my everyday life on Trenton Avenue. Upon entering the front door, a wooden staircase led to the second floor lounge which was furnished with tables and overstuffed but comfortable chairs and sofas. The lounge led to a screened-in porch at the rear of the building, overlooking the river. Next to the lounge were the locker and shower rooms. It was after practice, that Oscar tried, unsuccessfully I might add, to get me to acquire a taste for grapefruit juice.

After one practice session, Oscar discovered some of my sketches. He had a friend and fellow runner who also was an artist look at my drawings. The friends felt that I did have some innate talent. That afternoon, he took me to the Philadelphia Graphic Sketch Club where he enrolled me in an art class. He paid for my tuition and bought all of my equipment; including, charcoal, pastels, drawing tablets, and portfolio. Oscar paid for my art education for a long time.

I spent a lot of time in the Art Museum where I must have, at first, been an oddity. At first the guards eyed me with suspicion and kept a close eye on this poorly dressed urchin walking among some of the greatest art in the world. In time, they got to know me and I them. How can I explain the feeling? I just felt comfortable around these great paintings and statues. The vastness, the quiet, and even the odor of the huge halls made me feel that I was in a place of awe and devotion, not unlike a great church or cathedral.

A love of art museums has remained a part of me for all of my life. Where ever life has taken me, large city or small town, I have a tendency to gravitate to the nearest art exhibit. As for myself, I have become a fairly accomplished artist, in my own right, however, not to the degree that I would have liked. Rarely have I ever been completely satisfied with my work. What artist is ever satisfied? I always manage to find something that I could have or should have done differently.

The lower level of the boat house contained a storage area for the sculls or boats. I was always amazed at the way that they were so neatly stacked on racks. They were all polished to perfection. You would be hard pressed to find a smudge or the slightest flaw. It was no wonder that they seemed to glide through the water.

On several weekends, Oscar, along with his lady friend, Mrs. Lillian McCord and her son, Jimmy, would go on a camping trip to Beach Haven on Long Beach Island. He asked my parents if I could go with them. We would set up a tent on the bayside of the road. Long Beach Island in the 1930's was a desolate strip of land. Only the road separated the bay from the Ocean. There were no stores or houses along the strip. Aside from a couple of bait shops, there was nothing. We spent our time swimming, eating, and fishing. At least, we were trying to fish. On Sunday night, I would usually fall asleep on the way home. I can remember Oscar picking me up in his arms and handing me over to Dad who would then put me right into bed.

When Oscar took me to the Graphic Sketch Club for the first time for enrollment, I was nervous but anxious to see the inside of the building. As we entered through the vestibule, we turned left into what I recall was a church or chapel, complete with pews, an altar, stained-glass windows, candles, and a rook screen. I do know that even as a child, I was struck with a feeling of devotion and spirituality that I would not experience again until I visited some of the old churches in Europe, most especially in Lucerne and Rome. From there, we went to the art studios on the second floor. Here too, I have memories of being in awe of all that I was observing; the drawings, the statues, half-finished oil paintings, easels everywhere, the odor of paint, turpentine, thinner, chalk and the unmistakable smell of cedar from pencil shavings. Certain odors to this day can conjure up good memories of hours spent in those old studios. It took about an hour and two street car trolley transfers to get to the Sketch Club. After spending some of my time with Oscar, I would gladly make this trip later in the day. Later, I convinced Mr. and Mrs. Stevenson to permit their son, Howard, to join me in the art classes.

Oscar had signed me up and purchased the necessary equipment to begin taking lessons; portfolio, sketch pad, pencils, charcoal, art gum erasers, pastels, and a bottle of fixative. All of this to start a young boy for the hard and difficult streets of "Fishtown" on a new and exciting adventure in life. An adventure that would fill my life with satisfaction and fulfillment all of my days. Yes, I am still a dreamer and can get lost in dreams through writing or at the drawing table.

The passage from kid to teenager was often lined with obstacles and hurdles. One had to belong to a neighborhood group but not necessarily a gang. A transitional stepping stone could be any number of tasks; stealing donuts from a bakery wagon, leading a cop on a chase through an empty factory building, or running a gauntlet. We kids, of course, knew every alley and every abandoned factory in the area, including every hiding place. There really was no fear in getting caught because we could out run most of the burly Irish cops. "Running the Gauntlet" was something else. There was a stretch of Hope Street from Dauphin Street through Susquehanna Avenue to Norris Street. These two blocks of Hope Street were lined with homes of the areas black families. This was still the age of segregation, even in the North. Certainly, blacks experienced more freedom than in the South but still races did not mingle but had their own neighborhoods as did the Irish, Poles, Germans, and Italians. To be accepted and feel safe in any neighborhood, one had to be a member of the neighborhood gangs. Most of these were not violent gangs but more of a brotherhood of kids who supported each other, played together, and yes, did get into some mischief. One of the rites of passage for an initiate to enter into a gang was to "Run the Gauntlet," which meant running down the two blocks of Hope Street, in the dark of night. Hope Street was the only section of Kensington that was all black or colored. Members of the gang stood at both ends of the street to make sure that the runner ran the entire course. Actually, no one was going to get hurt but it could be quite scary running down the center of the street while eyes stared at you form the darkness. You could not see anyone, but you could feel their presences as your imagination ran rampant. The people living in the homes were probably thinking "What the hell are those crazy white boys doing now?" Their young boys, do doubt, had more to fear if they ventured into a white neighborhood.

I remember going to the swimming pool on Second Street before I could swim. As usual, the pool was overcrowded and everyone was yelling, screaming, and chasing other kids. The only place that anyone could attempt to swim was in the deep end of the pool. Like many others, I was running around the edge of the pool, being chased by someone, probably Howard Stevenson or Hooch Miller. As I ran past the deep end of the pool, a black kid gave me a shove that sent me flying into the deep water. I went straight to the bottom. I struggled frantically to get my feet on the concrete bottom in order to push myself up. Flailing legs and feet of kids treading water delayed my rise to the top, being pushed back down several times. Gasping for breath, I finally reached the surface. I was now faced with the challenge of getting to the side where I could hang on. My strokes were fast, frantic, and awkward, but I was swimming. This, of course, was how I learned to swim. When I got out of the pool, I made my way around to the deep end, and singled out the boy who had pushed me from a small group of black kids. I walked up to him and punched him squarely in the nose. He went sailing into the deep water. From that day on, Bowie and I would become good friends with a mutual respect for each other. Bowie was the only black kid who could or would venture into our neighborhood. He would often come over to our street and join in a game of ball. When members of our group would meet Bowie and his friends on Front Street, we would greet each other. We both had learned a lot from our encounter at the pool.

Another bright, sunny summer day. We had nothing else to do, so as on many other days, Clyde and I decided to walk downtown. It was to be a long walk but we had very little money and could not afford to ride the "El." The station was not busy enough for us to sneak on for a free ride. We walked down on Front Street, pass the old soup kitchen, to Berks Street. We engaged in conversation with some kids, about our age, playing on the sidewalk. After beating them in a game of marbles, with their own marbles, we returned the winnings and continued on our way, keeping our eyes on the gutter in hopes of finding some small change. Not much luck on a street littered with gum wrappers and cigarette butts. After making a stop at Drakes Bakery, to buy a couple of day old cupcakes, (the clerk threw in a couple of stale cakes), we continued on to Eighth Street. At Eighth and Race Streets, we took our time and looked into some store windows. We did a lot of window shopping in those days. Clyde and I stood gazing into the window of a pawn shop. The window was full of things that we could only dream of ever having: cameras, watches, diamond rings of many shapes and sizes, and radios, even portables, and all kinds of articles that could be hocked for a couple of bucks to satisfy the hunger for food, smoke, or booze. Most were never redeemed.

Next to the hock shop was a men's store. The window had men's ties and shirts, but what really caught my eye was the men's jewelry, "Swank" jewelry. In my mind, it just had to be pure gold. On one side of the heavy plate glass window, the yellow gold cuff links and tie tacks sat passively in velvet and satin boxes and seemed to take on life as the bright light of the sun created rays that bounced off of the yellow metal. The other or outside surface of the glass contained the reflection of two young boys, in worn hand-me-down and ill-fitting clothing, well-worn sneakers that had seen better days, hair in need of both combing and cutting, and dirt smeared faces with eyes glowing with anticipation of better days in the future when nothing would be impossible. Someday, I thought, I would have cuff links and a tie clip when I could afford a tie. Was I dreaming beyond my reach? Perhaps so, but maybe not. Dreams cost nothing and certainly could bring a few moments of happiness to young minds.

"Hey! Step right up."
"Come in a little closer, they won't bite."
"See the dancing girls."
"One thin dime will get you into the back room."
"She will take everything off."
We stood on the pavement peering into the Gypsy show. A girl was up on a make-shift stage, dressed in a skimpy colorful

costume and wriggling to the beat of some eerie Gypsy music. Men, young and old, stood with hands in their pockets, gazing at the girls, not missing the slightest movement. We laughed and tried to understand the fascination that held the attention of those guys.

"Hey! You kids, get the hell out of here," we heard the barker yell.

"Yeah, yeah," we answered as we slowly walked away.

Gypsies were in town at the time. Store windows were draped with dirty multicolored curtains. At the door sat some women, some fat, some skinny, some good looking, some ugly, but all were overly dressed in brightly colored dresses with bandanas on their heads, hawking their wares to passerby; palm reading, fortune telling, or whatever else that they might have to offer. There had to be more because some sat on a chair with skirts pulled up to their waists while others had breasts revealed. Running up the street, as we passed a fruit stand, we both grabbed an apple and scurried away as fast as we could, weaving in and out of the people on the sidewalk. Behind us, in the distance, we heard someone yelling.

"Stop those kids! Stop them." Could he mean us? Naw!

Our route finally took us to the "Troc Theatre." I had often heard Dad, Uncle Phil, Uncle Bill, in whispers, talk about going to the "Troc" on a Friday evening. Mom and my aunts stayed at home, of course. The Troc was a favorite burlesque theatre featuring a variety of strip tease artists, young girls, and some old, who made their living by taking off their clothes, bit by bit, to the beat of some raucous music. Naturally, the men only went there to see the comics, in particular Billy (Cheese and Crackers) Hagen, a very popular comedian, who when faced with a dilemma or a sexy, young woman, would turn to the audience and with a surprised tone would say, "Cheese and Crackers." This remark came to be his trademark. Clyde and I stood outside looking at pictures of past and present strippers; Sally Rand, Lili St. Syre, someone named Bubbles for obvious reasons, a scantily clad girl with a snake wrapped around her body, and another girl with a half-dozen white doves gently taking off pieces of her costume. Many of our later "Hollywood stars" both male and female began their careers in such small theatres as the "Troc."

In time, we were on Market Street. I was quite familiar with the downtown because of spending time there with "Oscar" on many Saturdays. We roamed around the department stores such as Lits, Gimbles, Wanamakers, and Strawbridge and Clothiers. We ran up the steps and rode down the elevator, making stops at the toy department of each store. At other times, we were escorted to the front door, as if we did not know the way. We did not steal anything or do any damage to the store. I guess that they did not like our looks.

"Do you have any change, Mister?" One of us would ask a well dressed man, especially one who was in the company of a young lady. Most wouldn't want to be embarrassed by refusing in front of the girl. We managed to collect a few cents, enough to buy a "Philadelphia pretzel" and a soda. Still store hopping, we came to Eighth and Market. There would not be another subway entrance until Second Street. The day had gone by fast and it was time for us to make our way home.

We entered the Market Street subway and went down on the train level. The station was crowded with office workers eager to go home. After waiting for a train to stop, and timing the stop, we ran and slid under the turnstile and got on a car just before the doors were about to close. There was no time for anyone to react and stop us. At subsequent stops, we would leave the car, run down the platform, and enter another car. At Second Street, the train came up out of the tunnel and after rounding a turn at Front Street, became the "Frankford El." Clyde and I got off of the "El" at Dauphin Street and walked the block and a half to our homes. I just made it home in time for supper.

There was a light tapping on the bedroom door. No answer.

A slightly louder but fervent knock.

No answer.

A still louder but hesitant knock, now accompanied by a quiet voice.

"Mom, Mom did you lock the front door?"

Still no answer.

Now a more persistent knock and again, "Mom, did you lock the front door?"

"Phil, will you go to bed?" The sound of Dad's somewhat irritated voice came through the wood paneled door.

"Ask Mom if the door is locked and the windows, too."

"PHILIP! Either go down and check for yourself or go to bed."

This dialogue was repeated on many a night. For some reason, Phil always had to be sure that everything was closed up tight before he could go to sleep. It was his constant persistence that brought about Dad's anger. Our parent's bedroom door was at the bottom of the staircase leading up to the third floor boy's rooms; therefore, it was convenient for Phil to make a final check before going up.

On Trenton Avenue, no one had more than the neighbors and no one could possibly have less, so there was never any reason to lock the doors. We were all in the same boat and no one had any cars, and it seemed that none of the neighbors were going to go any place. The Depression was at its worse and Dad was selling ice snow cones from a pushcart in order to eke out a living for his family.

I was about ten years old when Dad finally got a steady job at Harbison's Dairy. This enabled us to move up a step into a little better neighborhood but by no stretch of the imagination, a more affluent area. The most profound difference was that all of the fathers had jobs. We were not the poorest family on the block by any means. Our friends, the Fields family, had that dubious honor. Still, there was no reason for Phil to be so afraid that someone was going to break into our house. I would pity the poor soul who tried. But that was Phil, a consummate worrier. He was really a good brother and a very nice person who would help anyone in need. He just could not stop worrying. Phil worried about school, not having a job, having a job, not having a girlfriend, having a girlfriend. He worried about Mom and Dad, his brothers and sisters, and his friends. When he befriended someone, he was a close and constant friend. He should have been a priest. In fact, when he served as an altar boy, the parish priests wanted him to go into the seminary. I imagine that the lack of money was the reason that that did not come about. Phil was the only one in the family to be an altar boy. The rest of us just couldn't "cut the mustard" or meet the required standards.

At some point, Phil decided to learn to play the guitar. He was, no doubt, influenced by Sis's husband, Nick Schilk, who could play any instrument he picked up. Nick could play, and well, the banjo, piano, saxophone, and the piano accordion, all without having had any instructions. Phil never became a great guitar player, but he did become good enough to qualify as a member of the Greenwood String Band. This group would march every year in the Philadelphia New Year's Day Parade.

A gathering of some of the Mummers at our house on New Year's Eve became a yearly ritual. The furniture would be moved back against the wall to make a little room for dancing. Neighbors, upon hearing the music would just pop in, no one needed an invitation. Beer and food was provided by the party goers. The sound of the singing and music would reach a crescendo about midnight and then begin to taper off, stopping only when it was time for the bandsmen to report to the "New Year's Day Parade."

January 1st was and is usually a very cold day, but these men in their fancy costumes and heavy headdresses were not feeling any cold or any pain. There was no ruling against drinking, so most of the Mummers carried a small flask of whiskey under their costumes. Nearing the end of the parade, they were well lit and were in no need of any illumination to light their way. Besides the bump on his head that he received from Sister Marie Alphonse, Phil received another memento after one parade. Phil and a group of friends went into a downtown bar and they got into an altercation and Phil received a broken nose.

At the beginning of the parties, I was only about twelve years old. For some reason, when I was young, I had a predisposition to having a sudden and unwarranted bleeding of the nose. Perhaps too much activity or excitement would bring it on. At any rate, in the middle of these parties, I would be leaning back with a cold object or a piece of ice on the bridge of my nose to stop the flow of blood. Fortunately, by the time that I entered the service, I had outgrown this tendency.

Over a period of a few years, Johnny Roberts and I became very good friends. I spent many evenings at the Roberts' home and at the nearby "Light House," a neighborhood boy's club, where John and I would spend a lot of time boxing, playing "Ping-Pong," and shooting pool. John's parents were very nice people and welcomed me into their home with friendship and love. The Roberts family had come to Philly from upstate, a little town in the slate belt called, naturally, Slatington, Pennsylvania. Why they moved to Philly was a mystery to me. John's uncle drove around in a new red convertible and made several trips back to small town Slatington to display his good fortune. Their religion also was a mystery to me. I knew that several nights a week, religious meetings were held in their home, usually around the dining room table. Mr. Roberts was a sickly man and obviously retired, at least there was no indication of gainful employment. I never saw any family pictures displayed in the house. I did know that there was an older sister who lived nearby; however, I was never aware of any other relatives. It was a quiet household with Mrs. Roberts usually busy in the kitchen, preparing meals while Mr. Roberts sat in an upholstered chair and looked out the front window.

One Sunday afternoon, John told me that the family was going for a ride in his uncle's convertible and he invited me to go along. It was a warm, sunny day and we did enjoy the warm air brushing rather swiftly across our faces and through our long hair. Hair that was long not because of style or fad but because we simply were in need of an overdue haircut. Midway through the drive, John told me that they were on their way to visit his brothers. I had no idea that he had any brothers. They had never been mentioned. Eventually, we came to a stop at a gated entrance through a massive and high stone wall that surrounded "Holmesburg Prison." It was a bleak, somber, and gloomy place. Placed strategically along the upper portion of the wall, were gun towers. In not too many years, I would learn the effectiveness of just such machine gun towers as a deterrent to thoughts of escape. But for now, I experienced a cold chill as we entered the foreboding building. The inside was even less inviting and did not lend itself into bringing any joy or cheerfulness into our visit.

Guards led our group into an equally drab visiting room. A room that, except for a table and a couple of chairs, was absolutely bare. Not even a calendar was in view. The starkness of the gray paint-peeled walls was broken only by a small loud ticking clock. Sounds of voices could be heard in the distance, causing a din of combined sounds that made it impossible to recognize any intelligent conversation. The muffled sound of footsteps coming down a long corridor, stopped at the side door of the visiting room. We could also hear the occasional metallic clang as steel doors were snapped shut. The side door opened, two rather gaunt young men entered the room. I knew now that Johnny's brothers were not guards or members of the security staff. They were immediately embraced by their tearful parents. John had four older brothers. All were in prison. The four brothers had banded together into what was known as "The Quick Change Gang," who over a period of time were engaged in robbing stores. After robbing one store, they would get into a car and make a fast get away, make a quick change of clothing in the car, and proceed to another location to commit another robbery. These, I am sure, were armed robberies. Naturally, they were eventually caught and incarcerated. This was the destiny of many young men of the period, who without jobs, hung idly around street corners and in bar rooms. They would drink, talk incessantly, get into minor scraps, and occasionally require the police to break up a fight. One of Dad's oft repeated quotes was, "Idle hands are the tools of the devil, idle minds are the workshops of Satan." The two brothers that I met that day, in spite of the prison garb, appeared to be nice, intelligent, young men. Years later, one of them was closely involved in the development of a device that had a bearing on gyroscopes that were used on submarines during the war. The other brother, as our visit came to an end, gave Johnny and me a figure of a wooden horse that he had carved. The horses were beautifully sculptured and smoothly finished with a semi-gloss varnish. For my horse, I made a bridle of leather and a saddle that I carved out of wood and covered with thin leather complete with a girth fashioned from string and a couple of small rings. This horse, along with other precious belongings of mine, would disappear while I was away in the service. John's four young brothers were destined to spend most, if not all, of their lives behind bars. The visit was a short, controlled visit with guards always present and watchful. We left the drab and dreary scene and atmosphere behind steel doors and walked out into the bright sunlight. The trip back home was sad and quiet with very little conversation. John's parents had exhausted all of their finances in a futile effort to obtain the release of their four sons. I could now understand the moments of silence and sadness that I had sometimes noticed as I entered the Roberts' home.

After I came home from Oscar's one Saturday, I met Johnny Roberts at the Howard Movie House on Front Street. I cannot recall what the main feature was that day, but there usually was a first run movie (sometimes a double feature), "MovieToon News," a couple of cartoons, a fifteen minute comedy, and a weekly serial; Buck Rogers, Tom Mix, Clyde Beatty at the Circus, The Lone Ranger, etc. At intermission, we went back to the candy bar to buy a box of "Goobers" chocolate covered peanuts. While there, we got into a conversation with a young girl about our age. When the lights dimmed, signifying the start of the second-half of the show, we left the lobby with the girl tagging along behind. As we left the aisle to get seats, she put herself between John and me. Part way through the show, I felt something on my lap searching for something. It was her hand and I assumed that she was looking for some "Goobers" but the hand kept groping. Oh God! I wondered if Johnny noticed. In the semi-darkness, I managed a furtive glance over to him. I saw that her other hand was busy on his lap. After some time, and much apprehension, I bolstered up enough courage to softly and gently move my somewhat shaky hand across her leg seeking what I naively thought unexplored territory. As I inched across, my now sweaty palm settled upon Johnny's hand. He had reached the destination before me. When we left the theatre, the girl went her way and we went ours. We agreed that we would have to look for her again. Suddenly, I felt a hand on my shoulder. It was my brother Phil.

"What the hell were you two doing in there?" he sternly asked.

"We were watching the movie," I answered.

"Yeh! Well, I am going to tell Mom."

I knew that he would not because he would not talk to Mom about something like that. My fear was that he would tell Dan, John, and Frank. If so, I certainly would be in for a lot of kidding and would not be able to take communion on Sunday. How was I going to tell the priest? After a tense supper waiting for Phil to say something and knowing that he was enjoying my uneasiness, thank God that he did not say anything. I made my way to Holy Name Church. The church was crowded; in fact, all of the confessionals were full, with people waiting in line. There must have been a lot of sinning during the week. Oh good! Father Bopal was sitting in one of the pews hearing confessions. I would not have to go to one of the older priests. The older ones were usually very strict and scold or chastise you for any minor sin or infraction. Penance would be severe. I might be sent to hell. If a kid did not say penance and get absolution and forgiveness, he would wind up in hell. Going into a confessional box was not my favorite part of going to church. It was dark and scary. A child had to kneel, in the dark, where his head barely reached the screened opening in the wall separating him from the priest. The faint whispers of the sinner in the opposite side could be heard while waiting for the door to slide open revealing a dark figure behind a small screen. The dark shadow would listen to you recite your sins and then give you penance, usually a couple of "Our Fathers" and "Hail Mary's" depending on the deepness and degree of your sins since your last confession.

When my turn came, I took my place kneeling in the pew behind Father Bopal, the young priest known to be more forgiving and lenient. Father kept looking forward with his head slightly bent and his hand cupped over one ear.

"Bless me Father for I have sinned. It has been a week since my last confession."

"And what do you have to tell me, my child?"

"I fought with my brother, Father."

"And what else?"

"I disobeyed my mother, Father."

"And what else?"

"I used curse words, Father."

"And what else, my child?"

Fidgeting on my now aching knees, in a low voice I began to tell him about the incident at the Howard Theatre.

"Speak up son."

In a slightly louder voice, I continued with my confession.

I noticed him straighten up and rise slightly in the pew and with a voice that seemed to echo throughout the church, he said, **"YOU DID WHAT?"**

My embarrassment manifested itself in my getting hot and red from the neck up. I received five "Our Fathers" and five "Hail Mary's" and an Act of Contrition. I went to the back of the church and knelt down in an empty pew. Boy! I'll never get out of here with all of those prayers. I might as well say the whole rosary. On my way out, I stopped at the Holy Water font and nearly covered myself with Holy Water. Walking the streets back home, I felt holier and walked with a lighter gait. A burden had been lifted and I was blessed with the grace of the Holy Spirit, until the next time.

It was Saturday morning. I had gotten out of bed early, got dressed, and had a bit to eat. No school today, it was decision time. Should I go out to play with my friends, Clyde Dillon or Howard Stevenson, or should I walk over to Mrs. Glenn's house and spend some time with Oscar? I was sure that Mrs. Glenn would have some errands for me to run for her. She would pay me a few cents and then I could go to the Kent Theatre that afternoon.

The weather was nice and warm so I walked the eight blocks to her house on Norris Street. I fully expected Mrs. Glenn to open the door with her usual cheery, "Hello Joe." She did open the door.

I asked, "Is Oscar awake yet?"

With that, she started to cry and crushed me to her bosom. This was not like Mrs. Glenn. I remember thinking, "Is she drunk?" although I never knew her to take a drink. I knew the smell of people who had been drinking and I could not detect an odor. She continued to cry while trying to tell me something.

God! I just could not get away and I was being suffocated within the depth of her bosom. In between her sobs, I could hear her say, "Joe, he is gone." "Oh my God, Joe, Stan is dead." "Do you understand, Joe? Stan is gone."

I still could not quite make out what she was trying to say. I was relieved when her brother, Mr. Mercer, came into the living room. Sitting me down, he began, with as much compassion that he could muster, to explain what had happened during the week.

On the previous Wednesday evening, the runners of the Passon Athletic Club were going to practice in the park. Oscar, having had a severe cold, decided not to run but agreed to drive his car and clock the runners. As he began to cross Spring Garden Street Bridge, his car came to a stop. Oscar had loaned his car to Mrs. McCord's brother, who did not bother to refill the gas tank and also did not tell Oscar about it. The cars in the 30's had the trunk and the gas tank in the rear of the car. With a flashlight in hand, he started to look into the tank opening. As he was doing this, a car made the turn to approach the bridge and continued to drive over the bridge. The driver, not seeing Oscar or his car, rammed into both, pinning Oscar between the two cars. Both of his legs had to be amputated and he was in a coma until he died. Thank God that he did pass away because I do not think that he could have lived without his legs. He has never been out of my mind for all of these years. I also thank God for blessing me with the friendship of this kind and gentle man whose teaching and guidance have been and still are a part of me and who and what I am to this day.

Oscar was dead!

I just could not believe it. It couldn't be true. Mr. Mercer told me that the funeral would be held that afternoon and that they wanted me to be there. As the truth and reality of it all finally hit me, I began to cry. My friend and mentor for all of these years was gone. I left the house in some confusion and with tear-filled eyes, ran the eight blocks to my home, crying all the way.

As usual, Mom was always there for me. She saw that I had a clean shirt and tie to go and pay my last respects to the man who had meant so much in my young life. I walked back up Norris Street to the Fluer Funeral Home. Mrs. Glenn directed me to an empty seat next to her. Among the mourners were doctors, lawyers, engineers, and professional, and athletic acquaintances. Sitting among many of these important people from both Philadelphia and Camden, sat a tearful and lonely young boy, watching an important part of his life surely pass away.

Even though Oscar was gone, I continued to visit Mrs. Glenn for many years. While I was in the service during the war, I wrote to her regularly. I kept up the friendship with her until the time of her death in 1948.

The making and development of friendships throughout ones lifetime is an amazing and beautiful process. Some friendships are made on purpose, some haphazardly; some by happen-stance while others are developed over a long period of time and relationship. Which is the best and more lasting way? One way is no better than the rest provided that the two people want the friendship to last, have a mutual respect for each other, a knowledge that one will stand by the other in bad times as well as good, and an honest attempt to keep in touch regardless of circumstances and distance.

I have in mind my teenage friends of the 1930's and 1940's. Bill Molter and I started out at an early age. We were together in grade school at Holy Name. When seating was arranged in alphabetical order, since both of our names began with the letter "M," we were usually given desks close to each other. Most of the time, Bill was seated behind me. Bill always says that I copied from him, but I defend myself by reminding him of the difficulty of copying from a person seated in the back. Oh well! We both passed. After graduating from Holy Name, we both went to Penn Treaty Jr. High and then on to Northeast High School before entering the service. Much later, after three hard years of evening classes and study, I did finally graduate from Liberty High School in Bethlehem, Pa. All of his life, Bill lived on Martha Street which was one street over from Trenton Avenue where I lived. When our family moved to Arizona Street, about six blocks away, we lost contact for some time except while in class. On Arizona Street, I met and developed a friendship with bill Eckart, a neighbor. In time the Eckart family moved away to Mascher and Lehigh Streets. While visiting Bill, I met Johnny Roberts who would become a close friend and valued buddy and friend. I took Johnny around to meet Bill Molter and through him, we then met Joe Schum who also lived on Martha Street. In this way, the four of us along with Jim Kelly and Charlie Brown developed a brotherhood of sorts. Such a circuitous route can be the pathway to a long and lasting friendship. We really all grew up together. We played together, fought together, rode horses together, drank together, and entered World War II together. Joe, Bill, and I were inducted into the armed services on the same day and went to Indiantown Gap, an induction center, together. Over the past fifty years, the three of us have kept in contact and remain good friends to this day. I pray that it continues.

Many years later, Bill and I had the honor of being a part of Joe Schum's wedding to Marge Dwyer, a beautiful young lady who was also a student at Holy Name. She was in a class one year ahead of Bill and I. Since the classes were not co-ed, I really did not know Marge that well. Over the years, the Schums have remained my dearest and most cherished friends, in spite of the distance between us, they in San Diego, California and I in Bethlehem, Pennsylvania.

Starting at a new school, especially a public school was a new experience for Bill Molter and me. Neither one of us could afford catholic high school, so we decided to go to Penn Treaty Jr. High the following year. It certainly was different in public school. Instead of sitting in the same room all day, we now had to change classrooms every forty-five minutes. We now had girls in every class except shop. Girls in skirts and blouses instead of uniforms; girls, some with makeup; girls wearing silk stockings; and did I say short skirts; girls, short girls; tall girls; blonde girls; and more girls. How were we ever to get any studying or work done? Here we had homeroom, assembly, and study hall. Now instead of nuns, we were taught by both male and female teachers.

We did have a good year at Penn Treaty and did learn a lot. We both enrolled in wood shop and electrical shop and worked on projects together. Some subjects such as history, math, and english left us bored and complacent because what they were teaching, at the time, we had already studied in grade school. We could just sit back in class and still come up with a passing grade on the tests. Of course, we were not doing ourselves any good. We could have applied ourselves and made better use of our time.

Walking home from school one day, Clyde Dillon and I noticed two young girls walking ahead of us. One of the girls I had seen in school and felt that she was a pretty nice young lady. She was a shy but attractive girl with a dark complexion; dark, very long hair; exceptionally large dark eyes; and a very nice figure that was enhanced by a tight-fitting yellow sweater. Clyde and I managed to build up enough courage to approach them. Upon catching up to the girls, we asked them if we could walk home with them. By the time that we reached the corner of our street, we were well acquainted, having learned where they lived, their names, and a promise to meet again. That didn't take very long.

Ruth Rayner and Ida McAnny spent a lot of time with Clyde and I during the summer after we graduated from Penn Treaty Jr. High. Ruth's mother enjoyed having young boys around the house so she gave us free rein during the hot summer afternoons. We never did see Ruth's father. He was always away on some mysterious business. We suspected that he had a lady friend someplace. We teens would play games, listen to some baseball on the radio, or just hang around the house. We never caused or got into any serious trouble. Ida and I did, however, become very friendly and attached to each other. She lived, at that time with her parents and a younger brother in a small apartment on Cumberland Street. Ida also had an older brother who was either in the army or the CCC camp.

Even though Ida and I met by chance, I believe that her parents and mine did know each other. My brother, Phil, had been dating Josephine Meisensahl, a cousin of Ida's. John married Marge Meisensahl, also a cousin. I do not remember all of the particulars, but when it was time for John McAnny to come home, there just was not enough room for Ida and an older brother in the apartment. It was decided, I do not know by whom, that Ida should come to live at our house. Mom and Dad did get to love Ida and treated her like a daughter. She was always a pleasant and lovely young lady, easy to love and care for; however, the living arrangements were not good for a boyfriend-girlfriend relationship. She shared a bedroom with my sister, Betty.

Ida stayed at our home for well over a year until the McAnnys could find a suitable house. Ida and I saw each other at breakfast before school, during school, after school, all evening, and every weekend. Dad often slipped me some money to take Ida to a Sunday afternoon movie. Later when we both started to work, we were together before work, after work, and so on. We did continue to date after Ida moved out and went to live with her parents. We did eventually drift apart but we were still very good friends. She was there to see us off when Frank and I went into the service.

When I was working for Francis Denny Cosmetics, the average pay was around fifteen dollars for a forty-four hour work week. Our pay came in an envelope and usually consisted of a few small bills and some change. A raise of five cents an hour was not to be taken lightly. One of this magnitude was given only after some deep thought and soul searching by the employer and only to workers of high caliber. The recipient of such largess was told not to reveal his raise to any of his fellow workers. They feared that other workers would also ask for a raise.

I remember during one Christmas season, Ida and I were walking up Front Street where we stopped to look into the window of a local jewelry store. She expressed a desire for a wrist watch that was displayed prominently in the window, something that she had never owned. The watch had a price tag of $24.00, a sum that I could little afford after purchasing small gifts for the family. A few days later, when I was alone, I went into the jewelry store to speak to the store owner. After some haggling, he agreed to put the watch in a drawer and hold on to it for me. The practice of layaway was unheard of in those days; therefore, just striking such a deal was somewhat of an accomplishment. From that time on, every payday, after depositing a dollar in a savings account, I would stop at the jewelry store and pay fifty cents toward the purchase of the watch. By the following Christmas, I was able to pay off the $24.00 and present the gift to Ida. I suppose that all of this was a lesson in the importance of stretching a meager pay by the use of thrifty practices.

I believe that I was about sixteen years old when Frank went into the CCC (Civil Conservation Corp). The CCC and WPA

(Work Progress Administration) were two of President Roosevelt's New Deal programs. These programs put thousands of unemployed people to work. Instead of being on the public dole in the form of welfare, young men could work for the federal government and receive compensation. The WPA built roads, bridges, and parks that we still benefit from today. Artists were put to work painting murals that still exist in many public buildings. Members of the CCC went into a military-like life. They were billeted in barracks, had uniforms, and were supplied with meals. I believe that they were paid about twenty-five dollars a month. After Frank joined the CCC, he was sent to New Mexico for a year where he worked on forest conservation. I can remember Frank sending colorful satin pillow cases to Mom that were embroidered with scenes from New Mexico.

When he came home, Frank was not idle for very long. Within days, he found a job at Ewart's Cafeteria in downtown Philly. It was a very fortunate move for him because he made the acquaintance of another employee who would change his life. Jean McGovern came from a large Irish Catholic family in St. Anne's Parish. The destiny of this young couple was marked from the moment they met. Eventually they would marry and have a large family of their own.

Bill Molter and I were walking up Front Street under the "El." A very attractive and seductive young girl, with long, dark, and curly hair passed by.

"Hi Joe!" she called in a sweet and sultry voice.

"Hey Joe, do you now her?" Bill asked.

"Yes, I know her," I answered.

"Well, then, invite her to my party next Saturday," he said.

"No way," I replied, "I'll introduce you to her and you can ask her to the party."

I knew Letty and her twin sister, Joan. I also knew that they were somewhat on the wild side. They were identical twins and they loved to play tricks on people and try to confuse them. You never really did know for sure which one of them you were talking to unless they wanted you to know. Having had a few dates with Letty and been in their home several times, I knew just how wild they could be. A movie date was, at times, when you did not have enough money and the girl would agree to meet you in the lobby, then go to the dark balcony and spend a few hours trying to put your arm around her shoulders and if you were lucky, perhaps get a kiss or maybe even two.

We caught up with Letty and Bill extended the invitation. The Molter house was a small row home on Martha Street. The living room and dining room were no larger than 12 feet by 12 feet, and a very small kitchen with a shed in the back. A toilet bowl was in the comer of the shed. Parties here, due to a lack of space, could not be large or lively. There was always plenty to eat and some beer. No one really drank to excess. We usually wound up playing cards or shooting dice for pennies. After the party, we were to sleep at Bill's house on the floor.

Should I say that Letty put a spark of life into the party? She surely did. Music was playing and Letty began to dance. She stood on the table and spun to the rhythm of the music. The faster the music, the faster she would spin. It soon became quite obvious that she was missing some articles of clothing. There was a group of women sitting around the kitchen table. When I was in the shed, I could hear the voices of Mrs. Molter, Bill's older sister, Rose, and a couple of other women.

"Mom, did you see what that girl was doing?" asked Rose.

"Yes, I certainly did," replied Mrs. Molter.

"Why, she doesn't have any pants on," someone said.

"Who brought her to the party?" another voice inquired.

"Bill said that Joe brought her." I heard someone else say.

After leaving the shed, I meekly made my way through the kitchen, past the stern looks of the women and got Letty into her coat. Bill did not tell anyone that she was there on his invitation.

I saw that Letty got home safely and returned to the party. When I got there, the house was in total darkness. Apparently, the party had come to an early end. Assuming that the guys were playing a trick on me, I began to pound on the front door and calling for Bill to let me in.

With that, the upstairs window opened and Mrs. Molter's face appeared,

"Go home Joe McLaughlin! Just go home. The party's over."

I remember waking up the dark and quiet Dauphin Street on my way home and thinking to myself, Hm! I wonder what that was all about. Why did they stop the party?

Apparently, Dad thought that I had gone to school long enough. One Sunday, when I had returned from church, he informed me that he had made arrangements for me to talk to Bill Clark, a friend of the family, about a job for me. There was no question or discussion. I was to go to the Clark home that very afternoon. After talking to Bill, it was decided that I would report for work the following morning. On Monday morning, I very reluctantly prepared myself for my first job.

Bill Clark was the foreman at "Frances Denny Cosmetic Company" located at Seventh and Market Streets in downtown Philly. "Frances Denny" was the maker of very famous and expensive makeup products that were sold only in top rated exclusive stores. The plant was located in several third floor or lofts of a number of buildings along Seventh Street that were connected by several ramps. These were old dust covered interiors that were not the best of conditions for the manufacture of facial products.

Bill's younger brother, John, and I started out doing the most menial of tasks such as cleaning up, stacking boxes, and moving merchandise and product from one building to another. We were paid thirty-five cents per hour and were expected to work five and a half days a week for a total of forty-four hours a week. Boy! I finally had a steady wage. I could pay for the "El" ride to work, buy my own lunch, give Mom some money every week, have my own spending money, and still put a couple of dollars a week into a bank account. Perhaps working wouldn't be so bad after all.

I worked at the Seventh Street location for a couple of months when the company decided to relocate to a better building at 60th and Woodland Avenue. It was a far better place to work but it also meant another half-hour trolley ride. The new building was spacious, clean, and a nice place to work. There was even a rest and lunch area with tables and chairs, on the second floor. An unheard of benefit for employees, at that time. At first, I operated the filling machines for face and cold creams which were then leveled and capped by a group of ladies seated around a table. After that, I was made an assistant to Dr. Bascha, the company chemist.

In this capacity, I would obtain secret formulas from the chemist and then proceed to mix creams, bath salts, and face powders, then checking under an ultra violet light to ascertain the proper color. The odor from the perfumes that were mixed into these products also entered into my pores causing people on the "El," while traveling home, to look questioningly in my direction, especially during summer months when I would perspire. The aroma from the mixture of a variety of scents was unbelievable. Even at home, I was in for a lot of teasing. My brothers could not allow a chance like that to pass unanswered. No amount of bathing would or could remove all of the offensive odors, in those days, no man could afford to smell like that. It was better to have body odor. I certainly did not need aftershave or a deodorant.

There was a large open field between the plant and the backyards of a row of homes along 60th Street. Every day a lovely young Italian girl would come into the field to burn household trash causing quite a stir among the men in the building, including myself. Some, not including myself, would call out and make remarks about her remarkable figure. I could not disagree because she certainly was pleasing to the eye. I just stood back and admired the view. From then on, I did not eat lunch in the plant. I made it a point to cross that field every day at lunchtime, on my way to a corner store that was near her house, to buy something for lunch. I really don't know whether or not she saw me although I was hoping that she would. A few days of this and my efforts were fruitful. She came into the store, allowing me to start a conversation. This went on for about a week until finally Mae Marcino invited me to join her for lunch at her house. From that time on, I had lunch every day with Mae. This did not set well with the men at the company because I was depriving them of their lunchtime pleasure. Mae and I soon became quite close and began to date. She had just graduated from high school that spring and was taking care of her parent's home while she was making a decision to go to work or to continue on with her education. Eventually, I did meet her parents, who graciously invited me into their home. Her father was a professor at the University of Pennsylvania and her mother was a teacher in the school district. Trying to date and maintain a relationship really became difficult. The daily trip to work on the Frankford "El," the Market Street Subway, and then a trolley car up Woodland Avenue, took an hour and sometimes more depending on the weather and traffic. Sometimes, I traveled home, ate a burned dinner, got cleaned up and dressed, and then made the trip back to Mae's house, went on our date, and again made the hour-long trip back home. Sleep would overtake me on the return trip. Distance and time were not conducive to building a relationship of any kind. Falling asleep on the "El" in the middle of the night was not the wisest thing to do, although in those days one could feel much safer than it is possible to do today. Months of this routine prompted me to seek employment closer to home.

In time, I managed to get a job at Cuneo Eastern Press, which was a publishing house for Life and Look magazines, many comic books, periodicals, and other books. I started out moving skids of paper and pages of magazines from one machine to another. Then I was put on a cutting machine. This machine cut and trimmed the three sides of "The Red Cross First Aid Book." The cutter was located at the opening of a U-shaped table where a group of women seated around the table would wrap the stacks of books prior to shipping. As the stacks left the machine after cutting and trimming, I would place the stacks on the table in front of the women. At times, one of the women would, on purpose I am sure, knock a pile of books off of the table. When I bent down to retrieve the scattered books, several of the women sat there with legs apart offering me an unbelievable view, one that I had never experienced before. To the amusement of all, I would rise up with a complexion that could rival a coat of many colors. This job did not last very long. Many of us were laid off. On our final day of work, we were given our last pay envelope and released early in the afternoon. An older woman, she must have been at least thirty, asked me if I would mind walking her home. Of course not, why should I mind? When we got there, she then invited me up to her apartment where we sat at the kitchen table and enjoyed a beer and some pleasant conversation. Gradually, she moved closer to me. In my inexperienced mind, I had not the slightest idea that I was being seduced. I finally realized what was happening when her hand started to move uncertainly but surely up my thigh where upon I made a hasty retreat and bolted out the door.

Bill Molter and I managed to get a job at a hamper factory in the neighborhood. This job did not last very long at all. The pay was low and there was no expectation of doing better. The only memorable thing about that experience is that we met Jim "Killer" Kelly. Jim was welcomed into our circle of friends. He was really a nice guy but with one fault that became increasingly obvious as you got to know him. Jim was accident prone. If something was going to happen, it surely would happen to or with Jimmy. One had to be exceedingly careful while working with him, whether it be assisting him when operating a dolly, lifting boxes, or rolling 55 gallon drums that were tilted on the rim which made it easier to roll but could be very hazardous; thus, the nickname "Killer Kelly." Jim survived the war although it is beyond me how he did manage that but thank God that he did. Many years later, he took a job on the railroad which was the worst place for someone with an affinity for disaster. Fate was lurking in the shadows for the right opportunity for Jim to make a mistake. The dark lady of calamity, bided her time until in the end a fleeting moment of chance would present itself: One night, as he was uncoupling two freight cars, he lost his footing and fell, as the train began to move. The momentum caused him to fall to the side rather than straight down between the cars. This sideward movement saved his life; however, Jim did lose both of his legs. He and Bill remained in the neighborhood and were inseparable and loyal friends until Jim "Killer" Kelly passed away.

The three of us left the hamper factory and together found work at James Good Chemical Co. This was a plant across the street from Molter's, commonly known as "SOAPY." If ever a place was waiting for a fire, it was the "SOAPY" and indeed it did suffer fire on a number of occasions. The company manufactured soaps, resin, petrolatum, carbontetrochloride, and other chemicals. We operated a machine that filled fire extinguisher containers with carbon-tet, a compound that was, in later years, found to be a carcinogen. Filling 55 gallon drums with powdered resin petrolatum, an amber colored gel used in lubricants and medical ointments, much like "Vaseline," required two men at the hot vat containing the gel. When the vat became too cool for the compound to flow freely through a tube to the drums below, one man had to enter the huge still-warm tank and, with a shovel, remove the slow-moving gel from the sides and bottom of the vat. The other man at the top and outside of the vat, awaiting his turn to enter the tank, kept a constant vigil to see that his co-worker did not pass out from the heat. This person was, usually within a few minutes, covered with perspiration. If in the tank too long, he would indeed pass out. Working with resin was not any better. There was a small two-story building outside and away from the main building. It measured about ten feet by ten feet. The upper room contained a hopper and a grinding machine that pulverized the chunks of resin that was fed into the machine by the man on the upper level. The man below would fill 55 gallon drums with the powdered resin. Bill and I would usually work as a team, taking turns at each level. We did wear a mask, but I seriously doubt that a mask was really any help. Our clothing, hands, hair, including eyelashes and brows, would be covered with a thick coating of a sticky gooey mixture of resin and sweat. When Mrs. Molter walked by one afternoon, she didn't even recognize her own son.

Our next adventure into gainful employment was when our whole band of friends were hired to work at Harbison's Dairy. Both my dad and Bill's father worked at the dairy. All but Joe Schum went together to work at Harbison's. Joe already had a good steady job at Swift's Meat Packaging Co. It was a good day for us but I fear a sad one for Mr. Richie, our foreman. We were all full of mischief and pulling pranks on, not only each other, but also on poor Mr. Richie. He did have some difficulty in keeping us in line because he never could complain about our work. We always did our job assignment properly and in haste which allowed us more time to horse around. To get to work at the dairy, we were required to join the Teamsters Union. Only a few years before that, the union was engaged in a battle with the dairies to represent their employees. The battle was long and fierce. At times, union men would overturn milk delivery wagons and empty milk cans causing precious milk to flow down the streets and into the storm sewers. The dairy owners were forced to give in to such tactics, leading to a closed shop where workers were compelled to join the union.

As a youngster at the Malta Boat Club, Oscar tried to get me to acquire a taste for grapefruit juice, telling me that it was good for me. At the dairy, Dad encouraged me to drink buttermilk. It also was supposed to be good for me. Dad drank a quart of buttermilk every day. That was not for me. Bill, Jim, and I would each drink half of a quart bottle of chocolate milk and then mix the remainder with a pint of heavy cream. I am sure that Dad disapproved, however, if anything was going to finally put some fat on my bones that surely would. It didn't.

Our jobs at the dairy were mostly menial. When necessary, we had to clean and scrub the pasteurizing room. On certain days we had to arrive early in the morning and start to work in the ice house where it was required to move 100 pound blocks of ice, chop the blocks into small chunks, and load the pieces onto the delivery wagons. Just another one of my bitter experiences with the cold. I never seemed to get used to it. Our primary responsibility was to stack the empty wooden milk crates when they were returned by the wagons on their return. Here again is where we drove Mr. Richie to exasperation. We would stack the crates in rows of eight to ten crates high, leaving a space in the center where we would hide after pulling a stack in after us to close the entrance. We remained as quiet as a church mouse as Richie searched for us. I know, it was a terrible thing to do, but we were not much more than kids. Bill and I remained at Harbison's up until we enlisted in the service.

While we were in the Army, the Teamsters Union ran periodic letter writing contests for servicemen. The winner of these contests would receive twenty-five dollars. Whenever I found myself getting short of cash, I would sit down and compose a letter to the union with praises for the union activities interspersed with a wide sprinkling of patriotism and flag waving, most of which I did truly feel and believe. Within a few weeks, I would receive a check in mail call for twenty-five dollars.

It was a cold Sunday morning in December, a very good day to go horseback riding. The animals would be frisky today. I had gone to mass at St. Boniface Catholic Church at Norris and Diamond Streets. St. Bonnies was a beautiful old church in a mostly German parish, where Mom had gone to school. All of her children attended school at Holy Name, a predominately Irish parish. It had been some time since I had last gone to Mass. I had been neglectful about going to church ever since I started to work. I was anxious to go riding so I hurried home and changed into riding clothes; western shirt and pants, a heavy jacket, and cowboy boots. Bill Molter, Joe Schum, Charlie Brown, and John Roberts had similar outfits. We met at our house which was more conveniently located near the York-Dauphin Street station of the "El." it was a rare sight to see a group of young guys in western outfits walking in our neighborhood. It did require a little bit of guts and courage, however, we never did have any trouble. Certainly, some people on the "El" eyed us with some suspicion and curiosity but were hesitant to say anything that would warrant any action on our part. We got off the train at Frankford Avenue and Torresdale, got on a trolley going out Torresdale to Welsh Road. We had to walk a good distance out Welsh Road to "Chat's Riding Stable." Cowboy boots were not made for walking and Joe Schum, even in boots, still retained his usual bouncy walk with his head popping up above the rest of us, at every step.

Chat welcomed us to the stables. He knew that we were all experienced riders except Charlie Brown who usually managed to hang on to the animal's neck and begged us to slow down. We had been coming to Chat's for some time so he would permit us to ride his better horses. He also knew that we treated his animals with respect and would not overwork- them and return them to the stable covered with sweat and lather. Most of us worked at Harbison's Dairy and knew the enjoyment of riding but at the same time, we were aware of the horse's limitations. Joe Schum did not work at Harbison's but shared our respect of horses and mutual love for riding. We often helped around the stables and if some riders failed to return on time, Chat would send us out to locate them and bring them back. We knew all of Chat's horses by sight and by name. We were also familiar with every path in "Pennypack Park" and the Park Police were familiar to us. On this particular day, Chat had given us his favorite three-quarter western ponies. They were small, very fast, and had an incredible ability to, with the slightest tug on the reins, plant all four hooves on the ground and stop on a dime, almost unseating the rider from the saddle. They were wonderfully trained animals. We had proven ourselves to be, not a gang of inner-city thugs from "Fishtown," as we no doubt appeared to be at the beginning, by the horsy set but a group of capable and responsible young men. I did enjoy riding in the spring and summer with the crowds, hikers, fishermen, and just every day people out to enjoy a day in the park, but I think that my favorite time, despite the cold, was riding on a day with a light snow fall. The gentle sway of the horse, the soft crunch of the dried fallen leaves, under the thin blanket of snow at each step of a hoof, the quiet rush of the flowing water in the creek, all combined to lull one into momentary daydreaming. Very few people would be out and I would encounter an occasional rider or park guard. I would ride along, feeling the warmth of the horse underneath me and get caught up in a reverie of thought, only to be broken by a snort of the animal, accompanied by a gush of vapor emanating from its wide nostrils. Lonesome? Perhaps, but still a chance to gather one's thoughts and clear one's mind. A therapy of the mind and soul, recognized long ago by the cowboys of years long gone, while performing the lonely task of riding the herd or tending the grazing cattle in the grasslands of the old west.

When we had finished riding for the day, we began a leisurely trip back home, stopping at the "Horn and Hardart's Cafeteria" for lunch where some diners seemed somewhat reluctant to sit near us. From there we decided to take in a movie at the Midway Theatre at Kensington and Allegheny or "K and A" as it was commonly known to anyone from Philly. As we found seats in the balcony, we did notice people in nearby seats, after some discreet whispering, get up and move to another section of the theatre. I realized that we did smell a little horsy, but that certainly did not call for such rudeness. Yes, we did reek of sweat, horse, and no doubt a little manure. If the feature film were a western, we could, as we made our way up the aisle, add an element of odoriferous reality.

Later on, during the show, we became aware of some loud talking and nervous movement throughout the theatre. Some movie goers were moving about and others hastily left the building. Not knowing what was going on, we got up to leave. We walked past the candy stand where two friends of mine were working. I stopped to talk to Ida McAnny and her sister, Millie. We asked them about the sudden commotion.

"Didn't you hear?" asked Millie.

"Hear what?"

"The Japanese have bombed Pearl Harbor," she said.

"So where the hell is Pearl Harbor?" someone asked.

"I don't know," Millie said. "But I think that it is somewhere in the Pacific."

"That shouldn't bother us. Those Japs wouldn't dare attack us, besides there is a Japanese ambassador in Washington right now signing a peace agreement."

"What we have to worry about is those damn krauts."

"Who knows where they will strike next. Oh well, that's their problem. The people in Europe will have to deal with that."

"Yes! We have the Atlantic on one side and the Pacific on the other. The oceans are too wide so no one could make an attack on us."

Walking along Kensingston Avenue, the conversation continued.

"Even if it does mean war, we can lick their Jap asses in no time at all."

"The Japs are like Chinks, ain't they?"

"Naw, the Chinks, at least, know how to run a laundry. The Japs only know how to copy things and make cheap junk."

"Yea! Even their boats are called junks."

"How can they even shoot a gun? They are all near-sighted little dwarfs who wear coke-bottle glasses."

How naive we were. New words: black-out, draft, GI, Wac, new phrases; "Kilroy was here," "Rosie the Riviter," "Loose lips sink ships," "Uncle Sam needs you," new places; Tarawa, Saipan, Iwo Jima, and Guadalcanal, were soon to become commonplace in our society and language. The war would go on for years, changing the lives of everyone, rich and poor, young and old, city bred and country born. Untold millions of lives would be lost in the coming years; all because of the greed and self-importance of a few madmen.

That night, the family gathered around the kitchen table to discuss the events of the day and just what they would mean to us, in the coming days. Which and how many of us at that table would be called into the service? How soon would all of this take place? Mom as Mom would, sat away from the table and with folded hands in her lap, appeared to be listening, made few comments. She still had memories of World War I. The glistening in her eyes betrayed the tears that were building up as she contemplated the thought of one or more of her sons, now sitting at her table, going off to an uncertain future in a war. Little did she know that in a year or two, she would be placing, in her front window, a banner with five stars, depicting five sons serving in a war, in places that she had little or no knowledge of and had never heard of their names or location. In the next four years, Mom and Dad would turn gray and age twenty years. Phil and Dan, being the oldest, would be the first to go. Frank would be drafted next, and I volunteered to go with him. John, married with two children, would be the last son to be called to serve his country in World War II. Billy would later serve in Korea.

Very soon I would be going into the Army. That would be the end of riding for awhile unless I were able to get into the cavalry, however, even then, horses were giving way to tanks and motorized vehicles. A young neighbor had shown some interest in buying my riding clothes and boots. It would be quite some time before I would be using that outfit again, if ever, so I agreed to sell.

One last ride was a necessity. I did not contact Bill Molter or Joe Schum because I wanted to ride alone. I rode the "El" and a trolley car to Pennypack Park. The short walk to "Chat's" stable always seemed much longer when walking in Western boots. The cold winter day brought a chill and redness to my cheeks and awareness that this would be a good day for a ride. The horses would be frisky and ready to go. When I reached the stables, Chat came out of the tack room and greeted me with an unusually cheery, "Hi Joe, what are you doing here today?" I say cheery because his demeanor was usually caustic, gruff, and hard. Chat was very protective of his animals and anyone returning a horse puffing and covered with lather was in for a very rough verbal bawling out. He would make no attempt to restrain his anger and the unfortunate culprit would know immediately and with certainty that he would no longer be welcome at "Chat's."

I explained to him why I happened to be there on that cold weekday when no one else was around. It was my desire to have one last ride before going into the service. When I made an approach to enter the stable, Chat stopped me.

"Wait here Joe," he said, "I'll get a horse for you."

A short time later, Chat came out of the stable leading a beautiful chestnut stallion. Obviously, this was not a rental horse but one of Chat's favored animals. The horse stood there proudly displaying his arched neck, blaze face, long flowing tail and mane, deep broad chest, and wide flaring nostrils. He nervously moved back and forth and pawed the hard frozen ground in anticipation. In truth, this was not a horse that Chat would entrust into what he deemed, incapable hands.

During the first few minutes, horse and rider engaged in an initial but eternal struggle to determine who would be in control. He would pull against the reins in an effort to wrest them from my hands and then throw his massive head back only to be stopped by the martingale running from the cinch to the head strap of the bridle. He constantly attempted to move in his own direction or would walk sideways. He only enforced my determination to stay in the saddle and assert control. After settling down, we rode along the creek in harmony as we both enjoyed the cold that even to me was invigorating, a cold that was broken only by the heat from the body of the animal beneath me. The park was empty except for an occasional rider or a mounted Park Policeman. We had a quiet ride that encouraged thought and contemplation. Thoughts that were broken only by the gentle ripple of the water flowing down the stream. The horse's ears would perk upright to the scurrying sound of a chipmunk or a squirrel frightened by the snap of a twig under the hoof of the horse.

We rode past he "Devil's Pool," a rapidly spinning whirlpool, according to the legend among the kids who frequented the park, had no bottom but swirled, spun, and drilled its way to the center of the world where it joined with Satan's own underworld River Styx, one the rivers of Hades across which the souls of the damned were ferried.

The clouds began to darken. A light dusting of snow flurries began to fall. My thoughts ran the whole gamut of experiences and relationships, past, present, and future. Was I doing the right thing? Phil and Dan were already in the service. I thought of jobs and the future. My future. Was I going anyplace? Apparently not. I was now adding to the worries and anxieties of my parents. Could they possibly get along on Dad's pay while we were all away? The horse shied to the left almost unseating me from the saddle. Something must have spooked him. Probably an animal running across the brown, dried leaves. He settled down and we continued on our way. Surely, I should be able to spend some time in the same outfit as Frank. Who the hell am I kidding? There was no guarantee. We could be separated. I thought about school. My thoughts now seemed to be running rampant and amok. What about girlfriends who had been a part of my life? Would I see them again? They would no doubt be married by the time that I would be home again. Why did I decide to enlist? Was it out of patriotism? I truly don't know. Everyone else was going to serve and I suppose that I also wanted to be a part of the crowd. Did I think that war was fun and games and adventure? A guy could get killed. Some us would not be coming home. Boy! How I wish that Oscar were here. He could advise me and ease my troubled thoughts. "Oscar! Why did you leave me so soon and with so many unanswerable questions and imponderables?" The snow was getting heavier and was piling up on the path. The hundred of naked tree limbs were reaching up to the darkening clouds, like bare arms beseeching them for an answer to my torment and dilemma. Why did I always feel different than my brothers, street friends, and buddies? Why did I think differently than they? They could accept life and whatever it dealt them and cope with it. I could not accept street ways and life as it was without questions. Oscar instilled in me the desire and ability to think differently but without the education and knowledge to know why. A soft cloud of warm mist emanating from the horse's nostrils, gently rose and brushed across my face like a soft damp caress. Maybe we could send some money home to Mom. I wonder what we will have to pay for in the Army. Toothbrush and shaving kit, I guess. Is war just like we saw in "All Quiet on the Western Front?" I should have talked to Uncle Bill. Mom and Dad were starting to age already with just Phil and Dan gone. John, even with two children, will probably be inducted soon. My God! That will be five of us in the Army. Why us? If the war lasted long enough, it was possible that even Billy could be called up. That would make six. Surely the war could not last that long. As I started to lean forward in the saddle to pat the horse's neck and softly whisper words of encouragement into his ear, I saw flakes of snow landing on his head and neck; flakes that immediately melted and disappeared from the body heat of the animal. The branches of the Evergreen trees started to gently bow from the weight of the thickening snow, as we passed by. It was getting difficult to see through the veil of white. Why was I looking for an answer? There seemed to be no satisfactory answer. I had turned eighteen and was now eligible for the draft. Sooner or later I would be receiving a notice in the mail. By enlisting in the Army, I would be throwing myself into a life and environment that was completely alien to my beliefs. In the silence of the snowfall, the comforting squeak of the leather saddle appeared to be much louder than usual. I released my grip on the reins and gave the horse its head. It instinctively knew that I was relinquishing control and turned toward the stable. He broke into a gentle canter as I eased back into the saddle. He slowed down and picked his way through the deepening snow. The struggle was over. What was done was done. There was no turning back. The die was cast.

"How are we going to tell our parents?" Bill asked.

"I have no idea." I answered.

Bill Molter and I had, after many discussions, finally made our decisions. We were going to enlist in the Army. Frank and Joe Schum had received their "Notification of Induction." It would be just a matter of time before Bill and I would be drafted, therefore, we felt that we both should enlist.

At that time, Bill and I were working at Harbison's Dairy. Dad was working in the washroom, where the milk wagons and trucks were taken for periodic washes. The room had large sliding doors which Dad kept closed because of the water and constant dampness. Dad slid the door open in answer to my knock. It was then that I told him that I was going into the service. I tried to explain to him, that by doing so now, perhaps Frank and I could serve together and help each other. It proved to be a very difficult time for Pop, as it would be for any father, forced to realize that more than half of this family would be going off to war. With tears in his eyes, he accepted my decision but told me that it was up to me to tell Mom.

Telling Mom was one of the hardest things that I would ever have to do. I knew just how much it would hurt her. Her whole life was devoted to her family. Now, her world seemed to be falling apart. With five sons in the service, the next three years would be sad and lonely years for her. No amount of words and explanation could soften or lessen her sadness. All of my efforts were futile. The only thing that made it a little easier was the fact that Frank and I would be together.

CHAPTER THREE

INDUCTION

CHAPTER THREE

INDUCTION

February 8, 1943 was the date of our induction. We were to report to the Police Station at Trenton Avenue and Dauphin Street. There were, perhaps one hundred of us, many of us who had been schoolmates. Add five or six family members for each inductee, and it was quite a large number of people. The McLaughlin group included Frank and me, Mom, Dad, our sister Betty, and our brother Billy, Ida McAnny, and Jean McGovern. The group was paraded or marched up Dauphin Street to the "El" station at Front Street. I remember that it was garbage day so we had to avoid bags of the stuff as we proceeded up the street. Hopefully, this was not a precursor of things to come.

We were taken to 30th Street Station, where we boarded a train going to Indiantown Gap, an induction center located near Harrisburg, Pennsylvania. Frank was the last to board the train. We had to pull him into the last car as the train was leaving the station. He had prolonged his goodbyes with Jean until the last minute. As the train pulled out of the station, the windows were thrown open and everyone tried to get a chance to lean out of a window to wave a final farewell. All of these young men were in a joyous and jovial mood; laughing and joking, singing, and playing cards, all attempting to give the appearance of a carefree bravado.

This was a group of teens and young men; some good students putting off their education to answer a call to duty, some were toughs who should have been in reform school, most were from poor families, some who could and should go on to become lawyers, doctors, or leaders in society, some street wise and tough but honest, raised on movies that glorified war and heroes of World War I. Upon arriving at Indiantown Gap, we were taken to a large building to undergo examinations, both physical and mental. As we were herded down the street, we were greeted by catcalls from the "veterans" who were hanging out of the windows in nearby barracks.

"Hey! You guys are in for it."

"Wait till you get those needles."

"Yeah, that corkscrew needle shoved up your ass."

"Keep in line you rookies; you look like a bunch of girls."

In the course of the examination, we were to endure an endless variety of questions and embarrassing probes.

"How far did you go in school?"

"Do you like girls?"

"Do you like boys?"

Suddenly, a hand and finger was pushed roughly into your groin. Someone shouted, "Turn your head and cough." What the hell did coughing have to do with your balls?

"Bend over and spread your cheeks," someone yelled.

Oh no! They aren't going to shove something up there, was my first thought. At this point, we did not know what to think or to expect. At the command to straighten up, we did so with a sigh of relief. We were checked from head to toe and everywhere in between.

After lunch, we were taken to the supply depot to be fitted for a uniform. Did I say fitted? Forming a long line that was hurried past a long table, articles of clothing were tossed at us as we called out our shirt size, pants size, and shoe size. Size really didn't mean a thing. The GI's behind the counter didn't even look at the sizes. I guess that they were ahead of the times with "One size fits all."

Poor Bill Molter, that day he became the butt of some jokes around the camp. Out of all of the hundreds of recruits getting uniforms, Bill was the only one who was issued pants that were made out of World War I horse blanket material. They must have itched terribly. No amount of pleading from Bill could bring about an exchange.

That night, we were assigned to a barracks that was equipped with double-decker bunk beds. The room was abuzz with excitement as men exchanged stories about their individual experiences during the day. We started to make acquaintances through conversation and yes, even arguments. Before hitting the sack, we had to shave, shower, and see that our new uniforms were properly folded and hung. Tired as we were, no one was going to fall asleep very fast that night. It was during that sleepless period of the first night, that I would pose the question to myself many times in the next three years, "What the hell am I doing here?"

The next day we would get the much feared shots. After breakfast, we were ordered to prepare for more physical examinations by removing all of our clothing except our socks and boots. After donning our stiff and new raincoats, everyone marched down the camp streets to the dispensary. The cold February air rose up from the bottom of the raincoat and was trapped inside. That cold air swiftly drove away any erotic thoughts and softened one's sensuality. Johnny Rudolph looked like a raincoat going down the street under its own power. John was less than five feet tall, so the coat not only reached the ground but dragged along behind him.

Medics, sitting on stools, yelled at the recruits as we were herded past, like cows in a stock yard.

"Ok! Soldier, skin it back, milk it forward."

"Don't be bashful, push it back."

"This one has to be circumcised."

"Don't be shy; move along, we don't have all day."

This was the first day of many "Short Arm Inspections" that we would endure during the coming years. I got the feeling that some of these medics really enjoyed their job. Next, we were told to go back through the doorway. As the recruit entered the room, his eyes were drawn to the pictures of some naked girls on the wall. While his attention was focused on the pictures, a hypodermic needle was jabbed into both of his arms. The immediate sensation was one of searing pain, followed by sore muscles. Both arms were sore all day long and into the night, making it difficult to roll either way in bed. That night, the barracks echoed with moans and groans. Although we expressed disbelief, we were all relieved to have avoided the much talked about and feared "corkscrew."

During these days, we experienced our first taste of regimentation. We were told when to sleep, when to get up, when to eat, when to dress, when to go to the latrine (a new name for the bathroom), and when to get a shower. All of our needs, not our desires, were provided for us. We didn't even have time to think, all day long, until we rolled into our bunks at night and the lights were turned off. After everyone had settled down, we could escape into our own private thoughts; thoughts of home, family, or perhaps a special girlfriend; thoughts of known past or of the unknown and unpredictable future. No one would dare think that obvious but unthinkable thought, that some of us, with no way of knowing who, would not be coming home.

At this point, our group did not know if we were going to stay together or not. Everyone was in a different barracks, except Al Cummons, a friend from school and the drum and bugle band, who slept in the bunk below mine. Al and I were to become very good friends and buddies in the next year.

After about four days of indoctrination at Indiantown Gap, we were herded or should I say loaded onto a train, with our duffle bags and all of the clothing and equipment that we had been assigned. We may have looked like soldiers at this point, but we certainly still had a lot to learn. It was at this time that we lost track of Bill Molter. He was shipped out in a group that was going to the infantry. Frank, Joe Schum, Al Cummons, and I all boarded the same train.

Rumors were spreading rapidly throughout the train. It was not a sleeper, therefore it was assumed that we were not going far, still some men were saying that we were going to California, then Texas, then Arizona. it was all mere speculation because no one really knew. The train did, however, head south. We passed Washington D.C. Everyone started to settle down and relax. Card games were started. Craps were being shot in the aisle. The train continued south. It looked like we would end up in North Carolina. Meals began to be served in the mess car. The sun had gone down and darkness had finally hidden the passing country-side. By now, most of the unlucky gamblers were broke and cursing their bad luck. Not being able to see any identifiable signs along the route, we had no idea as to our location or direction. Eventually the train did start to slow down and come to a stop. Someone said they had seen a sign "SAVANNAH."

"Hey, we are going to Florida."

We all conjured up visions of sunny Florida with palm trees, beautiful girls, and sun shiny days. The train was only stopping for fuel and water. So we thought. We just sat there in the darkness. After waiting for who knows how long, an order came down for us to get our duffle bags and to detrain. We were then told to line up and answer roll call. Next we were loaded onto 2 ½ ton trucks. By this time, we were all beginning to sweat in spite of the cool night air. We arrived at camp around midnight and soon realized that this camp must look much better in the dark than it could possibly look in daylight. Someone bellowed orders for us to get out of the trucks and line up. This is where we separated. Al Cummons and I went into one group, Joe Schum went into another, and Frank into still another. The NCO, Sgt. Jarvis, told us that we were in Camp Stewart, Georgia. Never heard of it. Where the hell is it?

Each man was then assigned to a one-story barracks. Al and I managed to get bunks that were side by side. We placed our shoes and belongings next to our bunks. Eventually the excitement, the squabbling, and talking subsided and I fell into a restless sleep. I must have gone into a sound sleep at some time because someone managed to steal my new dress shoes during the night. I had to use my first months pay to buy another pair. During the first month, when everyone else was dressed for retreat, I had to wear my rough combat boots.

The morning after our first night in camp, we were awakened by the sound of a bugle and some noncom yelling at us to get up, with a phrase that we were to hear frequently in years ahead.

"Let go of your c—ks and grab your socks. Reveille in half an hour. Chow in forty five minutes."

We rushed to the latrine, washed up, brushed our teeth, and then ran back to the barracks to get dressed. Who the hell ever said that the South was warm? We were freezing. It was then that I discovered that my dress shoes were missing. After dressing, we rushed out to the parade ground, lined up, and waited for roll call. There in front of us, stood Sgt. Jarvis in a pair of brand new dress shoes. I had no doubt that they were mine. Who could I report the theft to?

For the next thirteen weeks, we were subjected to "Basic Training." We were taught how to sit, stand, eat, and yes, how to salute. Marching was not too difficult because I did have some training in the Boy Scouts and in the drum and bugle corps. We were not permitted to leave the camp for thirteen weeks, during which time the outfit was drilled in military procedures and discipline. Our platoon sergeants were Sgt. Jarvis, a southern regular army man, and Sgt. Vick, an American Indian. Both were arrogant and ruthless noncoms who enjoyed ordering and pushing people around, especially Yankees. I wish that I could say that they were only doing their job but they seemed to seize every opportunity to belittle someone in order to enhance their own self importance. We were in for a rough thirteen weeks of boot camp.

We soon discovered that half of the outfit was from big cities in Pennsylvania; Erie, Allentown, Bethlehem, Scranton, and Philly. The other half was made up of country boys from Tennessee. We were going to find it very difficult to get along. There were numerous fights and arguments and even some stabbings. It would take months for any friendships to evolve.

The location of the camp did not help the situation. Camp Stewart was located in the Okefenokee Swamp in the southern part of Georgia. Part of the swamp was filled in with sand, asphalt roads were laid, single-story barracks were built, a flag was raised, and it was called "Camp Stewart." Mosquitoes were as large as bees and had a voracious appetite. Snakes of all kinds were to be found in every part of the Camp. On our first hike, we hadn't gone twenty feet into the swamp when we encountered a huge rattlesnake curled up and basking in the sun as it filtered in through the tree tops. To us city boys, it was not a pretty sight. One of the Tennessee boys trapped the snake and skinned it.

Finally, after thirteen weeks of basic training, we could have a pass to go into town; however, the pass was limited to just one evening and not overnight. We all had looked forward to going to town and being able to mingle with civilians. I had taken a shower and put on my new dress uniform. I experienced the same feeling that I had as a child, when I had gotten dressed in my new scout uniform. Along with Joe Schum and several others, we ventured into Hinesville, Georgia. An asphalt two-lane road ran from the main gate to the town. It was only a couple of miles; therefore, we walked to the town. A couple of miles were nothing after all of the hikes that we had marched. Both sides of the road were lined with tents housing all kinds of businesses; a souvenir store, mind and palm readers, some merchants sold food to the unwary young GI's, most of the tents displayed girls out front hawking their wares. The town was a cross road of two dirt roads. At the intersection was a small jail, a bar (other bars were conveniently located along both sides of the narrow streets), a photo shop where every GI went to have his picture taken in his new uniform to send back home, a souvenir store where you could buy anything from a handkerchief to a satin pillow case with pictures of Camp Stewart, Ga, pictured on it. These were just like the ones Frank had sent home to Mom when he was in the CCC camp in New Mexico. The only civilians that we encountered were the people who were trying to separate the young, naïve, and homesick boys from their money, as little as it was. It soon became clear why we didn't get an overnight pass when we saw signs on front lawns that openly proclaimed,

NO DOGS OR GI'S
ALLOWED

From then on, we avoided Hinesville and spent most of our evenings at the camp PX where, at least we were not exploited. At the PX, we could buy beer, food, and just about anything that we wanted, even cameras, at a reasonable price. We only left camp when we could manage to get a weekend pass to Savannah. All over the South, we came upon signs that were unfamiliar to us Northern boys. Signs that read, NO COLORED, WHITES ONLY, and drinking fountains that were to be used only by white people. This was how the South was and would remain for some time to come.

When we finally completed our basic training, our company was informed that we would remain together to form a new Anti-Aircraft Battalion under the command of Lt. Col. Gage. The new outfit to be known as the 490th AA Battalion would be supplied with 40 mm Bufors anti-aircraft guns. We would remain at Camp

Stewart to train and practice. Firing practice usually took place on a nearby beach where fire could be directed out over the ocean. Our target was a long sleeve that was towed by a plane. Those poor pilots did take a chance because some gunners did freeze up and bursts of flack would come dangerously close to the tail of the plane.

My brother, Frank, was placed in A Battery along with Bill Miller and a couple of other friends, Joe Schum went to C Battery and Al Cummons and I were assigned to B Battery.

Battery "B" was scheduled to go on a full day hike of 25 miles, with full pack. As usual, Capt. Williams was at the head of the column. He was determined and would never give in to fatigue. We could tell just how tired he was getting by the position of his helmet liner. At the start of a forced march, his liner would face full front on his head. After a few miles, it would be cocked at an angle to the right of his forehead. Later, it would be at a 45 degree angle. At the end of the hike, his liner would be facing completely to the rear with his gas mask pack riding high on his chest.

At some point of this particular hike, it became necessary to cross a narrow but fairly deep river. Pvt. Peter DiFalco, not being able to swim, aired his concern, and so we placed Pete in between Pvt. Slick and me. A rope was stretched tightly across the river just above the water. The column began to cross the river by moving hand-over-hand along the rope while keeping their M-1 rifles out of the water. Not too difficult a task if you followed instructions. As we made our way across, Pete became more frightened until in midstream, he panicked and went under. Slick and I hastily removed our packs and went down after Pete. Together, in a concerted effort, we were able to get DiFalco to the other side of the river. He hadn't taken in a great amount of water, therefore he seemed to be alright except for being somewhat scared. We continued, after a short rest, on with the march without any further incidents. The three of us were to become good friends and buddies until being transferred to different outfits.

Our bugler, Al Cummons, was a friend of mine from back home. We had lived in the same neighborhood, went to school together, and both were members of the American Legion Drum and Bugle Corps. I could not pretend to be any good at blowing the bugle. Al was very good with the horn; therefore, he was made the "B" Battery bugler. The CQ, charge of quarters, would awaken Al before anyone else. Al would then, while still half asleep, grab his bugle and go out on the company parade ground, which was right next to our barracks. At times, because of the excessive heat, he would stand there stark naked and play reveille. When finished, he would return to his cot. Since he had gotten up before any of us, he was permitted to go back to bed for a couple more hours.

After a night on the town in Savannah, one weekend, a group of us returned to camp somewhat under the weather. Our first stop was the latrine where most were in a desperate need to relieve themselves, while others had their heads close to the hoppers. Al, still being awake and lively, jumped up on one of the toilets and started to sing and dance. Within seconds, the bowl began to move and with a loud crash went tumbling, along with Al, to the concrete floor. Attaining rapid sobriety, we made a fast exit and headed toward our barracks. While in formation, at reveille the following morning, everyone was reprimanded by Capt. Williams, who threatened to withhold all passes until the culprit was found and made to pay restitution for the broken hopper. Back in his barracks after breakfast, we took up a collection. When we had a sufficient amount to pay for the damages, we gave it to Al, who went directly to battery headquarters and confessed to Capt. Williams, of his part in the previous night's activities. He then presented the money to the captain to order a new toilet. A few days later, after a new toilet had been installed, Capt. Williams presented to Al, for his honesty in admitting his guilt, a war bond in the amount that we had collected. Al always seemed to come up smelling like a rose.

As a range setter, I was positioned at my station, behind the "Direction Finder." A man to my left was to estimate the elevation and one on my right would track the lateral movement. It was my responsibility to determine the range or distance of the target. This information was fed into the 40 mm Bufors Anti-aircraft gun. We, along with the equipment, were in a dugout about five feet deep. The 490th was on an aerial practice range at Fort Fisher. We were firing rounds at a sleeve some distance behind a tow plane. I was looking through my scope, observing the blast in the sky, ready to make any necessary changes in our calculations. I spotted three good shots, when suddenly, there was a loud explosion and I could see nothing but clouds of black smoke through my scope.

"Oh my God, what the hell was that?" I thought.

An inferior round of ammunition had failed to go completely into the breach. The breach block had come down, with a force, in the middle of the shell, causing an explosion that ripped apart the gun. Both hands of the loader were severely burned and cut. Not knowing what had happened, the crew just wanted to get out of there as quickly as possible. I remember, climbing up on the edge of the dugout, to my waist, and hanging there. Momentarily, I froze. I could go neither forward nor backward, no matter how I tried or how much strength that I exerted. My feet just hung in midair, not giving me any leverage to push. Forcing my fingers into the ground and taking what seemed to me like an eternity, I was finally able to pull myself out.

After all of the excitement had died down and the injured had been taken to the hospital, Capt. Williams asked for volunteers to go back on the firing line and man another gun. Even though still shaken, the rest of us asked to go back. We were, however, minus a loader. Al Cummons, our bugler volunteered to take the loading position on the crew.

That night, after chow, the gun crew gathered around a fire on the beach. The sky was clear and filled with untold number of stars. The sound of the surf could be beard, beating repeatedly against the sandy beach but was interrupted by the loud voices of the GI's as they excitedly discussed the events of the day. The captain approached our group and asked Private Cummons to stand. He then proceeded to commend Al for his courage in volunteering to join the gun crew after the explosion. At that moment, Private Cummons was promoted to Corporal Cummons. The rest of the crew that had been manning the gun at the time of the explosion got a thank you. Once again, my buddy, Al, came out on top. There really weren't any hard feelings about it, in fact, everyone took it as a joke and it was a subject for laughter for a long time, even by Al Cummons.

A call to report to Battalion Headquarters was rare. Why was I singled out to report there? I couldn't recall any infraction of the rules that would warrant such a call. When I entered the headquarters building, a sergeant directed me to a small office in the rear. Coming to attention, I saluted and reported to a strange captain who was seated behind a desk. I knew that he was not a member of our battalion. The captain introduced himself as an officer in intelligence and informed me that I was to be a member of G2. I did not volunteer for this duty and wished to decline the offer. Apparently, I had been recommended by the previous G2 noncom. The captain told me that I had no say or choice in the matter. He continued by outlining my duties. I was ordered to covertly search out and report any subversive or un-American activities or talk within our unit. I was to make a monthly report, by way of self-addressed and stamped envelopes, to an insurance company in Savannah, Georgia. The insurance company was a cover for the intelligence group, I was told to tell no one of my association with G2 and it was quite obvious that the captain would deny ever having met me.

I did tell my brother, Frank, about the meeting because I was very apprehensive about the whole thing; however, I did not reveal my orders to anyone else. While performing my regular duties, I did keep my eyes and ears open and was aware of all that was said and done. Even the officers were under scrutiny. I felt like a spy and found it very distasteful and contrary to my character and personality. I did make some rather innocuous monthly reports, having found nothing that I would consider to be suspicious. The only incident that I found was of one young man of Pennsylvania German descent who openly made numerous pro-German remarks. So many that he was called, in a humorous way, "The Nazi" by his fellow GI's. I felt that his remarks were so honestly open that they did not warrant reporting. Hell! In spite of my Irish surname, my middle name, Otto, made my partial German descent obvious. What could be more German than Otto? People of Japanese descent were being placed in internment camps in California but not people of German or Italian descent. I later got to meet many Japanese-American soldiers who fought with the 442nd Infantry Regiment in Germany. They fought gallantly and honorably throughout World War II. The young Pennsylvania Dutch soldier, whom I will not name, was eventually killed in action somewhere in Europe by the Germans while fighting for his country. My intelligence activities ceased when the 490th was transferred to Camp Davis, North Carolina.

CHAPTER FOUR
490th Sp BATTALION

"Bill Molter and Joe" Graduation 1939

CHAPTER FOUR

490th SP BATTALION

After many months of training on the 40mm guns, the 490th was finally beginning to resemble, if not a fighting force, at least a defensive one. The boys from Pennsylvania were at last getting along with the boys from Tennessee. Not great friends as yet but on friendly terms. In the Army manner, someone at the top had decided to make a change. The 490th AA Automatic Weapons Battalion was to become the 490th SP Automatic Weapons Battalion. This meant that we would now be a self-propelled outfit, where as before our 40 mm Bufors had to be towed to a position and be dug into a pit before it was ready to fire, now the weapons would be mounted on a half-track, a vehicle with wheels on the front and tank like tracks on the rear. We no longer had to rely on 2 1/2 ton trucks for transportation.

The day finally arrived. Our platoon went to the camp motor pool to be assigned to our new equipment. Boy! What a sight. There on the lot were rows, almost as far as the eye could see, of new olive green half-tracks. Each battery was assigned sixteen half-tracks, eight with 37 mm cannon, two 50 cal. air-cooled machine guns, and eight vehicles with four 50 cal. air-cooled guns on a revolving turret. The first platoon was to have the 37 mm cannon and the second platoon was assigned the 50 cal. machine guns. I was the squad leader in the second platoon. Pvt. Joe Stanley was my driver, Pvt. Ed (Masie) Masiejczyk from Philly would be the gunner and two other privates would act as loaders. The guns were covered with cosmoline, a very thick protective grease. We spent hours, long into the night, cleaning this grease off of the guns and other gear. It really was an impressive sight to see all of these weapons lined up in one place. To us, a bunch of eighteen and nineteen year old boys, it certainly looked like a formidable force. Who would dare challenge us? We really did have a lot to learn but we were very young. John (Pappy) Kent at thirty was the oldest man in our battery. We did have some sessions of introduction and indoctrination to familiarize ourselves on the use and operation of these new guns and vehicles. All of the 40 mm guns and the trucks of the old 490th had to be cleaned and greased before being turned into ordinance.

I was assigned to attend classes on the use, maintenance and operation of the 50 cal. air-cooled machine guns. We were required to take the guns apart and to reassemble them until we would literally do it in the dark. In fact, our final exam was just that, in the dark. At the end of the studies, I returned to my own outfit, arranged to have classes set up to instruct the squads of our platoon to see that everyone was familiar with these new weapons. Because of this training and teaching, I was to be classified as an expert on the 50 cal. machine gun. The 490th was the first self-propelled anti-aircraft unit in the army and was used henceforth as a cadre to instruct and train officers and men assigned to other newly formed self-propelled battalions.

One Monday, upon returning to camp from a three-day pass, I discovered that the second platoon was not in camp. My platoon had gone out to a firing range, leaving me the sole member of the second platoon in camp. "B" Battery was called out for close order drill. The first platoon fell into position and was called to attention. I, as the second platoon, fell in behind the first. The young lieutenant proceeded to put the men through their paces with a series of commands: "Platoon ATTENTION-N-N-N, right face, forward MARCH, to the right flank MARCH, to the left flank MARCH, to the rear MARCH, to the rear MARCH, first platoon cadence count, whereupon the entire platoon of some forty men called out at the top of their combined voices,

"ONE, TWO, THREE, FOUR - LEFT, RIGHT, LEFT, RIGHT."

"SECOND PLATOON, CADEN-N-N-CE COUNT."

This command was followed by silence.

"SECOND PLATOON, CADEN-N-N-CE COUNT."

With a start, I realized that the order was for me. I called out as ordered, "One, Two, Three, Four-Left, Right, Left, Right."

"SECOND PLATOON, I CAN'T HEAR YOU, LOUDER. SECOND PLATOON CADEN-N-N-N-N-CE COUNT." "YOU CAN DO BETTER THAN THE FIRST."

Marching behind the first platoon, I drew myself up to my full five feet eight inches, took a deep breath and shouted out as loud as I possibly could without losing my voice,

"ONE, TWO, THREE, FOUR - LEFT, RIGHT, LEFT, RIGHT."

"That was much better, Second Platoon, but you can and will do better the next time."

After my platoon returned from the firing range, Lt. Hand, a West Point career officer, approached me and said,

"Congratulations Corporal, I understand that you represented our platoon admirably, thank you."

"Thank you, sir." I replied.

A compliment from Lt. Hand was not to be taken lightly. For the next week or so, I was facetiously referred to as "Second Platoon Mac."

On another occasion, I along with Frank Wyatt, who was also from Philly, returned from a leave to find that the whole battery was away on a bivouac. We had no way of joining the outfit until a supply truck would go out to the bivouac area. We went to the Battery Headquarters and reported to Mr. Willard, the effeminate Warrant Officer. He told us to meet the next supply truck at sixteen hundred hours (four p.m.). While waiting, Frank and I amused ourselves at the nearest PX, the Post Exchange. Of course, we missed the supply truck. Mr. Willard was furious. He ordered us to spend the following day cleaning and scrubbing the headquarters building and to meet the truck in the afternoon. The following day, we completed our required chores as ordered, and again retired to the PX. Once again, we lingered over beer and amusement and again missed the truck. Mr. Willard came sashaying into the PX and with a fiery red face that was indicative of a top about to be blown, threatened to have both of us demoted. The next day, he was our shadow. He followed us everywhere and had us scrub the headquarters again under his watchful eyes. When the supply truck was loaded, by us I might add, Mr. Willard informed us that he was going to drive the truck himself and make sure that we reached the bivouac area. The three of us boarded the truck and were on our way. A few miles into the trip, he calmed down, loosened up, and started to get somewhat overly friendly. Down the highway, he spotted a roadhouse and suggested that we stop and have a beer and a bite to eat. Since he was in charge, we could not decline and eagerly accepted his command without question. It was a typical sleazy roadhouse with beer stained tables and floor, neon signs behind the dirty bar and all over the walls, idle rednecks seated at the bar, some half-drunk asleep, and country music blaring from the jukebox. We had not finished eating when two young girls came over and sat down at our table. As we became engaged in a conversation, Mr. Willard shot up as though hit by lightning and ordered us back into the truck. Frank and I reluctantly made a rather hasty exit. We only traveled a short distance when the truck came to a stop at a second roadhouse. The situation was almost identical to the previous one. Again, we were approached by a couple of young ladies, oops, girls. Mr. Willard dashed out of the place without saying a word, leaving Frank and I stranded in the middle of nowhere. We spent the next few hours at the bar, until well after dark. After we left the roadhouse, we made our way, somewhat unsurely, across the asphalt road. We sat down on the side of the road and waited for a lift. Eventually, we saw some headlights approaching. We stood out on the road and stopped the vehicle. It was a 2 ½ ton army supply truck on its way to the battalion camp. The driver agreed to take us to our outfit and told us to climb onto the back of the truck. I began to climb up over the side, threw my leg over the wooden side panels, and put my foot right into the middle of a crate of eggs. The eggs, complete with broken shells, seeped over and into my boot. Tomorrow, someone was going to be short of egg rations.

When we got to the camp area, there was no way that we could locate our platoon through the dark unfamiliar woods. At least not until daylight. Someone loaned us a pup tent but we could not even manage to put the thing together. I lay down on the damp grass, looked up at the rapidly spinning stars that were moving in all directions, and clutched the ground in an unsuccessful and futile attempt to stop the Earth from rotating. The following morning, Frank and I reported for duty, some three days late. Mr. Willard, in his report stated that Cpl. Wyatt and Cpl. McLaughlin were assisting him in camp maintenance for the past three days. There was no mention of our little misadventure of the previous day.

A show was going to be presented in the mess hall at Camp Davis for the entertainment of the men in our battery. It was a show that I had been looking forward to seeing for some time. A member of our platoon and a friend of mine, Pvt. Walter Hartenstien, had been a hoofer or song and dance man in civilian life. He and his partner, his sister Betty, had performed on stage in theaters and clubs throughout the Northeast. Walt arranged for Betty to bring a troupe of entertainers to the camp to perform for the men in the 490th with Walter as the emcee and star of the show. Once again, I was suffering one of my attacks of the flu or a severe cold. There I was lying on my cot, in the darkness of the empty barracks, sneezing, coughing, shaking, and going from hot to cold with a fever. I attempted to prop myself up by the open window so that I might hear the tapping of dancing feet, music, and applause, as the sound of laughter and gayety traveled through the dark night across the deserted parade ground. This would have been a welcome relief from the drudgery and daily regimentation of Army life, but alas, I was to be denied any participation in the joviality of the night. After the show I could see, in the brightly lit open doorway of the mess hall, some soldiers mingling with members of the cast while others headed across the field to the Battalion PX for some beer. I forced myself away from the window, closed it, and curled back into my own sick and miserable self.

Prior to the war, women were not only expected to but were destined to take a lesser and subservient role in all walks of life. Rarely could a female aspire to a life other than raising children and keeping a house. Young ladies of the more affluent upper class were educated and trained in the social graces, dancing, painting, playing bridge, crocheting, needlepoint, and the proper manners of a society that engaged itself as a life of leisure and frivolity. These young ladies were preparing themselves for their coming out at the annual Debutante Ball. They were taught all of the niceties required to attract a young man of wealth and family position. Girls in the working or lower class were forced to leave school early, as were boys, to stay at home and help to raise their younger siblings, learn to sew, cook, and keep house. The needs of a wartime environment quickly changed that old time way of thinking. More and more of our young men were going into the military, enlisting or being drafted, leaving jobs open in the burgeoning wartime industry. Women were leaving somewhat dubious comforts of home and hearth and taking jobs in factories. Some were accepting jobs in government and in the military while others worked in shipyards.

The term "Rosie the Riveter" was to become synonymous with the role of women in the war effort. Women were enlisting in the WAACs (Women's Army Auxiliary Corps), the WAVES (Women accepted for Volunteer Emergency Service), and the WASPS (Women's Air Force Service Pilots). It was not until many years later that the WASPSs were given the status of being a part of the military and veterans. Girls could only aspire to become a nun, a nurse, or perhaps an airline stewardess. Except for a few daring female pilots, a young lady wanting to enter into aviation had to become a stewardess which also required a degree in nursing. The girls serving in the WASPs released young male pilots for combat duty overseas. They would become ferry pilots, flying planes from base to base and factory to air bases not only throughout the country but also overseas. Others flew planes that towed target sleeves. They performed this very dangerous task every day for inexperienced kids like us manning powerful weapons such as the 40 mm and 37 mm canons and 50 cal. machine guns. Frank was a machine gunner in a turret with four 50's on a halftrack. I never did get the opportunity to watch him perform because he was in another battery and usually practiced on another section of the beach. The 490th engaged in anti-aircraft target practice at Tybee Island, Fort Fisher, and the beaches along the coast of North Carolina. Our guns would take aim at the white sleeve gliding behind a tow plane and attempt to pepper it with flak. On more than one occasion I observed the glow of tracer bullets slowly inching closer to the tail of the plane, requiring a crack on the helmet of the erring gunner. At times, an inexperienced gunner would freeze at the controls of the guns and turret, gripping white knuckled to the controls, erratically sending bullets into the sky in all directions. We had to forcibly open the hands and literally drag the gunner from his seat. Those brave young women were risking their lives, every day, for us to receive much needed training. There were times when, upon landing, the pilots found more bullet holes in the fuselage of their planes than they found in the target sleeve. It was not until 1979 that congress gave the WASPs recognition as veterans and these women did not receive any medals until 1984. The war opened new doors of opportunity for the women of this country, both rich and poor. Doors that would never again be closed.

Since the end of the Second World War, women have rapidly entered into commerce and business in untold numbers. They have filled jobs in stores and factories. Many women have become CEO's of major corporations, captains of industry, congress-women, senators, attorney general, secretary of state, and I certainly envision a time in the not to distant future when it will not be beyond the realm of possibility, a woman president of the United States.

A small group of the GI's was making it's way across a large parade ground that separated the 490th from the camp theater. The group included Joe Schum and David Jones from Battery "C," Bill Miller, and my brother, Frank from Battery "A," Al Cummons and I from "B" Battery. We had just seen "The Sullivans," a movie about five brothers who enlisted in the Navy and were assigned to the same ship. That ship went down with the loss of many men, including all five of the Sullivan brothers. After that disaster, the service adopted a policy that discouraged the assignment of family members to the same ship or organization. Somehow, Frank and I slipped past that ruling; however, we did not serve in the same combat unit.

It was a beautiful clear night. The moon was full and there were no clouds in the sky. We all were enjoying the walk and the warm night air and also the conversation that included no small amount of kidding among friends. Our demeanor was friendly, carefree, and light as we discussed the movie and other topics. As we neared the battalion area, we heard the popping sounds that we all recognized as gun fire. The unmistakable glow and arc of tracer bullets passed over the one-story barracks. As Al and I got closer to Battery "B," we could hear the shouting and cursing that accompanied the confusion of our fellow GI's attempting to arm themselves and mount the half-tracks. I could see Capt. Williams trying to get some order out of all of the confusion. He was yelling out commands and offering an occasional kick to the butt of any reluctant private. Most soldiers meet a fear of combat in a foreign land. We received our baptism of battle in the good old U.S.A. in the Okefenokee Swamp in Georgia.

The reason for all of this sudden activity was and is questionable in the minds of members of the 490th. To my knowledge, no official report was made. I can only speak of what I saw and heard. Rumors were running fast and furious; an entire black outfit had raided the supply depot and went AWOL (absent without leave) into the Okefenokee Swamp, a black girl was raped by a white soldier, a white girl had been raped by a black soldier, the outfit was scheduled to go overseas; therefore, the whole outfit went AWOL. Which or any of these reasons were true, I really do not know, but I do know that a black outfit did go into the swamp and the 490th was ordered to go into the swamp and to apprehend and return to camp all of the members of this mutiny. It took several days to round up all of them. A few of the more violent men were put into a Georgia sweat box (a box made up of a wooden frame covered with tin and barely large enough for a man to stand). The sweat box would be placed in the sun. Anyone, spending some time in the hot confines of the box would swiftly lose all ability and desire to fight. They would be removed all limp and covered with sweat. News of this episode was quickly hushed up. The only civilian who knew about it was Walter Winchell, a famous correspondent and newscaster. Even Winchell was uncharacteristically silent about the whole affair.

Every Friday evening a convoy of 2 ½ ton trucks would roll into Savannah. After parking at one of Savannah's famed squares, the trucks would unload their cargo of anxious GI's looking forward to a weekend of fun and frivolity. For many of these kids, and that is what they were, it would be the first time to be on their own and away from parental restrictions. Accompanied by loud yells and screams, the crowd would disperse in various directions. Some would head for local speak-easies and bistros, others would go to dance halls or brothels, still others, including Joe Schum and I, would go to the Savannah Hotel or the DeSota Hotel. At either place, we could spend hours mingling with other soldiers and some civilians. Drinks would flow like water in the Savannah River. Laughter and loud conversation filled the crowded smoke filled lounge. In due time, young good looking southern girls would enter and join in the fun, some latching onto the arm of a shy but willing GI. The mood was anything but quiet albeit peaceful until later in the evening when the boys began to feel their drinks. After that, an altercation could break out over the slightest provocation, even between friends.

The good citizens of Savannah feared this invasion as much as they did Sherman's march to the sea. They did permit their young daughters to attend dances at the YMCA or the Serviceman's Canteen but woe to those who brought home a GI or who had the temerity to fall in love with a Yankee. These wild nineteen or twenty-year old young men, just recently given their freedom from strict family home life and even stricter parents, and finally after thirteen weeks of military life under the watchful eyes of domineering noncoms, were finally let loose upon a city that did not welcome them with open arms or affection. They were met with open palms of greed waiting willingly for the free-flowing dollars. The GI's were all searching for the same things; good food, female companionship and drinks. All were in plentiful supply in Savannah. Our favorite haunt was the DeSota Hotel where we could spend the night drinking, singing and just having a good time letting loose after a week of taking orders. Usually, one member of our group was assigned the task of finding suitable lodging for the weekend. One week, it was my turn to find and secure rooms. I went over to "Battery A" to see my brother, Frank, before leaving for town. I had not spoken to him for some time; therefore, I was unaware of recent events. Jean McGovern, without the knowledge of her parents, had come down to Georgia to be with Frank. Naturally, she couldn't and wouldn't stay with him unmarried. They had made arrangements to get married in a Catholic church that Saturday. They both wanted me to be present at the ceremony. I could not refuse, so I told Joe Schum that he would be responsible in acquiring rooms that weekend. After the wedding, I would meet Joe and our buddies at the DeSota. The wedding was a rather fast marriage rite with only me, Dick Kruse, and his wife in attendance. Immediately after the ceremony, the married couple went on their way to wherever married couples go in Savannah. I went to seek out my friends at the hotel. As usual, we spent the night singing, drinking, and just plain letting loose. Several times, during the course of the evening, I asked Joe if he had gotten a room for us. He assured me that everything had been taken care of and that I should not worry. At the end of the night, which was about two in the morning, we left the lounge on unsteady feet and Joe led the way to our waiting beds. He took us down some narrow dark streets. They really were dimly lit alleys lined with old brick houses reminiscent of eerie fog laden streets of London. Inwardly, I was glad to be a member of a group walking together. Eventually, we came to a very old large house where Joe walked up a few brick steps to a landing and an unlit ornate double door. It seemed apparent that the occupants had gone to bed. Schum did not bother to knock but led us into a dark vestibule. The outward appearance was deceiving because when we entered the inner door the place was an absolute bedlam. Scantily clad girls were screaming and chasing equally undressed GI's down the hall and into rooms. It made little difference whose room they went into. We stepped into a room that, during better times, had been a lovely formal dining room. The only pieces of furniture were folding canvas cots not unlike our own cots back at camp. This was to be our sleeping quarters for the night. There were sufficient cots to accommodate all of us. Pocket doors, that separated our room from what had been, at one time, the living room, were slightly ajar with a pair of ladies panties hanging in between. I went over to close the doors. While doing so, I caught a glimpse of the dimly lit interior. Couples were engaged in a variety of sexual positions and activities. Our good buddy, Joe, had gotten us a room in a house of ill repute or more aptly put a whore house. No one in our group took advantage of the offerings of the house. We were more concerned about losing our wallets and watches than we were, in some cases our virginity. Our alcoholic intake did not prevent us from having a sleepless night. There was always the fear of being rolled during the night. I, for one, slept with my wallet firmly under my head.

I remember the following morning very clearly. We were all young naïve kids feeling our oats and looking for a good time, totally unaware of the historical significance of Savannah. We did not frequent antebellum homes, galleries, or museums. Instead, we headed for the nearest Walgreens drug store and restaurant for breakfast. I ordered bacon and eggs which were accompanied with an unappetizing looking side dish. This was the first time that I was introduced to grits. To us Yankees, what the hell were grits? I did not like them then and never did acquire a taste for that tasteless dish. Was it cereal? Was it vegetable? Who knows? I still don't.

Sometime after Frank and Jean were married, I, along with other buddies from Philly, had gotten a pass to go home. At the end of my leave, Aunt Cass gave me a bottle of liquor to take back to Georgia and to have a toast with the newlyweds. Dear Aunt Cass was Mom's younger sister; however, she was completely different. Where Mom was shy and reserved, Aunt Cass was very outgoing and fun loving. She was self-supporting and single, but by no stretch of the imagination could she be called an old maid. She was a little on the stout side, but always well dressed and well groomed. Whenever she was between jobs, she would come to live with us. We did have a full house but there was always room for one more. Most of the time, she had her own apartment. She and Jack Flood, a Pennsylvania State Trooper, were friends and companions for twenty-five years before finally getting married. Unfortunately, Aunt Cass passed away just two years after the wedding. By the time that our train reached Washington D.C., the bottle just had to be opened. A group of my buddies shared its contents and the bottle was empty before we were not too far south of Washington. Frank and Jean never did receive the gift from Aunt Cass.

The group from Philly was feeling no pain when we finally reported back to camp. Our outfit happened to be out on the Infiltration Course at the time. We were ordered to get into our fatigues, grab our packs, and to report to the course at once. The "Infiltration Course" was laid out in such a way that a GI had to crawl under a barbed-wire barrier that was stretched about eighteen inches above the ground. The ground was pock-marked with shell holes. Dynamite charges would go off as you made your way across the course. On the opposite end of the field, 30 cal. machine guns were set up to fire live ammunition just above the barbed wire screening. The best thing to do was to dig your face into the dirt and mud as far as possible.

Jack Founds, Rudy, myself, and a few others from Philly, still somewhat inebriated, digging our fingers into the dirt and hugging the ground, cautiously inched our way forward under the wire as the shells burst around us. The staccato sound of the machine gun fire above our heads had an immediate sobering effect on all of us. The urge to stick one's head up and to look around to see what the hell was going on, disappeared. As I moved forward, I was kicked in the head by the foot of the soldier just ahead of me.

"Hey! Watch where the hell you are kicking," I yelled.

As he turned his head to face me and to offer an apologetic, "I'm sorry soldier; I didn't mean to kick so hard." I recognized Lt. Col. Gage, our Battalion Commander.

The 490th had completed training and was combat ready; however instead of being sent overseas, the battalion, having been the first self-propelled anti-aircraft battalion in the Army, was to be used as a cadre to instruct and train officers in the use and maintenance of half-tracks and their anti-aircraft guns. These officers were destined to command fresh troops in new self-propelled battalions. The 490th was also the oldest outfit in Camp Stewart, so the powers that be also decided to locate our outfit outside of the camp proper. We were assigned to a large weedy field near Richmond Hill, Georgia, a small village near the camp. Jean and a girlfriend were fortunate enough to obtain a room in Richmond Hill; therefore she was close to Frank.

When we arrived at the field that was to be our home for several months to come, the first duty of the day was to hack down all of the weeds and clear the field, after which a mess tent and a latrine had to be constructed. Our living quarters were to be our pup-tents, measured and lined up in a straight row. Each GI had in his gear a half of a tent and some tent pegs. To form a tent, one had to team up with a buddy and his half of a tent. We were going to be sleeping together for some time; therefore, it was necessary to pick someone with whom you could get along. Each man of course, slept in his own sleeping bag.

I was supposed to team up with Pvt. Peter DeFalco. Since the incident of crossing the river, Pete and I became fairly good friends; however, only in camp. Pete seemed to have his own circle friends off base. He and I pulled guard duty together, trained together, and did KP (kitchen police) together. On the day that we were to set up camp, word came down that Pete was to be transferred. He spoke fluent Italian and was being sent to Italy as an interpreter. For some months, I was kept informed of Pete's whereabouts through a series of correspondence with his sister in Johnstown, Pennsylvania. Gradually, information about him became less and less. In my letters, I would pose questions about him; however, in his sister's reply, she would write of ordinary inane objects and ignore my questions. Suddenly, the letters came to a stop. I would write but receive no answer. Eventually, I too stopped writing.

When Pete left the 490th, Al Cummons suggested that he and I should bunk together. This was a good arrangement since Al and I had known each other for years back home. We went to Penn Treaty Jr. High together, were in the same drum and bugle corp., and went into service at the same time. Al, being the Battery bugler, had to be the first one out of the sack every day, which meant that I was never late for reveille.

I would hear nothing of Peter until a few years after the war. He was to become an accomplished dancer at the Ethnological Dance Center in New York City.

Battery "B" was assigned to do guard duty at several gates to the camp. We had to pull four hours on duty and eight hours off. Johnny Rudolph and I shared duty at the same post from 12 to 4 a.m. There was little activity during these early morning hours except for several GI's without passes trying to sneak back into camp; however, we still were required to stay alert. For two young Philly boys, every sound and ruffle was cause for alarm. At least we were not completely alone as we were pulling duty on the dark deserted beaches of Georgia. We could only gaze at the sky full of stars for so long before becoming completely bored; therefore, Johnny and I spent hours reminiscing about our childhood at home, roaming the streets of North Philly. We came from different neighborhoods but areas that were in close proximity, therefore very much alike. We discovered that we had many mutual friends. One morning, after having morning chow, Sergeant Caporelli, our Sergeant of the Guards, gave Rudy and I the job of policing the area around the guard post. This duty required us to clean the grounds of all debris, gum wrappers, and many cigarette butts. We were doing quite well until we came upon Cpl. Barr lying on a cot and basking in the early morning sun. Rudy asked him to get up so that we could complete our task and clean up the mess that he had made around the cot. He refused and remained on the cot. After several requests and refusals, Rudy took hold of the side rails of the folding bed and upended it, tossing the corporal onto the ground. When he recovered from the shock, he came charging at me with his head down, like a raging bull. When the angered NCO got close to me, I stepped aside, put my hands on his back and pushed, using his own momentum to send him flying into a nearby concrete drainage ditch. I followed him into the ditch, got a good hold on him, raised my tightened fist ready to pummel him when I heard the voice of Sergeant Caporelli yell out, "Don't hit him Mac, he can have you court martialed." My arm and fist remained in midair. The relationship between Cpl. Barr and I remained rather testy until I was promoted to corporal and we were on equal footing. This was, however, the beginning of a friendship between Johnny Rudolph and I that would last for three more years in the Army, in the States, and in Europe.

Back at camp, one day, after noontime mess, a young lieutenant lined us up outside of our barracks. He separated us into pairs and attempted to educate us in the use of the machete in self-defense. I must admit that we treated this training rather lightly and with humor. As pairs, one GI was to wield the machete, stretching his arm out full length to measure the distance to the belt buckle of his partner, then swinging his arm from side to side, barely nicking the brass buckle. The swinging would start out slowly and rapidly increase. Places would then be reversed. The lieutenant then began to instruct the men in self-defense against a machete wielding enemy. For the demonstration, he chose Pvt. Jack Founds. The officer was going to disarm Jack when he swung the weapon. He stood there in a defensive position with legs spread apart, arms extended and hands waiting to move. Jack began to swing the machete in a fast moving arc. The tip of the knife caught the Lieutenant between the fingers of his right hand sending blood all over the ground.

Another buddy of mine, Tom Nelson from Philly, while stationed at Camp Davis, North Carolina, joined me in weekend passes to the city of Wilmington. While walking through the city park, we began a conversation with two young girls and spent a pleasant Sunday afternoon gently rowing and circumventing the lake under Spanish moss covered trees that grew along the banks. It was a fairly warm and clear November day. We acquired the girls' addresses and a promise of a date the following Wednesday night, providing that we both could get a pass into town. Wednesday was Thanksgiving Eve so we had no trouble obtaining a holiday pass. In anticipation and promise of what could be but probably wouldn't be, arrived at the address that the girls had given to us. We were in our dress uniforms and felt quite confident. In answer to our knock, the door was opened by a boy of about twelve years of age. He told us that the girls had gone to church. I said that if he would direct us to the church, we would gladly escort the girls back home. The church was not very far from their house, therefore Tom and I decided to walk. We came to a rather dark street with not a soul in sight. We saw a light coming from a building midway down the narrow thoroughfare. As we approached the white painted frame building, we could hear voices raised in the singing of hymns. All of the windows of this somewhat dilapidated structure were painted white with areas of paint scratched away. To Tom and I, it appeared to be what we thought would be a "Holy Roller" or a Southern Negro Church. We looked at each other and shook our heads. No! Our girls would not be in there. We climbed up and peeked in through a scratch in one of the windows. Sure enough, our two friends were sitting in the third row, enthusiastically joining in the "AMENS" and "ALLELUIA BROTHERS." The preacher asked each member to stand up and tell the congregation all that he or she was thankful for on this joyous Thanksgiving Eve. The girls, of course, along with other members, rose and called out their blessings amid loud "AMENS." After some discussion, Tom and I decided to go in and join the service. I led the way, walked up the wooden steps, opened the door, and entered the church. Tom slammed the door shut and remained outside. Standing there in the middle of the aisle with all eyes turned toward me, I could hear Tom outside in a fit of uncontrollable laughter. I had the uncomfortable feeling of being completely naked as all eyes in the congregation were riveted on the red-faced embarrassed soldier standing alone in the rear of the church. I could vaguely hear the preacher beseeching me to come forward and join the service.

"Come forward brother."

"ALLELUIA, ALLELUIA."

"Come forward brother, AMEN, AMEN."

The girls were in the center of the aisle, reaching out to me. Discretion being the better part of valor, I decided to share a pew with them. After the service, I was treated like a new member of the fold and was lavished with food and drink (non-alcoholic) and pleasant conversation. I can not recall having any dissatisfaction or unpleasant memories of the event, even though I was forced into it.

Not long after that, while out on gun practice, Tom received orders that he was being transferred out. He had to return to our Battery area immediately. He told me that he had some extra khaki clothing that he would not be able to take with him so he would leave them in my foot locker. When I returned to camp and looked into my locker, there were no khakis, and my wrist watch was gone. I never saw Tommy Nelson again; however, it was not the last time that he would have an impact on my life. While I was stationed in Germany, I received a letter from Mom saying that Tommy had come to the house for a visit. He told Mom and Dad that he had seen me in England in a hospital and that I had suffered from shell shock. Certainly, I had been in

England for R and R (Rest and Recreation) but not in a hospital and surely not in a shell-shocked state.

The half-tracks were rolling. We were heading out to the firing range for practice. Unlike our usual practice, anti-aircraft fire over the ocean, this was going to be ground level firing at tank targets. After leaving the paved highway, we moved along dirt back country roads. It was the dry season in Georgia so the rapid movement of the tracks created huge dust clouds that we had to drive through. Our uniforms, equipment, and faces were covered with the thick dust. When we drove past small tenant farms, black families came running out of their shacks to yell and wave to us until the ever growing clouds of dust finally obscured our vision, which was limited at best.

Upon reaching the bivouac area, the first order of the day was to dig a hole large enough and deep enough to bury our vehicles over and beyond the track levels. A ramp also had to be dug to facilitate the backing of the half-track into the pit. The exposed portion and the guns had to be camouflaged. Each member of the squad was required to also dig and cover an individual foxhole. Masie, our gunner, seemed to be lingering over the completion of his foxhole. The rest of us were digging and covering the vehicle while he was engrossed in his own personal task. As squad leader, I finally ordered him to help us, which he did, somewhat reluctantly. I must admit that he did a great job of concealing his foxhole although it was much closer to the half-track pit than I desired. We spent the entire day preparing our emplacement. We preferred to sleep out on the ground rather than in the confines and hard surfaces of the armor plate of the track.

The following day was to be a "General Inspection." Captain Harold Williams arrived with his Executive Officer, Lieutenant Clifford Hand, a competent officer and leader and a West Point graduate, to make a preliminary inspection before the General's arrival. I had my squad line up in front of our vehicle. The officers checked the squad and proceeded to make an inspection of the half-track and the site. They checked the 50 caliber machine guns, the gun turret, the ammunition, and then they slowly walked around the emplacement looking for the slightest infraction of the rules. Capt. Williams was making the inspection as

Lt. Hand followed behind making notes on a clipboard. Our crew continued to stand at attention. Suddenly, the silence was broken by a loud thud and the voice of Lt. Hand yelling out, "Oh, my God!" Capt. Williams had fallen right into Masie's camouflaged foxhole. When he rose up from the deep hole, his head coming into view, his helmet was twisted on his head, and he was covered with greenery and tree branches. Without showing any signs of emotion, he asked, "Who belongs to this hole?" When I told him, his only reply was "Very good Cpl. Masiejczyk, very well covered." There was no further comment or discussion.

Later that day, the inspection team returned with a General. Now was the time to make a good impression and get points for our Battery. Sgt. Ben Harness, now our platoon sergeant since our beloved Sgts. Vick and Jarvis had been transferred out, gave the order for our squad to "fall in" in front of the half-track, which we did rapidly and in practiced order. Then he gave the command to mount the vehicle and take our required firing positions, according to the drill. Pvt. Joe Stanley behind the wheel, Masie jumped into the gun turret, two loaders stood by the ammunition cans, and I, as their squad leader, took my position behind the turret to direct fire. Masie, assimilating fire, rotated the gun turret and raised the guns in mock battle. I felt that we were conducting ourselves quite well. The General observed our every movement then made a remark to Sgt. Harness.

"Very good drill, Sergeant." "I see that your gun turret can revolve a full 360 degrees."

To which our esteemed non-com replied, "Oh no Sir, it can turn more than that."

Our Battery eventually moved out and headed for the firing range. When we arrived there, we lined the half-tracks along a rise some distance away from a wooded area. Several feet into the woods was a track along with a number of targets simulating enemy tanks, slowly moved among the trees. We spent several hours taking turns at practice, firing our guns at ground level targets. At the end of the day, the general decided, on a whim, to have the entire battery fire in unison. This meant that eight half-tracks with two 50 caliber machine guns and eight tracks equipped with four 50 caliber guns would fire at the same time into the woods. Each gun could fire six hundred rounds per minute with every fifth round being a tracer bullet. Naturally we did as we were ordered and subjected the targets and the surrounding woods with a tremendous fire power that immediately set the dry trees ablaze. We would spend the next three days fighting a forest fire.

Shouts of "GERONIMO" seemed to be coming from every area of the Battalion. A notice had been posted on the bulletin board asking for volunteers to join the infantry, the airborne or the paratroopers. The blue and silver infantry badge, the airborne insignia, and the way that the paratroopers tucked their pants into the top of their combat boots was an inducement, to any patriotic and gung-ho young soldier, to join their ranks. Pillows and mattresses were piled outside on the ground, next to the two-story barracks. Men were on the roofs of every building. With a short run and a sharp and loud yell of "GERONIMO" (the shout that the paratroopers would make as they made a jump from a plane), the GI' would jump off of the roof into a stack of mattresses below.

I had no intentions of volunteering for anything; therefore, I did not join in this sophomoric patriotism. Bill Miller, Dick Kruse, Jack Founds, and Frank were among those requesting a transfer. This was where my brother and I disagreed and went our separate ways. Eventually, we both would end up in France, Belgium, and Germany, Frank in the infantry, and I in the Field Artillery. I know that I rode many more miles than I could have possibly walked.

The 490th was scheduled to go on maneuvers in Arkansas. The entire outfit was first sent to Camp Polk, Louisiana. After loading and securing the half-tracks on flatbed cars, we boarded a troop train that left Camp Polk and headed north to Camp Chaffee, Arkansas. It seemed like a long circuitous trip, like most military routes, accompanied with the usual excited banter, dice, and card games. As we approached Arkansas, the weather turned dark and dismal. A slight downpour turned into torrential rain. On our arrival at Camp Chafee, we had to unload our equipment and store the half-tracks in the camp motor pool. All of this was done in pouring rain. The rain continued. We had to set up camp and put our pup tents in a large open field that was three feet lower than the surrounding land, with an embankment on all three sides. Since the ground was completely saturated and muddy, we could not dig a small trench around the pup tents to take away the rain water. Day after day, the rains continued. By now, everything was soaked. The whole area was nothing but mud. We could not train, we could not march. We ate in mud, we worked in mud, we played in mud, and we had to sleep in mud. When we were not out in the rain, we were miserable in our damp pup tents. While at Camp Chaffee, I did get to see John Roberts, my boyhood friend from Philly. John was stationed at Chaffee and was heading overseas. During our visit, he asked me to go to see his girlfriend, Mary Miller, if I got home. The chance of that, at the time, seemed to be impossible. I told him that I would do as he asked. We talked over old times, like the fun that we shared with Bill Molter, Joe Schum, Jim Kelly, and Charlie Brown. The times that we spent horseback riding, the parties we had, and shooting darts. I think that this short visit was good for both of us. I was not to see Johnnie again until after the war and after a lifetime of experiences. Did I say that the rains continued for several more days?

Our Battery Headquarters was set up in a garage in the camp motor pool. The First Sergeant came to our tent and ordered me to go to Battery Headquarters as soon as possible, without giving me details. When I reported there, I was informed that I, along with several others, was going to go home on leave. It was still raining when I put on my waterlogged dress uniform and packed up my waterlogged clothing into my waterlogged duffle bag and slogged through the mud and puddles toward the truck that was headed for the railroad station.

I left there with Johnnie Rudolph, who lived near Holy Name Church. We were both soaked to the skin and had a very damp ride, however, we did not allow that to dampen our joy in getting home. When we finally did reach Philadelphia, John and I headed for the nearest dry cleaning shop on Broad Street. We sat, half-clothed, in a shoe repair booth and waited for our uniforms to be cleaned and pressed.

While on leave, I did go to visit Mary Miller. When I went to her home, her parents informed me that Mary was in the hospital but was to be released the following day. I bought some flowers and headed to the hospital. Her long flowing brown hair covered the pillow as her dark beauty was enhanced by the stark whiteness of the hospital bed. Mary and I got along quite well from the start and dated for the rest of my leave. I believe that John forgave me. After the war was over, I was best man at his wedding, when he married someone else.

Near the end of my furlough, I received a telegram.

P232 23/22 4 EXTRA=PHILADELPHIA PENN 22 616P
CPL JOSEPH O MCLAUGHLIN=
1932 E ARIZONA STREET=
PREVIOUS INSTRUCTIONS CANCELLED PD ON EXPIRATION OF FURLOUGH YOU WILL REPORT TO CO 604TH AA GOUP CAMP POLK=
CO 490TH AAA AUTO WPNS BN S/P, NORTH-CAMPOLK LA 221915Z

With the telegram in hand, I went to seek out Rudy and our buddies to find out just what was going on. They all received the same message. For what reason, none of us were able to find out, the 490th had been disbanded. Everyone in the 490th was to be transferred to camps all over the country. Most of our friends, we never saw again. Some went to the Pacific, some went to Europe, and others never did return home. Some to this day rest, somewhere in France, under a well, manicured lawn, beneath a white cross, lost in a multitude of crosses stretching across French soil.

Tent city, Georgia   Joe with cup

1st. Platoon halftrack with 37mm. cannon and
twin 50 caliber air cooled machine guns.

My squad, on 2nd. platoon halftrack 222 with four 50 cal. air cooled machine guns. I am kneeling on the right.

Tent city, Georgia

Chow time

1st Sgt. Schnur   Caperelli John Kent Joe

CHAPTER FIVE
627ᵗʰ FA BATTALION

CHAPTER FIVE

627th FA. BATTALION

Upon our arrival at Camp Polk, we were placed in a casual outfit that was made up of men who had no particular assignment. We really did not have much to do except to wait around to be assigned to a unit. For weeks we were virtually on our own. The only thing that we were required to do was to answer the roll call at reveille, be on time for chow, and attend retreat. Other than that, we could sit around and read, swim in the camp pool, and occasionally join in a period of organized exercise. I did spend a lot of time, in the ring, boxing with Walter Graham from Erie, Pa. At first, not answering to anyone was a treat, but after a couple of weeks we began to get bored and lazy.

Eventually, we did receive orders assigning us to the 627th Field Artillery Battalion. I was placed in a battery commanded by Capt. Yakowitz. At least now we had a home. It took quite some time for us to become friendly with a new group and to familiarize ourselves with entirely different equipment. Compared to our 37 mm cannons, these 105 mm Howitzers were really huge guns. I did not particularly like the idea of working on these guns. For some reason, I was given the title of Instrument and Survey Man, whatever that meant. The 627th was to be my home for the duration of the war.

Near Camp Polk was the small town of Leesville, Louisiana. Leesville! What can I say about Leesville? It was a small town, although larger than Hinesville, Georgia. An article in "Readers Digest" had named Leesville the town with the most venereal disease in the country. Intolerance and bigotry ran widespread and rampant. Finding a place in town, on a weekend pass, was not just difficult but almost impossible. Here again, we saw signs everywhere that were prominently displayed on front lawns with the admonishment,

"NO DOGS OR GI'S ALLOWED"

A three or four-story building served as Police Headquarters and Town Jail. Early Friday afternoon, all of the street girls in town were picked up and put into jail. Come early evening, the town would be overrun with young soldiers anxious to have a good time and spend their money. The townspeople were more than willing to oblige them. Many of the GI"s would gather on the lawn in front of the jail house and call or whistle to the girls at the screened-in windows. The girls would then call out their names and the amount of their bail money. Any interested soldier could go into the station, pay the bail, and spend the night with the girl. These transactions were repeated on Saturday evening and must have been a very profitable business for the town.

One of my buddies could not or would not pay out any bail money. After dark, he and two others climbed up the side of the building on a downspout, cut through the screening on the window and entered the cell, where they spent a few hours with several of the girls. Fortunately, they were able to make it back down the rainspout without being detected. Years later, he would become a member of the social set in the main line of suburban Philadelphia. He did not want to hear about his earlier escapade. When reminded of it, he did not deny it but just passed it off. I wonder why?

The 627th FA Bn. Was sent to Camp Callen, near San Diego, California. The battalion was to continue field artillery training and to receive training in beach landings and island hopping. It seemed like good duty. We could enjoy the beautiful beaches of Southern California, the sights of San Diego (in a way a nice quiet town but sometimes a wild Navy town), and trips to Hollywood and Tijuana, Mexico.

In addition to being involved in these trainings, I also, as an instrument and survey man, had to get training in surveying. Along with Sgt. Webb, my instructor, we spent many days surveying the hills around La Jolla. The area was beautiful and the weather was perfect. I, being naive, enjoyed every moment of it, not realizing that this was preparation to be, in reality, a forward observer for an artillery outfit. To make a survey, one had to be close to and in sight of the enemy forces, complete a survey, call for fire for effect, ascertain by sight where the shells were landing and then make corrections as necessary.

Apparently, we were slated to go to the South Pacific, because we had been issued all summer clothing and equipment. Our training was based on all summer operations. We were making numerous practice landings on the beaches of Southern California. The 627th was getting into shape and working together as a cohesive unit. This, however, was not to be. As the army sometimes does, we were suddenly and rapidly loaded on a train and shipped to Fort Dix, New Jersey, where we were equipped with winter gear in preparation for immediate embarkation for Europe. We were to be replacements for the ill fated 106th Division and artillery was needed for the invasion of Germany.

During beach landing exercises at Camp Callan, the 627th FA sustained its first casualty. It was a perfectly clear day full of bright sunshine and cloudless skies. The waves were a little high and strong but nothing to be concerned about. The beach was full of activity as troops landing on the shore attempted to secure a foothold on the beautiful white sandy beach, just north of San Diego. Shouts and curses filled the air. This was not one of our best or most pleasant days on the beach. Why were we involved in beach landings? Surely the big guns would come in later after the beachhead had been secured, but here we were. Several landing craft loaded with fully equipped GI"s were coming in toward the shore. Suddenly, a wave hit one of the craft and turned it sideways to the shoreline. The next wave came in with a force, hit the boat and capsized it, tossing everyone on board into the water. Most of the men, although thoroughly soaked, managed to reach the shore safely. The driver of the landing craft was tossed out and hit his head on the metal framework of the canopy covering the driver's position. He was knocked unconscious and drowned in the boiling surf. Ironically, his home was only about ten miles up the coast.

After months of training in California, for island hopping in the South Pacific, we boarded a train for New York. Our immediate destination was Fort Dix, New Jersey, where we were to get shots for overseas duty and to exchange our warm weather khakis for cold weather gear. We all knew that we were headed for Europe where we may or may not return and since we were so close to Philadelphia, Joe Beitz, and I were determined to see our parents one more time before shipping out.

"Hey! Beetle, where the hell are you?"

"Sh! Mac, be quiet, he answered."

We had made it to the fence, where Beetle found an opening. After slipping through the hole, we began to make our way down the highway. We had not gone very far, when a taxi came along, on its way back from a fare, to the main gate. We stood on the side of the road and hailed the cab. There were no lights along the road and the night was so dark that the cabbie, at first, did not see us. He finally came to a stop some distance down the road.

"Where are you guys going?" the driver asked.

We told him that we wanted to get the nearest bus to Philly.

"There won't be another bus until much later in the night." He said.

We tried to explain to him that we had to get to Philly and that our unit in Fort Dix was waiting to be shipped overseas. Since we were so close to Philadelphia, there was no way that we were going to ship out without seeing our folks for the last time.

"Are you guys crazy?" the cabbie yelled. "You will be charged with desertion not AWOL."

Seeing that we were determined, he finally said, "Ok, but I will take you home." "How much will the fare be?" we asked.

"Never mind about that, we will talk about the fare later." he answered.

He drove us all the way to Philly. We went to my house first where I could spend a little time with Mom and Dad. My God! They seemed to have gotten so much older since my brothers and I had gone into the service. Dad now had gotten gray and appeared to be very nervous. I noticed a perceptible shaking of his hands. Mom was even more quiet than usual. She said very little but kept holding on to me as though she would never let go. After a very tearful goodbye, we went to Joe Beitz's house on Frankford Avenue. Joe had a short visit with his parents, and then we headed back to Fort Dix. The cab driver dropped us off at the hole in the fence, shortly before daybreak. We made it back in time, thanks to God and that wonderful cabbie, wherever he may be.

We spent the next three days at Fort Dix, getting shots, more physicals, filling out insurance papers, being fitted with new uniforms and fatigues and a great number of things necessary to prepare us for overseas duty.

The day finally came. Filled with a variety of emotions, outwardly showing signs of bravado and patriotism to our buddies while inwardly, each of us suffered pangs of anxiety and fear of the future. Would we return safely or return wounded, without arms or legs or perhaps not return at all? I am sure that any man who is headed for combat harbors such fears and thoughts. If he does not, he is either a fool or a dreamer. Unlike the movies, there were no bands or crowds of people to see us off.

With full gear, M-I rifle and duffle bag, we boarded a ship in New York Harbor. The ship, "GEORGE WASHINGTON," a German luxury liner that had been captured in World War I and converted into a troop ship, that twenty-seven years before had taken Harry Truman across the Atlantic to fight another war in Europe. The ship held about seven thousand fully equipped troops. As we headed out to sea, each of us tried to get a final look at the New York skyline and the Statue of Liberty. Thousands of men were unbelievably silent, sharing individual thoughts with no one. These were street kids, students, future doctors and lawyers, toughs, sons of officers or congressmen, all headed towards an unknown destiny.

The first day out, I suppose by design, we did not have much time to think. The day was filled with activity; bunk assignment (mine, one of four, one above the other in the hold), calisthenics, and boat drills. Boat drills seemed to be a waste of time. Who the hell were we kidding? There weren't nearly enough life boats to handle all of the men aboard this ship. Getting on deck; in normal circumstances was, at the least, difficult; during an emergency, it would be absolutely impossible. If this ship were to go down, most of the men on board would be lost.

Depending upon where your bunk was located, men were jammed together in tight quarters. The air, a combination of body odor, sweat, cigarette smoke and breath and other unpleasant smells, was stifling. As usual, gambling took up most of the free time. The occasional opportunity to go out on deck was a welcome relief, as was my one tour of duty on KP (kitchen police), a welcome relief from the boredom. A day on KP was filled with work; peeling spuds, washing dishes, scrubbing pots and pans, swabbing the deck, cleaning grease traps and cleaning tables. All of this was done continuously due to the vast number of meal times and the amount of men to be fed. Even eating was a task. As the ship would sway so also, your tray or plate would move down the table. You could be eating from the tray belonging to the man next to you.

I was able to go out on deck that first night. Even though the ship was loaded with men, there was an eerie silence on this dark starlit night. There was, of necessity, a total blackout, with no smoking or lights of any kind on deck. At sea, the sky appears to hold many more stars than you would see in the city. I was able, with no difficulty, to pick out Orion, Ursa Major, Ursa Minor, and Polaris, no small task for a boy who was brought up in the city.

Being the Corporal of the Guard one night, afforded me the time and opportunity to enjoy some moments of quiet contemplation and a chance to enjoy the silence of the night that was broken only by the rushing of the sea against the ship as it made its way through the dark water. Other ships were silhouetted against a moonlit sky. At the bow, where the ship easily cut through the ocean, the water appeared to give off an iridescent glow. It was one of the few times that you could lose yourself in thought and still be alert. My tour of duty ended much too fast and I had to return to the familiar and aggravating sounds in the hold. There were always the ever present sounds of snoring, someone breaking wind, heavy breathing, cursing, and the occasional sound of a creaking bunk as someone attempted to relieve inner tensions and frustrations by self-gratification. All of this, a symphony of moans and groans, accompanied by the aching metallic sounds emanating from the hull as the ship plowed its way through the waves of a now calm but always a dangerous and threatening ocean. A threat, not only of the possibility of a sudden storm, that could change the gentle swell of the waves into a raging, life-threatening and turbulent boiling sea but also of the possibility of a sudden encounter with one of the many German U-boats that were prowling the North Atlantic in search of Allied vessels, sailing from the United States to England and Europe.

The morning of the second day, I went out on deck. What had been an empty sea the day before was now filled with ships of all shapes and sizes, for as far as the eye could see. This was said to be the largest convoy of ships to cross the Atlantic Ocean, up to that time. Looking in every direction, I could see nothing but ships, all around us, even to the distant horizon. The troop transports were completely surrounded by war ships as a safety net, against an attack by German vessels.

On Sunday morning, we were able to attend services out on the deck. It was a multi-denominational service with a priest, a rabbi, and a minister in attendance. It was a bright sunny day in March, so after the service, I went back to the fantail, to relax in the sun. For some reason, the movement of the ship seemed to be less pronounced back there. This was a large ship and I was fortunate, because I did not experience sea sickness during this voyage.

Sailing across the sea, at night, during war time necessitates a complete blackout. No smoking on deck was permitted. There can be absolutely no lights of any kind. Even the smallest flicker of light can reveal your position to any passing enemy ship or submarine. In the middle of the night, about halfway through the trip, everyone had settled down for the night. Talking and gambling had finally stopped. At last we could go into a sound and undisturbed sleep, at least for the next few hours, before being awakened. Suddenly, everyone was shaken by a series of loud thuds and the ship seemed to lurch. There was a limited amount of confusion but for the most part, all of the men on board began hastily to get dressed and grab a lifejacket, hurried on by the sound of sirens and horns, then by the sound of depth charges. Apparently, a German U-boat had managed to slip through the safety net of war ships. A rapidly spreading rumor was that one of our vessels had been sunk by a submarine before it too was sent to the bottom of the sea. There was very little sleep for the remainder of the night, even after the all clear signal had been sounded.

After twelve days at sea, we finally reached the seaport of Le Havre, France. The fastest way to unload all of these men was by rope ladder, my least liked activity. It involved climbing over the ship's railing with a full backpack, all of our gear, including a gas mask and M-I rifle and then try to make our way down the rope ladder that was in constant motion, trying not to step on the head of the GI below, while at the same time, being rushed by the guy above you. The rope would swing away from the ship and then crash back against the side of the ship, as it rolled in the water. Upon reaching the bottom of the ladder, you were met with the task of removing yourself from the skin burning rope and boarding a rapidly rolling landing craft. All of this was accompanied by loud yelling, screaming and cursing when someone's fingers were smashed under the boot of the man above. We were then shuttled to the dock by the landing boats.

When we were all dockside, our platoon was called into formation. Our lieutenant, feeling that perhaps he had been a little too rough on his men in training back in the States and being aware that the possibility of retaliation, in a combat situation, was very real, made an impassioned plea for everyone to understand that his actions were for our own good and survival. Most of these men were cognizant of that fact but there was always a chance of one person capable of carrying a grudge and seizing the opportunity to act upon his ill-feelings.

From LeHavare, we were sent to "Camp Lucky Strike" at Etratat, on the coast of France, to await the arrival of our rolling stock; trucks, jeeps, and big guns. Lucky Strike was a semi-permanent camp, made up of large pyramidal tents placed on a wooden platform with a pot belly stove in the middle, surrounded by canvas folding cots. It was here that I reached a point of realization. This was no longer fun and games. Months of training were now over. This was no longer a bloodied nose outside of school, fighting with rules attached or with gloves in a ring, no longer settling disputes with words. I no longer had Dad to go to in a time of crisis; no longer could I rely on my brothers to back me up. I did have a feeling of being alone. Could I measure up? Could I stand alone? Would I, at the final moment, freeze up and not be able to move? Would I, when coming face to face or perhaps even eye to eye, be able to pull the trigger or would my finger stiffen up to the point of immobility? Could I react, when life and death was the final outcome, and be the first to take action? Could I, upon coming into a close conflict with another human being, use my bayonet and then place my foot upon the chest and struggle to remove a stuck blade from the gaping and bloodied wound? Could I, would I? All of these and many other thoughts ran through my mind. Certainly, during many months, I had been trained by competent and able officers and non-coms. Or were they really competent and able? Most of them were civilian soldiers just like me. The majority of the officers were ninety day wonders, just out of OCS (Officer Training School), with no actual combat experience. Did I have self doubt? I certainly did. It took some time and effort to remove these thoughts from my mind.

This spell was broken by Rudy when he asked me to go to the movies with him. The show was being shown at a large open adjacent field. Everyone sat on the evening dew covered ground. While we awaited the beginning of the picture, we were engaged in all sorts of conversation. Someone called our attention to some smoke rising from the vicinity of our tents. I made a casual joking remark to Rudy that it looked like the smoke was coming from his tent. We eventually decided to go to see what was happening. Sure enough, it was his tent that was burning. Rudy lost all of his equipment and personal belongings. He had to requisition all new gear.

"Oh God! I am cold. Will this never end?"

"I am glad that I crawled into my sleeping bag last night. I wonder what time it is? It must be the middle of the night. I remember the snow covering the ground. Boy! It is snowing again. Why do I feel so warm? Who the hell is that snoring? If any krauts are around, they sure as hell will hear that. God, I'm shivering again, someone must be shaking the bed. Oh well, I might as well go back to sleep. I could not find the slit trench anyway."

"Cold, cold, cold, that is all that I feel. No, there is something else. It feels as though someone is sitting on my chest. It is the weight of the heavy snow that had piled up on top of me during the night. That's funny, I am shaking like hell but I seem to be sweating. I can sense the salty taste of sweat on my lips. My lips are dry as hell. I wish that Mom were here, she would know what to do."

"Hey Mac! Come on, get up." I could hear faint voices in the distance.

"Are you ok, Joe?" someone asked.

My teeth were chattering like mad, however, I did manage to say, "I'm ok, Mom is going to be here soon."

"Hey! He really is sick. He is delirious. We had better get him into a truck and get him to a medic."

The voices were hardly distinguishable, yet I knew that Art Grossman and Joe Beitz were there. I felt as though I were floating on air as they lifted me onto a truck. "God! I feel sick." I seemed to be floating in and out of consciousness for some time.

I was thinking, "Here I go again." "Sick again." As I lay upon the bed of the truck, I thought about the time that I was sick, back in the states, on maneuvers, in the back of a halftrack. I was on the bulletproof deck of the vehicle and had curled myself around the machine gun turret, trying to get comfortable. The angle-iron brackets, used to secure the ammo cans to the floor, kept poking me in the ribs and hips. Then too, I was seriously sick with a cold and a very high fever.

"Come on Corporal, drink this down. It might lower your temp." Doc Mickle, our medic said, as he attempted to get me to take some medication.

"That's ok Doc," I said. "Mom is going to chop up some onions and wrap them around my wrists and feet." Someone put more blankets on me. The truck was moving again and I could feel it bouncing along the road. We were somewhere in France, only God knows where. We were traveling under blackout conditions. How long I remained in this feverish illness, I really do not know but it must have been for days. I did eventually become lucid and coherent as the fever subsided. I asked the guys for something to eat.

"You son-of-a-bitch," someone said. "You scared the hell out of us. A couple of times we thought that we were going to lose you."

"Where should I begin?"

"What am I doing here?"

We are somewhere in France. I had heard that we were near a town, on the coast, called St. Nazaire. The Germans are about one hundred yards away. I can hear sporadic gun fire. It is the middle of the night and I am perched between the branches of a tree.

"What the hell am I doing here?"

I am a young twenty-year old kid who had never been outside of Philadelphia until I was eighteen. A kid who had dreams of better things, perhaps a better life, maybe a chance to become an artist. Yet, here I am in a foreign country, sitting in a tree, waiting to be shot at or even to be killed.

St. Nazaire had been an important dry dock and submarine base. It had also been knocked out of operation in 1942 by a British naval raid, however there was still a large German force holding out as a pocket of resistance. This force had to be taken or destroyed in order to secure the coastline. This task was given to the French 1st Army under the command of General Jean de Lattre de Tassigny. The 627th Field Artillery was assigned to the French 1st Army to assist in the bombardment of the area. We were to capture German soldiers who would not surrender and at the same time give assistance to the French in operating the 105 mm Howitzer field artillery pieces.

During the day, we had directed fire on the enemy compound. The shelling began around noontime when the Germans were in a mess hall. When the first shell hit the building, we could clearly see men come running out, with mess kits and food flying in every direction. The shelling continued for the rest of the day.

"Yes! What the hell am I doing here?"

"Hey Yank! Hey Yank!" I heard someone call, "Where are you?"

It is now night time and I am sitting in the tree, trying to be quiet while deep in thought and still alert. I am brought back to reality by the call of the two young Frenchmen who share my treetop home. They had gone to relieve themselves and were coming back through the woods with flashlights turned on. As quietly as I could, I told them to turn off the lights and to shut up or they would give away our position to the krauts. The two Frenchmen were assigned to me for instructions on how to make a survey, direct fire, make corrections, and relay that information back to the gun position.

By the way, the little trip through the woods to relieve themselves probably did give away our position. The following day, the tree was literally blown out from under us, sending the three of us sprawling to the ground. Did the Germans have us spotted or was this just a coincidence?

The engagement of the 627th at St. Nazaire earned us our first bronze battle star.

"Ok you guys, take off your fuckin clothes," a sergeant bellowed. "You're going to get a fuckin bath."

"Yeh, you sure are dirty, Bill."

"Hey Rudy, you don't have to shoot at the fuckin Krauts, you could stink them to death."

"Who the hell told you that you smelled like a fuckin rose?"

"Me Mudder, dats who."

We were in a rear bivouac area to get some rest and a much needed cleaning. We did not have a bath for quite some time and were a scruffy looking lot, covered with dirt and grime and all in need of a shave, all with various lengths of facial hair and beards, and some, if not all, carrying extra company, lice.

At that point, the battery was lined up, bare-assed naked and headed for the woods where the engineers had rigged up a multiple make-shift shower from galvanized pipe. The overhead pipe had a series of holes drilled into the underside of the pipe. The shower was located on the banks of a cold, fast, flowing river. Water was pumped from the river, through the pipes. Ten men could take a shower at the same time. Believe me, that water was really cold.

"Brrr! Christ, I'm freezing my ass off," someone yelled. Everyone was screaming, yelling, and cursing at the same time. The sound bounced off of the trees and echoed through the woods.

"Hey! Who's got the soap?"

"If you drop that soap, you're going to lose your cherry."

"What cherry? He never had one."

"Hurry up you guys, I'm freezing my balls off."

"Keep your fuckin shirt on."

"I can't, they took it."

"You're just jealous, cause I'm not cherry."

"Yeh! Yeh! Yeh!"

After the shower, we had to walk single file, down a path, with a split rail fence along both sides. We would then stop at a point between two medics armed with DDT spray guns. With closed eyes, we stood there to be deloused. Then we moved on to two more medics for a second shot of DDT. The whole body was now covered with white powder. Picture, if you will, all of these men walking around, stark naked, covered with white powder. Following this, we entered a building where we were issued new clothing. In spite of everything, it sure did feel good to be clean again.

We spent the rest of the day checking and cleaning our guns and equipment, reading mail, and writing home. Finally, a good night's sleep.

After St. Nazaire, preparations were being made for the first assault and the invasion of Germany. The 627th, along with other outfits, was to cross France as rapidly as possible. We were to act as replacements for the ill-fated 106th Division that had been completely wiped out as the 5th Panzerarmee, attempting to make a breakthrough at the "Bulge," surrounded the 106th and forced the surrender of 7000 GI's. At times, we could move fast because most of the Wehrmacht had been driven out. In some places, there were pockets of resistance., as the Germans attempted to halt our progress by blowing up bridges and destroying anything that we might be able to use. Snipers were hiding in what homes and buildings were still standing, after being subjected to aerial attacks and artillery bombardments. The streets were covered with rubble and most of the buildings were mere shells with partial walls standing precariously on foundations and with no interiors. The only living thing was the occasional rat scurrying among the rubble, in search of food.

While the convoy was en-route, I had no specific duty in regard to the vehicles and guns. My responsibility was to the surveying equipment only, therefore, I was assigned to be the jeep driver for Lt. Berndt. The lieutenant was a tall lanky Texan with a ruddy complexion and, I believe, delusions of grandeur. He carried a 45 caliber hand gun slung low on his hip, as a Texan should and he wore a World War I campaign hat with a wide circular brim and a pushed down crown. Was Lt. Berndt a good officer? He certainly was one of the best even though he was a little eccentric.

As convoy officer, it was his duty to patrol the entire length of the convoy, control and regulate the required distance between all vehicles and to maintain speed. This required patrolling the convoy repeatedly at breakneck speeds and a times, driving on the small narrow sidewalks of the very small curving streets, in very tiny villages. These ancient streets were built for carts and not for large trucks. At times, we would race ahead of the column, check out the route and make sure that the route signs were pointing in the proper direction. English speaking Germans, dressed in American GI uniforms would infiltrate our lines and change the road signs, to upset, and confuse our troop movement. They were quite successful at this ploy.

All activities, during this period, seemed to indicate the coming of the end of the war for the Germans. As we pushed forward toward the "Maginot Line" and the "Sigfried Line," the enemy was making last ditch battles and any allied soldiers, who were just unfortunate enough to be captured, were summarily executed, as was evident at Malmedy where many American soldiers taken by the advancing German Army, had been shot down and left in a field of blood-stained snow. This was done to instill fear into the hearts and minds of our men. Instead of fear, this brutality caused the Allied troops to fight more fearlessly and with vindictiveness.

While going through a small village, the Lieutenant decided to check out a number of buildings for snipers. Once again, I was to volunteer. There were very few buildings left standing with sufficient walls and interiors that could afford a suitable hiding place and cover for snipers. As we stepped across the threshold of a house, I had a strange and sudden feeling that I had been in that house before, at some time, albeit I had never been in that town in my life. Call it intuition or ESP, or anything else, I knew every room in that house and could see two armed men in a certain room of an upper floor. We were able to quietly make our way up the damaged staircase and into that room without being detected. My vision or insight enabled us to survive that day.

It became necessary for us to rig a homemade device onto the front end of our jeep. A five foot piece of angle iron with angled grooves cut out of one side was attached upright to the bumper of the vehicle. This was used to snag wires that the Germans had stretched across some roads at a height that would decapitate anyone riding in an open jeep.

We crossed the Rhine River and entered Germany somewhere near Strasbourg and crossed the Neckar at Stuttgart. Finally, we had set foot on the homeland of the "Third Reich." The convoy proceeded north through Stuttgart, a city that had been bombarded by our artillery and aircraft for days, leaving nothing but rubble. The bridges across the Neckar had all been demolished so we crossed over on bridges that had been hurriedly built by our engineers. Our column continued north, not stopping in Stuttgart.

Our destination was Heilbronn, a small city on the Neckar. As we approached the city, we encountered refugees, fleeing the city. Old women in long black dresses with scarves on their heads, carrying large bundles, trudged along the road. Younger women pushing baby carriages, had small children trailing behind them. Old men, carrying huge backpacks attempted to keep up with the younger people. All types of things; baby carriages, kiddie wagons, carts, and a variety of homemade conveyances, were used to transport their meager but cherished possessions. The line went on for miles. Some, of course, were Germans who had been bombed out of their homes, while others were displaced persons from other European countries who had been taken as prisoners by the advancing German army and used as forced labor in the German factories.

Nearing the city, we could see why the people were on the move. They, of course, wanted to avoid being taken by the Russians. A fear well founded because of the havoc and destruction their own troops had wreaked upon the Russian people during the German invasion. Heilbronn had suffered total destruction. Not one building was left standing. The streets were covered with debris; stones and concrete prevented any foot traffic on the sidewalks, glass from blown out windows, broken down carts and wagons, dead dogs and horses and abandoned guns and cannon. The smell of dead and burning flesh and the suffocating odor of a bombed out sewer system. Many of the buildings had been hit by incendiary bombs and the interiors were completely burned out. These blackened structures, with only the stone walls remaining, gave one an eerie feeling, even in daylight. There was not a home, store, or church left undamaged. There were absolutely no signs of life, not even a rat scurrying by.

We continued through Heilbronn and finally came to a halt in a residential area, on the far side of town. This is where we were to be billeted for some time. There were row homes there, erected in a U shape with a common open area in the center, that had not been touched by bombing. Either this was not a strategic war producing target or it had purposely been saved from bombing for future use by our troops. It was a community of stucco two-story buildings. The common area was used by all of the residents as a fruit and vegetable garden with the biggest and most delicious looking strawberries that I had ever seen. We were, however, not to eat the berries because they had been fertilized with human waste. The residents were evicted from their homes and we moved in. Where they went, I know not, but I suspect that they lived in the cellars of the bombed out buildings or went to live with relatives in nearby towns. Art Grossman, Larry Coons of Oshkosh, Wis., myself and three others were quartered in one house.

Our duty in Heilbronn was to capture German soldiers, Waffen SS troopers and Nazis. A large field on the banks of the Neckar River was selected as a holding area. At this time, prisoners were being taken by the thousands. Many were mere children, young boys of thirteen or fourteen, young members of the "Hitler Youth," who upon being captured, burst into tears. Some of these kids had shown to be just as deadly as any experienced soldaten. Other captives were women and old men who were pressed into service in this final but futile struggle. Most of the prisoners were regular army men. It was an unbelievable task to hold and feed all of these people. The field was surrounded by rolls of concertina barbed wire with only one opening facing the river. All of the prisoners of war, both men and women, were herded into this one compound with only the clothes on their backs. Toilet facilities consisted of a ditch in one corner of the field. By now, truck loads of soldiers were coming in every hour. The war was rapidly coming to an end and they were anxious to surrender. As they were being unloaded, some of our GI's became somewhat over-enthusiastic. Of course, when you take some boys out of the hills and give them a gun and a stick, the feeling of power is going to get out of hand. Some of these guards would use the stick to unload the truck more rapidly. I never saw a need for such tactics because we could very easily have been the prisoners.

Officers and men would, of necessity, guard this enclosure. I remember trying to keep warm by an open fire at night. A buddy and I were on guard duty at one corner of the field. We dug a hole in the ground and started a fire to keep warm. He had found some eggs and potatoes at a nearby farm. We then roasted the spuds on the hot fire and fried the eggs in our steel helmets. Mostly, I remember being cold, always cold. The small fire only gave temporary warmth. At least, the potatoes and eggs were a welcome relief after weeks of "K" rations.

Every night, someone would jump the barbed wire fence and try to escape to the river Neckar. Possibly, some made it, others were shot down before reaching the river. Corpses were piled up near the entrance to the enclosure, until they could be carried away for burial and as a warning to others not to attempt an escape. The war was nearly over so an escape was really a foolhardy thing to do. It could only mean recapture or death.

CHAPTER SIX
KRIEGSGEFANGENLAGER B-13

CHAPTER SIX

KRIEGSGEFANGFNENLAGER B-13

Eventually, the army engineers built a more permanent POW camp across the river on the other side of town. This new camp consisted of a series of cages or lagers on both sides of some stone covered roads. Each cage, capable of holding about three thousand people, was enclosed with a wire fence that was topped with barbed wire. Shelter was provided by long low canvas tents, erected over a rectangular hole in the ground about a foot and a half deep. This hole allowed for more headroom for the twenty occupants of the tent. A small wood guard shack was next to the gate, where we could observe all activities within the camp and monitor all people entering or leaving the compound. There was a large open pavilion-like structure, used as a kitchen for one pot meals, usually a stew or a soup. Immediately inside the gate, there was a wood and tarpaper shack to house the camp master, labor master, head cook, and the interpreter.

The move to the new camp was hectic. A long line of POW's snaked through the streets of Heilbronn. Many civilians stood along the sidewalks. An elderly man, perhaps seeing someone in the column that he knew, walked over to the prisoners to talk to someone. When he had finished his conversation, he tried to return to the sidewalk and was shoved back into the line by a guard who mistakenly thought that he was a POW trying to make an escape. He kept trying to get back to the pavement only to be stopped again and again. Hopefully, he was able to be separated from the POW's before reaching the camp.

Upon arriving at and getting settled in the new camp, a form of government had to be set up. Covertly, I am sure that a policing body was formed and judges appointed to a kangaroo court. Outwardly, I saw the election of "Eric," a stem but fair sergeant, to be the camp or lager master. "Tony," chosen to be the labor master, was a bull of a man with broad shoulders and a very small waist. He too was a German army sergeant. Tony bellowed rather than spoke and people moved upon hearing the sound of his voice. He was the perfect choice to be in charge of the labor gangs. Most of the inmates received two meals a day, however anyone who volunteered to be on a work crew, would get three meals. Tony reminded me of Victor McLaglen, a professional boxer and a motion picture star of the 30's and 40's.

A large group of men gathered at the gate. Some were calling out "arbeiten, arbeiten." The word had gotten out that anyone who worked would get three meals that day instead of the usual two. A tall, thin young man worked his way to the front of the group and asked for work. His command of English was better than ours with no trace of an accent. He gave the appearance of being very pushy and talkative. He told us that his name was George, however, I had my doubts, even about that. George was very sly and cunning. He was also forward and gregarious with an obvious ability to con people in order to get whatever he wanted or needed. Still, these traits were an asset when dealing with some of the other POW's. We needed someone to act as a go-between within the camp. Although we did have some reservations, George became our camp interpreter. In POW life as well as in military and civilian life, many Nazis and SS (Schutzstaffel) were able to talk their way into positions of power within the camp government. Even in POW camps there had to be a governing body or there would be chaos. Whatever George's affiliation, he was an invaluable help to us during his stay in the camp. Later upon pre release interrogation, George never returned to our compound. Apparently the U.S. authorities saw reason to detain him.

One morning, when I entered the compound, George came forward and told me that some of the POW's did not have warm clothing and were almost freezing during the night. He also informed me that some men who lived in the area told him about a clothing factory in a nearby town that had manufactured Luftwaffe uniforms for the German war effort. I requisitioned a truck and along with a couple of other non-coms, took George and several POW's to the factory. There among the rubble, we found four workable foot pedal sewing machines and bolts of blue Luftwaffe officer material which we immediately confiscated. We took everything out to the truck and returned to the camp. With these items, soldiers with some tailoring experience were able to make clothing for those people in need. Many, upon being captured, came to this camp with dirty and torn clothing. This singular act was to set me in good stead with these captive Germans and aide me in future dealings with them in attempting to maintain order within the compound.

The war was coming to an end. Not only were more prisoners being taken but it seemed that more men, on both sides, were now being killed as the fighting became more fierce. Lt Tuttle, our esteemed leader, volunteered Joe Beitz and I to search the bodies of fallen men for identification and then load them on a truck for burial.

A large old warehouse was turned into a temporary morgue. As we entered the converted warehouse, we could feel the chilling cold and dampness that went right to the bone. All of our senses seemed to be effected at the same time. This strange feeling was exacerbated by the very coldness of death that permeated the entire make-shift morgue. There were rows upon endless rows of bodies stretching the entire length of the building, lying there in silence. There they lay, like stiff, battered and torn little toy soldiers, discarded by some child, unwanted and no longer loved. The uniforms were covered with dirt and stains of dried blood. Some staring with sightless eyes toward the wooden rafters. None appeared to have an expression of pain. Were their last thoughts pleasant ones of home and loved ones? At a glance, it was obvious, that all were not "Volks Armee Soldaten" or "Waffen SS." Some were young men whose lives had been snuffed out, like a candle in a stiff breeze, in the prime of their lives. Young men who could have had a future in the arts, science, medicine, politics, or just become good craftsmen. Men who, under different circumstances could have served their country in untold numbers of beneficial ways to the advancement of mankind, into a better and far more rewarding future. Others were old men who really should have been enjoying their twilight years, and young boys of thirteen and fourteen years of age, who should have been in school. These old men and boys had been thrust into the front to defend a dying Germany. Most had fought as ferociously as any hardened veteran and died on the first day of battle. These and many young American GI's who died in the last struggle were the true heroes of the final conflict. Were these the hated and feared enemy? As we stood there in the darkened gloom, lit only by the dust filled shafts of sunlight, shining in at an angle from the upper windows, each of us had our own thoughts.

"Why? Oh, why?"

Why was all of this necessary? To what end? To what purpose? What was accomplished? Did the loss of millions of lives, finally achieve a world and lasting peace? Was this, as the First World War was supposed to be, the war to end all wars? Could we, at last, go home to peace and prosperity without the fear of war? In a very short time, that dream would be shattered.

My eyes began to mist from the build up of tears. What a total waste. A waste of lives, minds, endeavor, and talent. What these men and others could have achieved will never be known, will never be realized. The tears forming in Beetle's bad eye created, momentarily, a dent in his usual tough exterior armor. He, like the rest of us, did have moments of tenderness.

After performing this task for several days, I remember that we could not even touch a slice of bread after scrubbing our hands countless times. We used a fork to pick up the slice. One day, as we attempted to load a corpse onto the tailgate of a truck, we dropped the body, leaving it with the back on the platform of the warehouse and the legs propped up on the tailgate. It was a most grotesque sight for even the most war hardened. Both Beetle and I were on the verge of becoming ill. I called out to the officer relaxing in a nearby Jeep.

"No way! Lieutenant no more, you can get someone else to do this job."

"Ok Mac, calm down," he said. "You had better go down to the compound and get some Krauts."

As I approached the lager, a large group of POW's surged toward the gate. Each man waved a hand above his head and shouted,

"Ich arbeiten, Ich arbeiten," "I work, I work."

Most prisoners received two meals a day. A prisoner who worked got three meals; therefore, many were anxious to do some kind of work, if not for the extra food, to alleviate the boredom of camp life.

I thought to myself, "Don't be that willing. You won't like the type of work that I have for you." I selected six men and led them away with my M-1 rifle trained on them. They faced me smiling and tried to indicate to me that I did not need a gun because they would not try to escape; they just wanted to work. They were not very happy when they saw what they were required to do; but they, albeit reluctantly, pitched in to the work at hand. There was some grumbling but it was in German; therefore, I did not fully understand what was said. It was probably best that I didn't. For the remainder of our time at the morgue, Beetle and I just acted as guards and supervised the detail.

It was a very common sight to see people, young and old, scavenging through the rubble of bombed out buildings for something of value or going through garbage cans in search of a bit of food. They would mingle near American facilities. This is where they were usually successful in finding something to eat. Enemy or not, it was heart rendering to see anyone in such dire need.

The German mark was virtually useless. Money was worthless until the issuance of occupation money. Everything was subject to bartering, inexpensive or costly. When walking or riding through the streets of German towns, villages, or big cities, we would meet someone willing to trade or sell anything.

"Hey Yank! You got any gum?"

"You have chocolate?"

"Hey Yank! You want my sister? Only two chocolate bars."

Anything was for sale, even their bodies and yes, I suspect, even their souls, just to satisfy the gripping hunger in their stomachs. The first days, weeks, and months after a defeat are terrible times for anyone. Once a population feels relatively assured that they will not be killed by the advancing occupation troops, there still remains the constant struggle for mere survival. There is no law, no order. Money is worthless. There are no jobs and little hope of finding help from anyone, friend or relative. Criminals are either released or escape from prison to prey upon honest people. Of course food is scarce. Much of the food supply has been destroyed or contaminated, looting is rampant, and, by and large, a great many of the people are looking out for themselves with absolutely no care or concern for anyone but themselves. Self-preservation is the rule of the day. Human rats are scurrying all over the rubble in hopes of profiting on the grief and sorrow of others. This, of course, was of their own doing. The Germans had brought this upon themselves by aiding, following, and giving adulation to Hitler as he led them down a path of total destruction. Was this to be a repeat of the days following the end of World War I, when one out of every four children died of starvation? The innocent will always suffer the most and the children cannot even comprehend what is happening to them. May God forgive us if we can not take care of the little children.

Screams of pain and terror broke the stillness of the night. We knew that the "Kangaroo Court" must have been in session and someone was being punished. With thousands of German POW's in the lager (camp), it was necessary to have some form of government and judicial system. Punishment was usually severe and swift. Any infraction or crime was, of necessity, serious. No one had much of anything; therefore, to steal from another soldier was an act of grand larceny. There was no such thing as petty theft.

On one occasion, Eric, the camp master, asked me to come into the compound. He led me to an area where there was a square of sheet metal on the ground. It was about five feet square. I had passed by it many times and thought nothing of it. Eric reached down and picked up the metal, revealing a hole or pit four feet by four feet and perhaps ten feet deep. There were two completely naked prisoners at the bottom of the pit, covered with dirt, urine, and their own feces. After four days in the hole with the sun beating down on the metal, there was not much life left in them. It brought back memories of the Georgia sweat boxes. Needless to say, I was horrified. I had the two men removed immediately and the hole filled up with dirt.

I arrived at the camp early one morning. George and I began to make the morning check of the fence. A couple of German non-coms came over to talk to George who turned to me and interpreted the substance of the conversation. According to them, a young soldaten was despondent because he had lice and took his own life. I could not believe it because everyone had lice at this point. They led us over to one of the tents. As I have said before, each tent was similar to a pup tent except much longer and made to house about twenty men. In order to gain more head room, they would dig a rectangular hole in the ground about a foot and a half deep, then place the tent above the hole, permitting more living space.

The boy's body was hanging at an angle into the tent. His arms seemed extended and bent, with his hands on the surface of the ground as though doing pushups or attempting to restrain himself. A wire attached to the apex of the tent was around his neck. His throat had been cut; however, the razor was inside of the tent, near his knee. Could this possibly have been a suicide? Not by any stretch of the imagination. We made inquiries throughout the camp to no avail. No one would tell us a thing. We had no alternative but to write it up as a suicide.

His body was removed and placed on a stretcher to be taken to the morgue, which was a converted barn located at the end of a make-shift road between the cages. The detail assigned this task usually had to wait in line to put the corpse into the barn because each body had to be examined and identified. It was a common sight to see groups of men sitting on the ground and leaning against the side of the barn. They would be eating, smoking, and joking as soldiers would. On the ground in front of each detail would be a stretcher bearing a corpse.

As part of the routine of changing the guard when we came to relieve the night shift, Cpl. Saeger and I, along with George, the interpreter, would tour the inside perimeter of the fence to check for any holes or openings in the fence. The night guard told us that he had noticed a young POW hanging around the fence and that we should watch for any attempt to escape. During the next few days, I did see him at the fence until finally he was met by a young girl. After checking, I found out that he had lived near Heilbronn and that the young girl was indeed his wife. Every day, they would spend an hour or so at the fence just talking and holding hands through the wire. The girl approached one of the guards and asked permission to bring a basket of fruit and other food for her husband. I told them that it was alright providing that I checked the basket before it could enter the compound. Every day she was there at a specified time, and I did search the basket for knives or guns. We could not afford to become lax or complacent.

After a couple of weeks, upon arriving at the gate with my squad, Cpl. Saeger told me that sometime during the night, the young soldier had tried to escape over the fence and had been shot down by a guard in the tower. He was dead and his body had to be taken to the morgue. Later that day, his wife arrived on schedule and it was up to me to tell her of the events of the previous night. As I was making a rather feeble attempt to justify what had happened, she dropped the basket and just stood there in somewhat of a daze. Nothing was said and no tears were shed. She stood there for some time in a state of shock, turned around, and slowly walked down the path toward the town. If only he could have waited a month or two, he would have been released. Another one of the sad turn of events during wartime and its aftermath.

We were riding in a Jeep early one morning on our way to B-13 for our tour of duty. The road between the compounds was extra dry due to the lack of rain. The Jeep created a thick cloud of dust behind us. Although the sun was low in the sky, it was obvious that it was going to be a clear, warm day. Usually, at this time of the day, the POW's were fairly quiet and just beginning to stir after a nights sleep despite the uncomfortable conditions. We could sense that something was different that morning. A mixture of voices, loud screaming mingled with roars of laughter, became louder as we got closer to B-13. The cage next to B-13 was a female compound holding a couple thousand women, young and old, who had been captured with weapons and therefore were treated as enemies. Apparently, this morning, they had decided to protest their plight. A couple of hundred of the women declared their dissatisfaction by removing all of their clothing and then standing near the fence. They just stood there, laughing and taunting anyone who drove by. There was nothing sexual or sensual about this scene. Many women and men too, were naked through no fault of their own when they were finally freed from the concentration camps. Even then, they managed to display a certain amount of dignity and decency although nude, disheveled, underfed, and skinny beyond belief. Whatever it was that enabled them to endure and survive such inhuman treatment, only God can know and understand. By contrast, these German women soldiers, albeit better fed and therefore better built, in there flagrant display of their nakedness, were disgusting. After being threatened with an immediate and complete internal physical, the women dispersed and redressed with little or no complaint.

The troops in Europe as well as the people back home had no knowledge of the horrors that were taking place in the concentration camps. There were a couple of hundred such camps throughout Europe. Some were not death camps such as Auschwitz, Bergen-Belsen, Dachau, and Treblinka; however, millions of people died in other camps from starvation, brutality, and overwork. Many worked in defense plants for the same people who were causing their slow death. Upon the liberation of the concentration camps, General Eisenhower issued an order that all troops quartered in close proximity to these bastions of horror and brutality must visit these camps and witness first hand what had been going on at these places for years. A camp in southern German, near Kassel, Ohrdruf, was full of slave laborers, who were near starvation. There were also numerous unburied corpses. Even "Old Blood and Gutts" General George Patton, when he came to see for himself, was reduced to illness and vomited. General "Ike" Eisenhower also ordered all German civilians living in the vicinity of these camps to go see these scenes of appalling horror. Many of them professed ignorance and were unaware of these tragedies. I found then, and still do to this day, that their total innocence was untrue and unbelievable. The odor that filled the air that they breathed must have been a clue. They must have seen truck loads of the starving near skeletal figures being transported to and from the factories. Still, I can also understand their reluctance to protest because had they done so, they too would have become an inmate at such a camp. Certainly they were terrified and reluctant to overtly question the Nazi regime.

As the war was coming to an end, there were tens of thousands of DP's or displaced persons roaming around Europe trying to find their way back home. The DP's were mostly men from other countries that Germany had conquered and had been forced into labor or made to join the Wehrmacht and fight for the Fatherland.

A large group of Hungarian soldiers were brought to our camp in Heilbronn to be fed and sheltered until they could board a train to return them to Hungary. They were a pitiful sight as they trudged along the road in their heavy, woolen uniforms, unkempt and bearded, hunched over from the weight of the packs on their backs. We lined them up in a row and had them remove the backpacks and bedrolls and place them on the ground. Just as everyone entering the camp, they too had to be searched for weapons. While in the process of conducting a search, we discovered three Waffen SS storm troopers among the group. They had donned Hungarian uniforms hoping to make their way out of Germany; thus avoiding punishment and perhaps retaliation. We sent them off to headquarters for interrogation and hopefully due process. We then searched the backpacks that were on the ground. Every one of the packs was stuffed with new shirts, pants, sweaters, silk stockings, and many cartons of cigarettes. It was no small wonder why the Hungarians were bent over from the weight of their burdens. In their travels, trying to find their way back home, they had looted many German businesses and stores. They no doubt felt that they were entitled to whatever they could take and carry. All of these things were confiscated and given to prisoners who were in need of clothing. Our original pity for this particular group of Hungarian soldiers was certainly misplaced. I am afraid that this experience made us somewhat skeptical of other groups of DP's that we were later to encounter.

SHIP 0800 WEDNESDAY

Roster of German Generals

Cage B 13

1

0800 WEDNESDAY

1 Bahn, Egmont	Gen.Maj.	81-G-411252	H	Hannover
2 Baumgartner,Richard	Gen.	81-G-413727	H	Salzburg
3 Friderici,Erich	Gen.	81-SP-70005	H	Bayern
4 Kotz, Richard	Gen.Maj.	81-SP-70015	H	Westfalen
5 Layers, Hans	Gen.Maj.	81-G-411254	H	Tirol
6 Lieb, Helmut	Gen.Lt.	81-G-411545	H	Hessen
7 Heidrich,Richard	Gen.Xxxx	81-G-411544	L	Hannover
8 Magerl,Dr. Heinrich	Gen.Vet.	81-SP-70021	H	Bayern
9 Meinhold,Guenther	Gen.Maj.	81-G-411258	H	Hessen
10 Michaellis,August	OT.Eins.Lt.	81-SP-73657		Oberbayern
11 Picker,Egbert	Gen.Lt.	81-G-411546	H	Oberbayern
12 Schlemmer,Hans	Gen.	81-G-411547	H	Sachsen
13 Schulz,Karl-Lothar	Gen.Maj.	81-G-411548	L	Hannover
14 Steets,Hans	Gen.Maj.	81-G-411549	H	Hessen
15 Trettner, Heinz	Gen.Lt.	81-SP-70017	L	Wuerttemberg
16 von Gablenz,Eckard	Gen.Lt.	81-G-411250	H	Sachsen
17 von Ihne, Victor	Gen.Maj.	81-SP-70020	H	Italy, Rome
18 von Ilsemann, Helmuth	Gen.Maj.	81-G-411550	L	Bayern
19 von Senger u. Etter-lin, Frido	Gen.	81-SP-70049	H	Goettingen
20 von Tschudi, Rudolf	Gen.Lt.	81-G-411552	H	Thueringen
21 Wehrig, Max	Gen.Maj.	81-G-411251	H	Wiesbaden
22 Zwade, Georg	Gen.Maj.	81-G-411256	H	Thueringen

MINE WASHED ASHORE

Make-Shift German graves

Horse drawn artillery

German occupation of Paris

Damaged German Ship

German cannon

Take ten

Viewing destruction

Horse drawn artillery

Letters from home

Destroyed buildings

German soldiers

Destroyed bridge

Disabled tank

NAZI Headquarters

German Occupation of Paris

NAZI Headquarters

German graves

We had not been told that we could expect any additional prisoners on that particular day. To us, the compound appeared to be filled to capacity. About mid-day, a couple of 2 ½ ton trucks slowly pulled up to the gate of B-13. As the POW's dismounted from the vehicles, it was quite obvious why we had not been informed. All of the soldiers were in uniforms of general officers. With all of the aplomb befitting their status, they were assisted by an aide in their descent from the trucks. One officer carried a little yapping Dachshund under his arm. The group of twenty-two generals included General Erick Friderici, General Hans Schlemmer, General Frido von Senger u.Etterlin, and the redoubtable General Richard Heidrich, the man with the dog, commander of the 1st Parachute Corp., at the battle of Monte Cassino, Italy. I was told that General Heidrich had two Dachshunds but one had perished in a parachute drop. I made the unforgivable mistake of treating these men like any other POWs. To me, in my young naïve mind, the war was now over and they, in spite of their braid, medals, and demeanor, were prisoners like any of the thousands of others in the camp. At their first mealtime, they stood in the chow line like everyone else. Indeed, I was taken to task for my unthinkable treatment of these men of renown. I had not assigned an aide to stand in the chow line and serve them their meals, and I had not supplied them with their own private and separate slit trench for their use when nature called. In the camp, each officer was to be supplied with his own quarters, an aide to attend to his every need, and a non-com to do his laundry and bring his food from the mess tent. We were expected and ordered to show these men all of the respect and courtesy due to a general officer. This was difficult for us to carry out after seeing all that we had seen in the past few months. They really did not have it so bad considering the condition of all of the people around them. Fortunately, the generals did not stay with us very long. Eventually they were taken away for interrogation and that was the last we ever saw or heard of them.

The Kriegsgefangenenlager (Prisoner of War Camp) at Heilbronn was made up of about fourteen enclosures or cages. My own squad was assigned guard duty at cage B-13 where about three thousand POW's were being held as prisoners.

Naturally, any group of people this large would include men of many talents and skills. Many of the men were not career soldiers, Nazis. or SS storm troopers but were ordinary citizens: businessmen, craftsmen, teachers, and artists who, upon the final hours of conflict, were given a rifle and sent to the front. Many others were teenage children. One young boy was only twelve years old and rather small for his age. Our platoon took him in as a mascot and fitted him with a cut down GI uniform.

In one of the make-shift huts, an elderly prisoner, obviously a teacher, scientist, and/or philosopher, sat surrounded by a group of younger men. He was rather short and somewhat stout with a gray, trimmed mustache and Van Dyke beard. He was expounding on some scientific theory. I enjoyed watching and listening to him, especially when he spoke in English, as he often did. He, along with others, had to undergo interrogation to determine what his contribution to the war had been and just what his scientific knowledge could contribute to the future peace. All of the prisoners were to be questioned before being released. Apparently, he was an important scientist because he was never returned to the compound. POW's who were found to be Nazi and Storm Troopers were taken way with no explanation, which was understandable considering the horrors of the concentration camps. The United States and Russia were engaged in a hunt for German scientists, especially men like Werner von Braun, who were rocket scientists. Little did we know that these men and their knowledge would eventually lead to the landing of men on the moon.

One prisoner, Johann Schopper, was an accomplished artist. When it became known that an excellent and well-known portrait painter was being held in B-13, our commanding officers just had to have a portrait painted by this man. Herr Schopper required some equipment and art materials. It was known, at this time, that I had some artistic knowledge. From small wallet-sized photographs, I had made a number of sketches of the wives and girlfriends of my buddies and some of the officers. Because of this, I was assigned to guard Johann Schopper on a trip to his home and studio in Nurnburg. A lieutenant, whose name I cannot recall, was in charge. When we arrived in Nurnburg, we were met by a joyous but tearful Frau Schopper. We spent a few hours there selecting and packing art material as needed. From the looks of this studio, it was quite obvious that this man was a great portrait painter. It was a typical artist studio with the smell of paint and turpentine throughout the rooms. Odors that reminded me of the Graphic Sketch Club back in Philly. Before returning to Heilbronn, we discretely permitted Johann to have a conjugal visit with his wife. We had recently done the same thing with Tony our tough Labor Meister. Before leaving to return to the camp, Johann gave a drawing to the Lieutenant and presented me with a signed drawing of a medieval castle in the city of Metz.

Our squad had orders to search all prisoners and to confiscate all weapons and cameras that we found. I was told to collect and store all confiscated material in a large box and to deliver the box to Captain Yakowitz. Guns had been taken earlier but this search did uncover many knives, bayonets, and cameras. The cameras were of a variety of models, some good and some bad, some old, and some fairly new. Naturally, I wanted a camera for myself. In our monthly allotment from the PX (Post Exchange) which included: candy, cigarettes, and toothpaste, a few Liecas, Ziess Icons, and Voightlanders would be for sale. After the officers got their pick, a drawing would be held to determine just who would be permitted to purchase one of the much desired cameras. My name was never called. Much to my chagrin, the recipients of these drawings was usually a GI from the hills of Tennessee or Kentucky who had no interest in photography. No amount of cajoling or offer of money could convince them to give up their chance to make a purchase. I had a good idea of what was going to happen to the carton of confiscated goods, so I removed a Voightlander reflex camera from the box. When I turned the box over to the captain, the officers made a search through the contents and took all of the better cameras for themselves. After doing so, the box was given back to me and I was instructed to distribute the remaining cameras to the non-coms.

Sometime later, I was assigned to drive the Captain to a meeting in a distant town We were driving through an area of countryside of unparalleled beauty, looking down into a lush green valley with mountains on all sides reaching to the clouds.

The hillside was dotted with small cottages but was dominated by a large, old medieval castle perched on the top. The officer ordered me to stop so that he could take some photographs of the scene. While he was busy taking his shots, I took out my Voightlander and proceeded to snap away. Upon seeing me, the Captain called out, "Hey Corporal, where the hell did you get that?"

With an air of innocence, I asked, "Get what, Sir?"

"You know what I mean."

I explained what I had done and he did not say a word. It was never mentioned again. Perhaps it was because it was I who was going to develop his film.

The road was dry and dusty. A group of GI's, riding in the back of a truck, was on their way back to their quarters. A young girl, walking her bicycle, was almost obscured by the cloud of dust stirred up by the truck. She was not missed by the young soldiers who began to hoot and call out to her.

'Hey! Wo gehen zie, fraulein?"

In near perfect English she answered, "I am on my way home."

I had the driver stop the truck. A couple of guys helped the girl get into the truck along with her bike. Everyone began to ask questions as once.

"What is your name Fraulein?" "Where do you live?"

Her name was Erica and she lived on the other side of the Neckar River, in the basement of a bombed out building. This was during the non-fraternization period, a time when GI's were not permitted to associate with the German people; therefore, we had to conceal Erica as we drove across the MP guarded bridge. A friendship between us would grow over the next few months. Along with English, Erica spoke several other languages. The building in which she and her mother lived had been hit by incendiary bombs and was completely burned out. There were no windows or roof, just a shell of a stone structure. The two shared a small basement room about six feet by eight feet, which was accessible only through a long, dark alley from the back of the building. It was furnished with homemade bunk beds, a chair, and a table. After I became friendly with the mother and daughter, I tried to take food to them when possible. That, in was not easy. Since we could not socialize, I could not cross over the bridge built by the Engineer Corps. After dark, I would make my way down the road leading to the river. At any sign of a light or an approaching vehicle, I had to jump into the bushes that lined the side of the road and wait for the vehicle to pass. Then I continued furtively toward the bridge spanning the river. Since I could not just walk over the wooden bridge without confronting the guards, I had to make my way up river to the bombed steel girder bridge that had been the main crossover before it was destroyed. The darkness of the night was broken only by the light of the moon as it appeared from behind a billowing cloud, casting shimmering rays of light on the rippling water. The moonlight also shown through the openings of the slanted steel, creating moving shadows on the river and giving the appearance that the whole structure was about to fall into the water below. Both sides of the bridge tilted down into the river, meeting in the water halfway across. To cross the bridge, it was necessary to go cautiously down the slippery metal of one side, jump over the water to the other side of the bridge, then climb up to the bank on the opposite side. I made this trip several times before the fraternization ban was lifted. Food and clothing were scarce. Of course, no work was available. Money was worthless. People were reduced to looking through trash, in search of bits of food. What little food and clothing that I could find or barter for this mother and daughter did help to sustain them. Did I aide an enemy, a young girl and her mother? I think not.

It was a Sunday morning and I did not have to pull guard duty at the lager. I had a couple of sweaters from the loot of the Hungarian soldiers, so I decided to take them along with some food over to Erica and her mother. They were happy to see me and of course what I had brought along. Their room was barely large enough for three people; therefore, after a short visit, Erica and I left to go for a walk. We strolled down a narrow road that ended at the banks of the river and watched some people boating and some hearty souls swimming in the cold water. The devastation of the town was hidden by the thick trees lining the river's edge. Here was a quiet countryside scene of people enjoying themselves along the banks of a slow-moving river; a scene that could have been anywhere in the world; a scene that could have been the subject of a painting by Renoir. At least here the signs of the recent war seemed to fade. Later, we went for a walk along a dirt path winding up the hill to the castle. The medieval castle was on the outskirts of Heilbronn. The path took us up to a courtyard that was surrounded by a shell pocked stone wall. As we entered the courtyard, I noticed three rather recent graves at the head of which were white crosses topped with worn and dented German helmets. Erica proceeded to give me a guided tour. Entering the courtyard from the other side, as Erica and I stood hand-in-hand, was a little old lady. She was dressed all in black with a black shawl over her head. When she came closer to us, in her stooped, aged walk, I noticed a bunch of flowers in her withered hand. Apparently, the flowers were to be placed on one of the graves. Placing the flowers at the base of one of the crosses, she knelt in silent prayer. When finished, she sat on the stone wall to rest before starting back down the long path. Erica and I were ready to leave and walked past her. We were about to greet her with a "Guten Tag" when she slowly raised her head and looked at us with the most steely-eyed look that I had ever seen and have not seen since. Was it hatred for me as an enemy? Was it hatred for Erica because she was with me? I will never know but I have never forgotten that stare. Losing the war certainly did create animosity in many of the defeated population, but their hatred was misplaced. The blame lay on the shoulders of the leaders who led them to these days of sorrow and despair. We turned around and headed back down the path, leaving the lonely, old women to her private sorrow and grief. This could very well have been my mother at another time, in another place.

At times, on a Saturday or Sunday, when I did not have to pull guard duty, I would take some food and clothing to Erica and her mother. I simply could not allow anyone whom I had befriended to go scavenging through trash and garbage cans. If the weather was nice, Erica and I would go for a walk along the river banks. There was very little that was available in the form of entertainment. Most people were engaged in mere survival. Time was spent just looking for food and warmth. There were no cafés or restaurants in operation. The occupation forces did provide some jobs for the civilian population; however, as more and more POW's were released from the camps, there were less and less jobs to be filled as the population of the towns grew. The United States government did its best to provide food for all of these people besides supplying food for displaced persons and for our own troops. The logistics of this operation must have been staggering. I found this to be true when Rudy and I ran the ration truck to the supply depot at Geissen.

One morning, Erica asked me if I would accompany her on a visit to a relative who lived in a nearby village. In hard times like these, no one was really safe walking the streets, so I agreed to go with her. Stray cats and dogs would roam the streets in search of food. Rats, well-fed on the carcasses of dead animals and people, had grown to the size of cats and were openly defiant and aggressive. They would confront a person without any indication of fear or of backing away. We walked through the debris covered streets. Stones, concrete, shattered window glass, and the broken interior of buildings covered the sidewalks and the streets. At some places, we had to very carefully climb over the rubble. When we neared one bombed out three-story building, Erica stopped.

"This is where I used to live," she said.

"Our stove is still in there. Do you think that you could get it for us?"

"Where is it?" I asked.

She pointed upward indicating a point on the upper floor. There was no interior to the building, so I could look straight up into the blue sky above. There, dangling from the wall and supported only by a long gas pipe, was the stove. I told her that there was no way that I could get that stove down without the help of a fire truck which, of course, was not available. We continued on our way to her aunt's house.

When we reached the house, or I should say, what was left of it, because the house itself was almost completely demolished. It was apparent that the family was living in the basement. Erica preceded me down the steps and into the dank smelling cellar. As I entered the doorway, through a haze of cigarette smoke, the basement was dimly lit by a single kerosene lamp on a small table. Around the table sat a number of German ex-prisoners who were still clothed in army uniforms. Apparently, they had just been released from a POW camp. Having just come in from the sunlight, I found it difficult to see clearly into the dark, smoke filled room. My first reaction was to reach for the Mauser automatic that I always carried in a shoulder holster under my jacket.

"Oh! Oh! What have I gotten myself into?" I thought.

A voice, in an attempt to speak English, came from the back of the basement.

"Hey, Mac, what the hell are you doing here?

When he stepped out into the light, I recognized one of the camp leaders from B-13. I later found out he was a cousin of Erica's. After he introduced Erica and I to the rest of the men around the table, we had a very congenial conversation with her relatives. Surely, it had been a very tense moment and I must admit that I was still uneasy and never did let my guard down. Thank God that my reputation at the camp preceded me. I breathed a sigh of relief when we left.

November 10, 1945, my twenty-first birthday, was a day like any other day. I had duty at the lager. This was the day when one was supposed to pass on to manhood. Unfortunately, I like most teenage young men, at the time, had made that transition much earlier during the very first day of combat. There is nothing that matures a person faster. A boy one minute; and in the time it takes to pull the trigger, a man.

I arrived at the camp, assigned guard duty to my squad and then checked the wire fence. George, our interpreter, came to the gate to give me a report on the happenings of the previous night, needed food supplies, men on sick call, and deaths. George told me that Eric, the lager master, wanted to see me in the camp master's hut. This was an unusual request, but I did not give it a second thought. Inside of the hut with Eric was "Tony," the camp labor master, a couple of cooks, and several other POW's. As George and I entered, I was greeted with a shout of "HAPPY BIRTHDAY" by all of these non-English speaking German prisoners. The cooks had made a cake and fashioned candles from some wax. One POW had made a small, wooden box with my initials carved into the side. A cobbler presented me with a pair of handmade riding boots. Someone had made a head of Christ from plaster-of-Paris and another artist took a German mess kit and engraved scenes around the camp on the sides and on the mess kit top. Using the Luftwaffe material and the sewing machines that I had helped them to obtain during the start of their time in the lager, a tailor made me an "IKE" jacket, shorts, and two pair of riding jodhpurs. All of these things were given to me in appreciation for the way that I and my squad handled some rather difficult situations within the compound. I felt that I was always fair in carrying out whatever was in the area of my responsibilities. A very memorable birthday? I have relived that day at some point during every birthday of my long life.

Inside of the fence, the POW's had constructed a large stone dial. It was within a ten foot diameter circle and made of white stones; a smaller circle with an upright pole in the center to cast a shadow registering the time of day. In the same area, they had also made a large waving American flag fashioned from colored stones. I have absolutely no idea where they managed to get the colors to dye or paint the stones. Ours was the only cage within the entire compound to display our flag in such a way, especially one that had been constructed by our recent enemies, without any urging on our part.

POW Hdq. Shack
Stone Sundial made by POWS

Stone Flag made by POWS

TONY
Camp Labormeister

JIM   BILL   JOE
ROY   WEBB

KREISGEFANGENENLAGER B13, HEILBRONN, GERMANY
SUMMER, 1945

After having breakfast, I was getting into a Jeep to go to the POW camp, when Larry Coons of Oshkosh, Wisconsin came looking for me.

"Hey Mac!" he called. "The Captain wants to see you."

'What the hell does he want?" I asked.

"I don't know, but he wants to see you right away."

When I entered the headquarters office, I was greeted by the somber and gloomy faces of Capt. Yakowitz, a lieutenant and the first sergeant.

"Ok Mac!" the top kick said. "Where the hell where you last night?"

"I was right here." I answered.

"Oh, yeah?" he bellowed. "Well, you were reported getting into some trouble with a girl last night."

With some apprehension as to what was to come next, and I might add, a little bit of sweating, I composed myself long enough to say, "What the hell are you talking about Sarge? I was here all last night and you know it."

With that, all three of them burst into laughter, the captain finally explained that I was to go to England for two weeks R and R (rest and recreation). I had orders to pack and leave that very afternoon. Two weeks in England without any money was not much to look forward to, so I tried to refuse.

"No excuse Mac," the Captain said. "You are going."

I explained this to my buddies, all of whom wanted to help. Art Grossman of Mount Carmel, Pennsylvania gave some of his money to me, took up a collection, and managed to get enough money for me to make the trip. All that I really needed was spending money. Lodging and food rations would be supplied by the service.

Along with the others, I joined a group of GI's on a 2 ½ ton truck to be taken to a train station where we boarded a French boxcar marked 40 hommes 8 chevaux, a 40 x 8. Those were freight cars that could carry 40 men or 8 cows. I got to see some of the countryside in relative peace, without looking for a Kraut behind every bush. Our destination was Fecamp on the coast of France, just north of Campy Lucky Strike at Etretat, where we had spent a couple of days after debarking from the "George Washington.'

We were to sleep that night in quarters used by transients shuttling back and forth across the English Channel. The beds were make-shift wooden bunks with mattresses stuffed with straw. They were also stuffed with fleas. I slept on the floor that entire night. Here again, like aboard ship, the sounds of snoring and other body noises mixed with different body odors was not conducive to a good nights rest.

Late the next day, we boarded a "Victory Ship," for a passage across the Channel. Rumors were circulating around that a number of these ships had broken in half in high seas. Even on the best of days, the Channel was not known for being calm. The day was cloudy and rainy; therefore, we could not spend much time on deck. For the most part, time was passed in the hold playing cards and shooting dice. The ship would rise to the top of a swell and then drop down to the bottom of a trough as the water surged from under the ship. All activity stopped as she moaned and groaned, and the creaking sound of metal against metal was heard throughout all of the decks. Fortunately, the trip only took a few hours. Our "Victory Ship" arrived in England in one piece.

We traveled by train, arriving in London late in the evening. After checking into a hotel near Grosvenor Square, having all of my papers checked and eating chow, I tried so get some shut eye. I just could not sleep. Perhaps it was a combination of the crossing, although I did not get much sleep on the ship, and just the excitement of the trip. Finally, I got up, got dressed, and went out for a walk. I only walked about a block when I heard someone call from the dark doorway of a corner building.

"Hey Yank, you want to get fucked?"

With a start, I turned toward the sound of the voice. There were two scantily dressed young girls in the darkness of the doorway.

"What did you say?" I asked.

"She said, 'Do you want to fuck?'" replied the second girl.

"No thanks," I answered, walking back into the night toward the hotel.

Why was I taken aback? Why was I shocked? I do not know what I had expected. I had been to Paris, where "La Femme de la Nuit" (Ladies of the Night) propositioned soldiers right on the street in broad daylight, even reaching down and openly caressing ones genitals or reaching under a table at a sidewalk café for the same purpose. It certainly did make it rather difficult to refuse. Perhaps, I expected it to be different in an English speaking country. All that I know is that hearing that word coming from woman speaking English rankled me. Certainly I had heard it used every day. Deep down inside, I knew that Dad would never tolerate such language. Cursing just was not allowed in our house and absolutely not in the presence of a female. We also knew that Dad would not say anything but that a slap in the face was forthcoming.

The following morning, after a good breakfast, I got my gear together and got on the first bus that I saw. I had no idea where it was going. The final stop was a small place called Southall, Middlesex. I did not get to see much of London until later.

I began to walk the streets of Southall without any idea about where I could find lodging. The best place to start, I thought, would be a local pub. On a side street, I saw a quaint-looking pub with a sign that read, "The Three Horse Shoes." As I entered, the place was as I had pictured it to be, with old rustic furnishings, a small bar, an old wooden floor, and not a sign of a modern establishment. It seemed to have stepped right out of the seventeenth century. Two early-day drinkers sat in the back of the room. At the bar stood an English soldier and sailor. Maureen Brady, the Irish barmaid called to them and asked them to come over and join us. She told them of my plight and suggested that they might help me find a place to stay. They agreed without a moment of hesitation. I was grateful for any help that I could get.

The three of us left the pub and walked down the street of the quaint village. We stopped to inquire at a few homes without much success. Eventually, we came to a small cottage with a flagstone path leading to the front door. The yard was surrounded by a white low picket fence. My knock was answered by a genteel looking middle-aged lady.

"Do you have a room to let?" asked the soldier.

"I am sorry, but I just do not have a room for anyone," replied the woman.

"Thank you very much" I said as I stepped off of the front stoop.

We turned and headed down the path toward the fence. As we neared the gate, the lady called to us.

"Hey Yank, come back here."

"When I joined her at the stoop, she asked, "Is the room for you or is it for those two Limeys?"

I explained to her that the room was for me and they were kind enough to help me find a place to stay during my leave.

"Ok," she said, "I have a room for you, but only you."

I was to learn later that she was Canadian and that she did not care very much for British servicemen.

During the next two weeks, I was to spend a pleasant and happy time at the home of Mrs. Alliston of 5 Stamford Close, Southall, Middlesex, England. I was treated like a member of the family. I went with Mr. and Mrs. Alliston to the local pubs at night. The locals would not let me pay for a thing, not even a drink. During the day, they guided me around the village and introduced me to some family friends. They even arranged dates for me with local girls. There was never a lack of companionship. I was the only American GI in the town and I was treated royally by the townspeople. Mrs. Alliston served me a breakfast of bacon and eggs every morning. Later, I found out that these were their monthly allotment of eggs. They sacrificed in order to see that I was properly fed during my stay in Middlesex.

I did manage to gain some respect and admiration among the habitués of the local pubs through my ability to shoot darts, an ability I had acquired, along with Joe Schum, Bill Molter, Jim Kelly, and Johnny Roberts, in Philadelphia saloons and on the boardwalk in Atlantic City. If you could drink ale or bitters and hold your own in a dart game, you were readily accepted into the local society.

I really did not get to do very much sightseeing having only spent a couple of days in London at the end of my leave. I did manage to enjoy what I had been sent to acquire, rest and recreation, thanks to the good people of Southall. Without them, I never would have known the joy of spending time with the people of rural England.

CHAPTER SEVEN

GOING HOME

GOING HOME - March 1946

CHAPTER SEVEN

GOING HOME

The 627th was to remain in Germany as part of the occupation forces. Those of us who had accumulated enough points to go home were transferred to the 401st. FA, Bn. in Langan, Germany. Johnny Rudolph and I were among that group. I had been offered a promotion if I would stay with the 627th for an additional six more months. Upon reading the written agreement, I noticed that nowhere on the document was the time limited to six months. I declined such an offer and began the first step toward going home.

After rejecting the captains offer to stay in occupied Germany for an additional six months, I was assigned to a group of non-coms destined to be transferred to the 401st. FA Battalion which was to return stateside in the near future. I found out about the transfer on the morning of our departure. I still had access to a Jeep, so I gathered up what food rations that were available and drove over to see my young friend and her mother for the last time. My visit had, of necessity, to be brief. They wanted to know where I was going. "Was I going home?" I told them what little that I could, that I had arranged for a friend to help them. We said our hasty goodbyes and I headed back to our headquarters. A short distance down the lonely road, I pulled over to the side of the road, turned off the motor and lowered my head down upon the steering wheel. I was a combat soldier and soldiers don't cry. Last November I had turned twenty-one and men don't cry. I had not cried since that day when Oscar was buried and that seemed like a lifetime ago. Certainly, I on occasion, had suddenly awakened in the middle of the night sobbing for no apparent reason but soldiers don't cry. As I bowed my head, it wasn't because I was leaving friends. I know it was a well-spring of pent up emotions and experiences that had built up behind a dam whose floodgates had abruptly burst open and spewed forth sights, sounds, and odors of death and destruction, months in a combat area, miles upon miles of starving bedraggled refugees and displaced persons, thousands of people in prisoner of war camps, hospitals and yes, morgues. All of these things seemed to finally erupt in the form of tears along that lonely road. I finally gathered my composure, arrived back at the house where I was billeted, gathered my meager belongings, and my duffle bag and joined my buddies in boarding the waiting 2 ½ ton truck; the truck that was to be on its way to some unknown destination and hopefully, HOME.

Also joining the 401st was a group of young GI's. These were Japanese-American boys who had been members of the 442nd Infantry Division, an all Japanese outfit. They were a fierce fighting unit that, it was rumored, did not take any prisoners. Their Japanese chatter on the radios thoroughly confused the Germans. The use of American Indians also caused the enemy to take indecisive actions. I became good friends with Bobby Oshiro of Maui, Hawaiian Islands. Bobby and I rigged up a darkroom in the basement of one of the quarters where he taught me the fundamentals of photographic development, something that I would use for my enjoyment many years later.

While at Langan, my main assignment was food and clothing rationing. Rudolph was my driver on many trips to Geissen where, at the supply depot, our 2 ½ ton truck would be loaded with meat, cheese, all types of canned goods, vegetables, and clothing.

Oh yes! I can't forget the bread, fresh baked round loaves of bread. The aroma filled the cab of the truck as Rudy and I drove back to the battalion. Each of us would munch on a whole loaf of delicious smelling and tasting warm bread. I can smell it now. A couple of ex-POW's, working at the depot, remembered me from B-13, so we managed to get a little extra food for our outfit. Upon our return to the battalion motor pool, Rudy and I would sort, cut, and ration out the supplies, according to the number of men in each battery. We were always in the good graces of the battery cooks who, hoping to get more or better food supplies, would give Rudy and me an early breakfast of bacon and eggs to start us off on our trip to Geissen. We arose early and eagerly, before anyone else, for this unbelievable breakfast. It really was far superior to powdered eggs.

Johnny and I were also in charge of the NCO Club, where it was our responsibility to furnish food, drinks, and entertainment. Occasionally, the cooks would ask us to arrange a private party, on a Sunday afternoon. The cooks would supply the food while Rudy and I, having access to liquor and champagne, would supply the drinks. On stage, at one impromptu party, were five young ladies in various stages of dress or undress. Bobby Bauman of Saxton, Pennsylvania, who resembled Lou Costello of Abbott and Costello fame joined them on stage and was in the middle of a comic strip tease act, when the Colonel and his staff entered the club. My first thought was, "Oh well, we have had it now so we just might as well continue." The officers sat down and joined in the fun, applauding with much more élan than we, had a drink and then left with a friendly, "Carry on."

The 401st was relocated to Butzbach where we were to guard a civilian prison. Believe me, this was different than guarding POW's who were just waiting to be released to go home and renew a life with family and friends. Butzbach is only a short distance north of Bad Nauheim, the headquarters of the 15th Army. On the 8th of October, General George S. Patton arrived to take command of the 15th. As ordinary GI's, we were totally unaware of the political circumstances behind his transfer of command. With all of the egotistical bickering and infighting among our military leaders, both American and British, it is amazing that we won the war. Each commander was making decisions solely for their own political advancement or aggrandizement, decisions that ultimately cost the lives of men at the front lines. Patton held the 15th in distain, considering it a paper army. He forgot to take in consideration that many men now serving under its command were combat veterans, including Nisei (Japanese Americans) from the 442nd Infantry Battalion, who had seen combat while serving in his own beloved 3rd Army and 7th Army. As part of the troops to be reviewed by the General, we were issued white belts and gloves and red cravats. Our helmet liners had to be lacquered to a high gloss and display our Battalion insignia on both sides.

Patton was very strict and demanded that all members of his command, officers and men alike, were neat, clean, and fastidious, even while in a combat zone. He did not ask of his troops anything that he would not do himself. He was not a rear echelon commander and would appear at any time or any place.

During the "Battle of the Bulge," Patton called Bill Maulden, a correspondent and cartoonist, to his office to protest Maulden's depiction of the GI's as slovenly, unshaven and unkempt, in his famous "Willie and Joe" cartoon in the Stars and Stripes Newspaper. The soldiers loved the strip and knew firsthand that Mauldin's version of the combat GI was more to the truth than General Patton's mental picture. We did not always have the luxury of soap and water, or an iron to press our uniform, or more importantly, the luxury of time to look to our personal grooming. Patton spent forty-five minutes chewing out the cartoonist and gave him a mere two minutes to reply. Thereafter, the General would not permit Mauldin anywhere near the Third Army.

A few months after taking command of the 15th Army, on December 9, Patton decided to go on a hunting trip in the vicinity of Mannheim. Somewhere near the northern suburbs of Mannheim, Patton's car was involved in an accident when his car slammed into an Army truck. He was thrown around the inside of the car and sustained a broken neck which left him paralyzed. He lived for twelve more days and died in a hospital in Heidleberg on December 21, 1945. It was a sad end for a military warrior who had hoped in all sincerity to die in a battle on a foreign land. He was buried along side the many soldiers who had lost their lives while under his command

The Rudolph family lived on Crease Street in Fishtown, not very far from where my family lived. Therefore, Rudy and I had a lot of things in common to talk about while on night guard duty or whenever we were assigned to other jobs together. In the town of Butzbach, Germany, we were billeted in the same room. The room had a potbelly stove in one corner, so we positioned our cot beds against adjacent walls with the heads toward the stove. We spent many cold nights in the warm yellow, red glow of that stove, talking about early days in Philly, what we had gone through during the past months and hopes and dreams of the future. Soon, we would be boarding a ship for the long awaited voyage home.

We talked about the time that he had been scheduled to be transferred out of the 627th. Since he was going to be transferred, he felt quite at ease in telling our platoon sergeant, Ben Harness, just exactly what he thought of him as a person and as a NCO. We had known Ben since our first days in basic training and as he moved up the chain of command. He had made some friends and also had made some enemies, but he was basically a nice, easy going guy. As luck would have it, and in the Army way, after Rudy's outburst, his transfer was cancelled. Any other NCO could have and would have made things very difficult for Rudy, but Ben knew him and just took it as a joke and laughed it off. Rudy had such a happy vibrant personality that everyone liked him.

Cpl. Lewis Bair of Lancaster, PA., Rudy and I formed a bond of camaraderie that exceeded all others while not excluding all others. We were like the rungs of a ladder with Rudy on the lower step, me on the middle, and Bair, being over six feet tall, on the top. We helped and protected each other. One evening, we were in a Beer Haus. It was a typical German beer hall with all of the sights and smells that were all too familiar to us. Bair and Rudy were occupied dancing with girls in the dance room that was next to the bar room. I was sitting at a small linen covered table, enjoying a stein of beer. Conversation was building as a couple vied for attention in English and German. I sat trying to block out the conversation and listen to the strolling female entertainer who, while playing a piano accordion, sang a variety of songs, including the well known "Lili Marlene" in German. Someone came running into the small room.

"Hey Mac!" He called out, "Rudy is in trouble in the dance hall."

A fight had broken out among some inebriated GI's in the dance hall. A fight that I suspect was started by Cpl. Bair. He loved to fight and while under the influence, it took very little to light a fire and inflame him. He just could not hold his drink. When sober, he was a calm nice guy, but with drinks, he became very aggressive and unruly. All through France and Germany, he carried a guitar that he loved to play as he sang songs of home. After a few drinks, I saw him throw his guitar to the floor and jump on it, crushing it under his feet. When he sobered up and realized what he had done, he sat down and cried like a baby.

When I went into the dance hall, I found a large pile of thrashing bodies in the corner of the room. After pulling a few men from the pile, I reached in and grabbed the smallest pair of shoulders that I could find and pulled. Rudy came sliding out from under the group and I helped him back to our table. He had come out of the melee with a broken leg and a broken ankle and was taken to the hospital. Bair had sustained only a few minor bruises

As Cpl. Bair and I entered the ward at the hospital in Frankfurt, we saw Rudy hobbling down the hallway on crutches with a cast on one leg. His ill-fitting hospital gown reached below his feet and was dragging along the floor in the same manner as his oversized raincoat would drag along the ground.

"Hey! Rudy, how the hell are you doing?"

"Where the hell have you guys been? I was expecting you a couple of days ago." He yelled.

"I had to requisition a Jeep and we both had to get permission from the Captain to make the trip." I answered.

"Ok, where is it?" There was no need to ask him what he was referring to.

The three of us went back to his ward, sat on his bed, and enjoyed the bottle of schnapps and champagne that we had smuggled into the hospital. Of course, we shared our wealth with the rest of the GI's in the ward. Rudy had to spend a few more days in the Frankfurt Hospital before rejoining our outfit. He was fortunate because in a few more days, we were scheduled to sail back home.

March 10, 1946, a damp, dreary day but one long awaited for by everyone. We were to be transported to the port city of Bremerhaven on the North Sea. When we arrived at the port, the weather appeared to be getting worse. The black rain laden clouds were hanging ominously low in the sky. Rains would surely begin before these thousands of nervous but happy GI's could board the ships; ships that seemed as nervous as the soldiers waiting anxiously on the nearby docks as they bounced in the choppy waters. I could remember crossing the English Channel aboard a victory ship. Although happy to at last be heading for home. I did board the vessel with some trepidation as all of the ships in the port bounced nervously to and fro in a sea that was growing more angry as the minutes passed. Like a bunch of cattle, we were herded onto the ship, and as I had expected and dreaded, we were directed to the hold, as far below as you could get. We were jammed in tighter than we were on the George Washington, a much larger ship. Again, the hammocks were in four tiers, one above the other. Duffle bags were stuffed into any available space. The ship could not provide any movies or any other form of entertainment. Free time, as on most boats, usually consisted of card playing, dice, or perhaps reading books that were passed around from man to man. Money rapidly changed hands. Transactions in Germany had been done in "Occupation Money" of which we were permitted to exchange only as much as we could have earned in the time that we were there. Men who had accumulated excess money through gambling or black-marketing, rushed to find someone who did not have sufficient funds to make his quota. The man with additional money would give one dollar for every two that a buddy would bring home for him. The last few days before shipping out were a financial whirlwind.

The first three days at sea were frightening as the storm came and gradually changed the ocean into one vast boiling cauldron. It was like crossing the channel once again but this went on for days. the little ship rocked back and forth, in a constant struggle to keep upright. We managed to get very little sleep because we expected the creaking seams to rip apart. Many GI's were moaning and groaning in their hammocks. The voyage was to take about fourteen days. Hopefully, conditions would improve. I remember sitting on the deck playing a game of poker when I suddenly felt a feeling of queasiness come over me. There was no time to offer any explanation. I got up and made a mad dash up the ladder to get out on the open deck where I leaned over the rail and emptied my guts into the sea. My stomach ached, my throat felt as if it were being torn apart as I gagged and coughed, my eyes watered and burned bulging from their sockets and my head throbbed. Would this never end? I continued to gag even after there was nothing left in my stomach to come up. I had often been sick, but this was so sudden and unbearable. I swore that no one would ever get me on a boat again. My only comfort was that I was not alone. The rail was filled with men with a series of vulgar epithets. This was my first and hopefully my last experience with sea sickness.

The storm finally abated and came to an end. The sea now settled down and was much calmer and we were permitted to go on deck in groups at assigned times. During this period, we could exercise, lay on the deck in the sunshine, or just have a smoke. At night, we were not sailing under blackout conditions, so we were able to go on deck for a cigarette or just enjoy the spectacle of a star-filled sky stretching as far as the eye could see. At least, we did not have to worry about Nazi U-boats.

The days began to pass very slowly and boredom became the rule of the day. Participants in the daily dice and card games became fewer as the lucky and rich became richer. Money was now scarce and cigarettes were now the popular medium of exchange. Even K.P was looked upon as a welcome relief. The trip started to become a voyage of frustration where even friends lashed out at each other at the slightest provocation.

At last, we were approaching the coast line of North America. A solid mass of GI's were out on deck anxiously awaiting the first glimpse of that all too familiar lady welcoming all to her shores. The scene was one of unnatural quiet. No one engaged in goodbyes but slowly withdrew into themselves. The sight of the Statue of Liberty was greeted with joyous uproar from everyone on board including the crew. Tug boats came out to meet us and escort our ship into the port. We were not greeted, as earlier returning troops had been. There was no flag waving or people waiting on the dock looking for loved ones or just to welcome the soldier's home This homecoming, for all of us was surely anticlimactic. Joy and exhilaration, directed toward homecoming forces, can only be exhibited for a limited amount of time by a populace who had already settled down into an existence of complacency. Johnny Rudolph and I gathered up our belongings and our duffle bags and disembarked. Then and only then, for us, THE WAR WAS TRULY OVER.

When we reached the end of the gangplank and walked on the dock, we were made to board a 2 ½ ton truck which was headed for Fort Dix, New Jersey. We would spend another few days at Fort Dix preparing for final discharge. After a series of tests, signing numerous papers, and indoctrination lectures that were supposed to ease our way into civilian life, we received out "Ruptured Duck" pin and our discharge papers. Rudy and I caught a train for Philadelphia. At last.

War is the most asinine of human endeavors. No one wins, one side simply loses more than the other, thereby being declared the "Winner." Did we win the Second World War? We certainly lost the peace. Just how long did we live in peace? Only a few short years after five brothers returned from the "war to end all wars," a sixth brother was called to serve in Korea. Then came Viet Nam. We had the dubious honor of being the greatest military power in the world, a position that we maintain today by default with the fall of Communism in Russia. More Russian people were executed and murdered during the reign of Josef Stalin, in the peace time years than were killed during the war. West Germany, with the help of the United States militarily and monetarily, has become one of the most powerful economic countries in the world. Who won the war? I wonder. The economic development of both Germany and Japan far exceeds that of many of our allies in the conflict. Are we, as a nation, goodhearted and compassionate or are we just plain naïve? I will leave the answer to that question to history and future generations.

As a child growing up in the "Depression," I remember a time when my father, along with many others, was without work simply because there were no jobs; children went to school hungry and with hand-me-down or torn and threadbare clothing, and with holes in their shoes, soup kitchens were the only source of a hot meal for many families with little children.

After a World War, Korea, and Viet Nam, ten presidents and sixty years, where are we? We surely do not learn from history because we, as human beings, still repeat the same mistakes. Politicians continue to promise us the same things at every election. We have put men in space and a man has walked on the moon but here on Earth, many thousands of jobs have gone out of the country to foreign shores solely to increase the "bottom line" and fill the pockets of a few. Once great steel companies have closed, causing thousands of well paid workers to lose their jobs and be forced to enter the low-paying service industry. It is almost impossible to find and buy a pair of shoes that were made in the United States. Does this bring about lower prices for consumer goods here at home? No way, in fact, prices seem to be constantly escalating. Only the designers and manufacturers seem to benefit and profit. The Unites States sends billions of dollars in aid to every country in the world, including the smallest island in the Pacific, while many families, here at home, live below the poverty level. Does this make sense? The politicians and economists, as long as they are living well, continue to tell the public about our great and thriving economy. Companies now engage in so called downsizing, a process by which a company can rid itself of competent long-term employees and pile more work on the remaining workers. Again, many Americans even those with college degrees are out of work. Our streets are filled with homeless people, many of the homeless are veterans. Children, once again, are going to school cold and hungry, and soup kitchens have found it necessary to reopen. Still, in spite of all the problems, we have the best and greatest country that has ever graced the Earth. Our freedom has been and always will be worth fighting for. May God bless America.

HEADQUARTERS
627ᵀᴴ FIELD ARTILLERY BATTALION

SUBJECT : Battle Participation Credits
TO   : Whom It May Concern

    1.   Corporal Joseph O. McLaughlin, 33583656, is authorized the following Bronze Service Stars while serving with this organization:

        Bz Sv Star: Northern France per Ltr AG 200.6
                      APGA ETGOUSA dtd 11 May 45.

Bz Sv Star: Central Europe per T X USFET dtd 2 July 1945.

Bz Sv Star: Rhineland per Ltr Hq USFET AG 200.6 APGA 6 Jul 45.

FOR THE COMMANDING OFFICER:

JAMES R COLLINS
WOJG USA 627 Fa Bn
Personnel Officer

March, 1946 was the time that Mom and Dad had been waiting for four years. The last of five sons would return from the war. The war years had taken its toll on our parents. Mom was about forty-eight years old and Dad was fifty-three, however, they had aged far beyond their years. Even though we were finally home, Mom did not seem to be very happy and she cried a lot. Perhaps it was just too much for her. Her health was not very good and she suffered from constant headaches. More often than not, she had a vinegar soaked cloth around her head as a remedy for those headaches. Whether or not it worked, only she would know. Both of our parents had become completely gray while we were away. Dad was no longer as jaunty as he had been, and his stature was somewhat bent. His eyes still retained some of their cheerfulness, but I could detect a little sadness in them.

Once again, since I was the youngest, Phil, Dan, John, and Frank were ahead of me. They had all come home before me, now it was my time to return. On the Friday after I arrived home, Dad wanted all of his sons to go out on the town with him. This meant making the rounds of all the local bar rooms. All of the neighbors would frequent the bars on Friday nights. This was to be a special night. Danny McLaughlin's boys were home and everyone wanted to join in the celebration. At each tavern, we would shoot some darts, drink beer and sing, harmonizing as we had done before the war changed all of our lives. Most of the drinks were "on the house" or were paid for by friends and neighbors. Needless to say, by the time that the bars closed, none of us were feeling any pain.

Coming home at about three o'clock in the morning, the six of us were walking down the middle of Arizona Street, arm in arm, with Dad in the center. At the top of our voices, we were singing one of Dad's favorite Irish tunes.

> Old Mamie Reilly, how to you to today?
> Old Mamie Rielly, I'm going far away.
> Oh! Won't you kiss me Mamie, before I go?
> Old Mamie, Mamie, Mamie Reilly
>
> Slide Kelly slide, Casey's at the bat,
> Old Mamie Reilly, where did you get that hat?
> And she lives down in our alley.
>
> That old oaken bucket.
> That old iron bound bucket.
> That moss covered bucket,
> That hung in the well.
>
> That old rotten toothbrush,
> That old rotten toothbrush,
> That hung in the sink.
> Old Mamie Reilly, how do you do today?
> Old Mamie Reilly, I'm going far away
> Oh! Won't you kiss me Mamie, before I go?
> Old Mamie, Mamie, Mamie Reilly.

As we approached our house, I noticed the window curtain being drawn back at the house across the street. Even at that hour of the morning, one of the neighborhood busybodies was furtively looking out. At the top of my voice, I called out, "It's OK now, Mrs. McCash, you can go to bed, the McLaughlin boys are all home." The curtain was rapidly pulled closed.

That was the last time that all of us went out together. The years of war had taken its toll on every one of us. We had all changed. I was barely twenty-two, but like my parents, aged far beyond my years. We were all to go our separate ways and to make lives of our own which, I guess, is as it should be.

The war was now over for us and most GI's would return home to a life not much better, if at all, than the one that they had before being drafted. Once again, jobs were scarce. The machinery of war and destruction was no longer needed in such great quantity. There just were not enough jobs for all of these returning young men. Many would pass their time away in saloons or standing on street corners. They were easily recognizable in poorly fitting civilian clothing with a "ruptured duck" (a discharge pin) in the lapel of their jackets. Most went into the service poor and came home poor. The promise of a better life would not be fulfilled until years later. Men from upper and middle income families did come home to the opportunity to take advantage of the "GI Bill of Rights" to get a better education and move up the income scale to a better way of life.

My four brothers and I were finally home. It must have been a tremendous burden lifted from Mom and Dad. John and Frank were married and out on their own. Even as kids, those two always did manage to find some kind of work. Frank now drove a truck and John found a job in a box factory on American Street. Phil worked occasionally and gave some money to Mom, however, he got it all back during the course of the week. He constantly went to Mom for money to go to the movies or for cigarettes or to go out on a date Dan was something else. Dan was Dan, one of a kind. He did not work, he didn't even look for a job. Half of his day was spent in bed. When he did get up, he would go out on a date with Marie, who not only paid for the date but gave spending money to Dan so that he could go to Elwood's Bar, after he took her home. The bar would close at 2:00 a.m. Then Dan and Elwood and some friends would go into the back room and play cards until seven or eight in the morning. Then it was time to go home and get some sleep. I often met him coming in when I was going out to work. Like most ex-servicemen, Dan belonged to the 52-20 club. This was unemployment money given to veterans at the rate of twenty dollars a week for fifty-two weeks. Dan added a little twist to his allotment. He wanted to save it for summer vacation.

I did collect for a couple of months, but only until I got a job at Sears and Roebuck on Roosevelt Boulevard. I worked in the shipping department. A couple of nights a week, I also attended art classes at the Hussian School of Fine Arts at Seventeenth and Market Streets. Most of the classes were nude life study classes which gave my brothers added material to rib me. At that time, I could lose myself in drawing and painting far into the night.

It was during this time that an opportunity presented itself. There was a corner combination candy and grocery store at the corner of Arizona and Jasper Streets. This store was owned by the father of a friend of mine. Dotty Lang's father wanted to sell the store. I felt that I could make a go of it, so I bought the store. I could work at Sears during the day and operate the store at night.

By the spring of 1946, most veterans had settled down into civilian life. Some would bear emotional and physical scars that would last a lifetime. Many emotional problems, like a delayed action devise, would not manifest themselves until much later in life. These were young men, kids really, who had been trained to survive and to kill for the past four years, being released into a so-ciety completely foreign to their acquired instincts. Some were able to cope with the change while others would never be able to adjust. The effects of the war on the youth of that period would last far into the next generation and beyond. For a long time, during the night, the screeching of the Frankford "EL" as it made its way around the curve at York Street, reminded me of screaming shells as they passed overhead on their way to wreak havoc and destruction upon German troops and positions. Was this one of the reasons why I left Philly? Probably.

War production had virtually come to a halt, and factories had not, as yet, converted to civilian production. Tons of war mate-rial, including large artillery guns, trucks, tanks, and Jeeps were being dumped into the Atlantic Ocean. With hundreds of thou-sands of service men returning home, there simply were not enough jobs available for untrained men. Idle hands and idle minds could only lead to trouble. Ex-GI's were walking the streets still in government issued clothes, not being able to afford civilian clothing. A proliferation of ill-equipped and incapable trade schools were opening up all over the country vying for the government money available under the "GI Bill of Rights." Much later, I did attend one of those schools to take a course in carpentry. Still later, I attended evening classes at Liberty High School in Bethlehem, Pennsylvania. After three years of classes three nights a week and studying at 5 o'clock in the morning, I belatedly acquired my much needed and desired high school diploma. I believe that I did appreciate it much more than I would have earlier.

I had no desire to go back to work at Harbison's Dairy, where I probably could have started to work immediately. I was not without a job very long. I went from business to business and factory to factory inquiring about employment. Being turned down time and again can be very frustrating and depressing. I, like many others, no doubt had the mistaken impression that being a returning veteran would entitle me to some kind of special treatment. What a mistaken idea that was. It is easy to understand why so many veterans opted to just rely on the "52-20 Club" and accept the twenty dollar hand out. I never had depended on anyone else and I was not about to start then. In my search for work, I came upon the huge Sears Roebuck building on Roosevelt Boulevard where I filled out an application and was offered a job. Apparently, Sears was a desirable place to work because of their profit sharing plan and an employee discount on all purchases. The Boulevard location, in addition to being a store, the building also housed a distribution center for the East Coast. I started to work in the shipping department where I sorted packages destined for stores located throughout the East. It was not a great job, but it did supply me with a wage and gave me the opportunity to develop new friendships. Meeting people other than ex-GI's, after three years of wartime, was sometimes pleasant but at other times it could be very difficult. We really had nothing in common to talk about with civilians, and most of the topics seemed so picayune, unimportant, and trite. It would take a long time to acquire and develop new interests. I worked at Sears for some months and met and dated a young female fellow employee who was very successful in helping me to acquire those new interests.

Two and sometimes three evenings a week, I would come home from work at Sears, eat a quick supper, and hurry off to classes at The Hussian School of Fine Arts. I was attending life study groups where we were free to draw and interpret the poses of nude models, both male and female, as we saw fit. During the class, the instructor would make suggestions and constructive criticism. The nudes, of course, were nothing like the voluptuous, slim, and svelte drawings that I had made for the walls of the mess hall back in Germany.

While in Europe, I managed to make a little extra money by turning small wallet-sized photographs of wives and girlfriends of fellow GI's into 8 x 10 sketches. The warehouse that had been converted into a mess hall needed some sprucing up. It certainly was drab and uninviting. A couple of spokesmen for the battery had approached me with a request to adorn the walls with some drawings. I was well aware that they did not mean landscapes or bowls of fruit or flowers. I drew a series of very beautiful nudes representing each month of the year The drawings were done to the exaggerated style of "Pette" and "Varga" girls. The nudes really did have an awakening effect on everyone during breakfast. They were mounted above the windows along both side walls of the mess ball. The officers enjoyed the light-hearted beginning of a long, long day just as much as the enlisted men. Everything was fine until the coming visit of the Battalion Chaplain. Our Captain, anticipating some possible embarrassment, told me to put some clothing, at least panties and a bra, on the girls. I refused to ruin the sketches by superimposing clothing on their beautiful bodies. I removed the pictures from the walls and gave them to my friends. I must agree that my drawings probably would have been inappropriate because the highlight of the chaplain's visit was to be a service in the mess hall.

Some of the models at the art school were thin, some muscular, and some quite heavy but all were composed, relaxed, and very confident in their nudity. Some would even read while posing. All were knowledgeable enough about the human form to change into a position that would accentuate a line or a muscle, upon request. Students merely had to make a suggestion, whereupon, the model very easily moved into the desired pose. I did have a natural talent, but I also had a lot to learn. Whenever I would come home with a portfolio of nude sketches, my brothers were delighted and also titillated, often making some off color remarks and questioning my ability to sit all evening in full view of a naked figure and still concentrate on drawing. How little did they know. Mom, on the other hand, stood in the background in silent understanding. Mom; in her silence, had far more knowledge and understanding than any of us gave her credit for.

Dan volunteered to take care of the store during the day. Most of the supplies were delivered in the morning. Many mornings, my reliable brother, Dan, would oversleep and miss the delivery truck, consequently, I would run out of supplies in the evening. Dan loved kids, therefore, every kid who came into the store with two cents, would get five cents worth of candy or a five cent ice cream cone. Very admirable on his part, but it played havoc with my receipts. Mr. Lang felt that he had every right to sneak into the store in the middle of the night and help himself to cigarettes or a loaf of bread. My brother, John, taught kids how to slip a wire under the frame of the pinball machine and rack up free games. On Saturday night, after closing the store, I would come home with the week's receipts which I then would spread out on the kitchen table for counting. Everyone gathered around the table to help me count and await their share. I never seemed to have enough to put back into the business. Needless to say, it did not last very long. After about a year, I sold it back to Mr. Lang. Fortunately, I managed to break even. I still feel that had we worked together, we could have gone into a business and made a success of it. Frank did want us to join together and start a painting and interior decorating business. It just wasn't to be.

It was at about this time, when I was walking past a furniture and upholstering store on Front Street, I noticed a living room suite in the window. I entered the store and ordered a sofa and two matching chairs for Mom and Dad. When the furniture was delivered, Marie went along with me to a fabric store to pick out some doilies for the backs and arms of the sofa and chairs. It was the first time that Mom and Dad had a new and complete living room set. They loved that set and enjoyed it for many years.

From the time that I started to work at Frances Denny Cosmetic Company, I tried to save a little of my pay each week. This was no easy task considering the amount of pay that I received. I started at thirty-five cents an hour for forty-four hours a week. At least fifty cents of my $15.40 pay each week went into a savings account at the bank. Dan and Phil believed that Joe always had money, therefore, he was an easy touch. They could always borrow some money from Joe. Of course, Joe always worked. After loaning money several times without seeing any effort to pay it back, Joe stopped loaning money. Then it was said that Joe was cheap or that Joe was tight with his money. It just took me some time to learn.

"Alright now, listen to me," said Dad. "Phil is going to bring Theresa's parents over tonight so I want you to be on your good behavior. Watch your language while they are here. I don't have to tell you that I want no cursing and be careful of your jokes. Phil wants all of us to make a good impression." We were grown up and had been through a war, but Dad would never tolerate cursing at home, most especially in Mom's presence and he was not about the change now. Theresa Hagen was the first girl that Phil had gone steady with in a long time. She, like Jean McGovern, belonged to an Irish Catholic family in St. Anne's parish. She was the only girl in the family; and as such, she was well protected. Her brothers, most certainly, were not destined to become priests or saints. They were honest but rough and kept in line with the knowledge that the breaking of any rules would mean answering to Gus Sr. Young Gus Jr. was always fighting, even with the cops. Fighting was expected and not an infraction of any rules. The Hagen boys were all tough Irish lads. The Hagens were by no means "Shanty Irish" nor were they "Lace Curtain Irish." They were just good, hard working people.

John and Frank were both married and out of the house; so, Dad's warning remarks were meant for Dan and me. Phil was somewhat unsure and apprehensive about us; needlessly, of course. He was afraid of what we might say. We could have left the house, but then the conversation might become inane and sink into the mundane. We had to be there to add a bit of lightness and frivolity to the meeting of these two families, who might in all likelihood become, by marriage, related. We had offered to go to a movie and stay away from the house as long as the Hagens were there, but Dad would not hear of it. He felt that, as brothers, we should stay at home to help our brother make a good impression.

Phil and Theresa, along with Mr. and Mrs. Hagen, arrived at our house around seven o' clock. After introductions, we all went into the living room where everyone became engaged in intensely formal and pleasant but uninteresting conversation. Phil was obviously on edge and just waiting for Dan to make some uncalled for remark. Mom served the usual pretzels, chips, peanuts, and beer. All those in attendance were beer drinkers so that did meet with the approval of the young couple. Phil, Theresa, and Mrs. Hagen were sitting on the sofa with Phil leaning nervously and slightly forward. I am sure that Dan and I added to Phil's discomfort by being perfect gentlemen. It was a hot summer evening and the warm air coming in the open windows offered no relief. The cold beer was refreshing but also added to the overall body heat that started to make everyone uncomfortable. After becoming more at ease, Mrs. Hagen, without warning, rose and scratching her sides and belly with her fingers, asked,

"Do you mind if I use your bathroom? I've got to get out of this damn girdle."

She did just that. She went directly upstairs and removed the confining garment and returned in outward relief. Needless to say, that incident broke the ice and we all relaxed and had an enjoyable visit for the remainder of the night. The conversation became light and humorous. Dan, with his usual carefree antics and quips, had everyone joining in laughter. Dad brought out his bones and clapped to the singing of many Irish songs. The evening turned out to be a success and the McLaughlins and the Hagens were to become friends. The following year, Phil and Theresa were married in St. Anne's Church.

Thoughts of their wedding remind me of John and Marge. They were planning to get married and had rented an apartment in a building just three houses down the street from our house. They had completely furnished the apartment with all new furniture. John and Marge had been decorating the three rooms for weeks, new living room set (we did not use the term suite), kitchen set, and the necessary bedroom set. It was tastefully illuminated with a variety of table and floor lamps. The marriage was not an elopement because everyone was aware of their plans. They had merely decided to take a bus to Elkton, Maryland. Elkton, at that time, was a popular spot for non-church weddings. The night before being married, John planned to spend the night in his new home. He invited me to sleep over with him. I jumped at the chance. I had never slept in a new bed with new sheets and blankets. We spent the evening in the living room listening to the radio and talking about his future. Little did we know what the next few years would bring. We stayed up as long as we possibly could because John had to get up early to meet Marge and catch a bus to Elkton. No one in our neighborhood owned a car and certainly not anyone that we knew. Our only means of transportation was either by bus or street car. No sooner had we settled down in the soft bed when I felt a slight twinge of pain in one of my teeth. I tried to be quiet, but that toothache got progressively worse as the night wore on, and developed into excruciating pain. I tossed and turned, moaned and groaned throughout the entire night. I am very sure that I prevented John from getting any sleep that night. The following day, a tired and bleary-eyed groom had to fulfill his promise of a wedding. While John and Marge were making their vows to each other, I was sitting in a dentist chair. What had promised to be a long, pleasant FIRST time in a new bed, turned out to be my FIRST time in a dentist office and my FIRST tooth extraction.

Sometime after we came home, Dad told me about an event that occurred before John was inducted. The telling of this tale affords me the opportunity to entertain some thoughts about my older brother, John. He was the comedian of the family, always laughing and joking and had an ability to bring some humor into a tense situation. John was, I believe the shortest of Danny McLaughlin's boys; but like Dad, he was as strong as an ox. Even as a kid, he always managed to find some kind of work to occupy his leisure time. Along with Frank and I, John shined shoes, ran errands, and collected cardboard and old newspapers. Upon leaving school, he obtained a job at "Father and Son" shoe store.

Later, he went to work at the "American Box" factory on American Street where he eventually rose to become the foreman and superintendent. Many of the laborers, both black and white, held John in high esteem for his fairness and honesty in his handling of labor relations. Certainly, knowing how to box and having an interest in other forms of self-defense contributed something to his ability to influence people. He was honest and hard working, however, his honesty did not prevent him from cheating at games such as Monopoly and cards. Playing at home, John was a consummate cheater and delighted in driving Phil mad with his slight of hand. One could never be sure where the cards were coming from, the top or bottom of the deck or from anyplace on his person. Phil would get so angry that he would throw away his cards and go stomping out of the room, leaving the rest of us in stitches because we all knew that it was going to happen.

Now to get back to the story, being married and supporting a wife and child, John was still awaiting induction into the service, as surely he would be when they started to draft married men. John and Dad stopped into a local bar at York and Jasper Streets to have a beer or two or maybe more. While they were standing at the bar imbibing, a young marine in full dress uniform entered. It was quite obvious that he was a new recruit fresh out of boot camp. As was the custom, during war time, the customers in the tavern would not allow a serviceman to pay for anything, food or drink. A glass jar was usually set behind the bar for a collection of money to pay the bill for anyone in the service of his country. John and Dad engaged in friendly conversation with the young man and set up several drinks. After downing a few drinks, he began to feel the effects and started to get a little testy. Looking around for someone to pick on and to demonstrate his newly found self-defense, he settled on John. He questioned my brother's loyalty and manhood. A sad mistake. He asked John why he was not in the service like everyone else. Dad attempted to appease the young fellow by telling him that he had already had four sons in the Army. All to no avail. It is always difficult to reason with a drunk. The Marine persisted and tried to put his hands on John, another mistake. Before Dad was able to see just what was happening the man in blue was sliding, on his back, across the beer-stained floor, finally coming to a stop under he pinball machine. John had gotten him into a hold and threw him across the room. In a few short months, John too was inducted into the Army and served bravely and honorably in the European Theatre of Operations; in fact, his unit, the 119th Infantry, US 30th Division, was awarded the Presidential Citation.

Occasional thoughts about Dan McLaughlin in these writings cannot bring forth the true character of such a complex person. Where I was a paradox of personality, Dan was a paradox in life. How many descriptive adjectives can be used to truly describe my older brother? Among those that quickly come to mind are; strong, tough, handsome (in a rough sort of way), charming, sincere, sly and cunning, lovable, impeccable, shy but forward, trustworthy but suspicious. This list is surely incomplete. He could have been a lover, a cop, perhaps a priest, and yet, he could have just as easily turned into a hood, a con man, or a gangster. He had the contacts and the opportunities to be any of these later in life. I am sure that the thought of Dad's disapproval did have an influence on his decision to try to be a good family man and father, which he truly was. For in truth, Dan was a good man and in spite of himself, a credit to his parents. Any description of Danny McLaughlin could be a novel in itself.

When as a child, as I related earlier, Dan took a hammer and hit Phil on the head, this caused a life-long rift between these two siblings. They slept in the same bed for many years, but never a word passed between them. It took a war to bring them, loosely and tentatively, together.

From what I can recall and what was told to me, when Dan was two and-a-half or three years old, he played with matches and set his pajamas on fire. He was severely burned and spent many months in the hospital where he was loved by the staff. Two nurses wanted to adopt him. These burns left him physically and psychologically scarred for life. The thumb and two fingers of his right hand were badly scarred. On his neck, a vicious scar ran from ear to ear. His right chest was one massive scar from shoulder to stomach with just a smear of color where the nipple should have been. As a child and brother, I don't remember having ever noticed these scars. Dan was just Dan, a lovable but naughty child and teenager. He was always getting into trouble and fights and was a constant problem for Mom and Dad, who showered him with love and affection. Our parents loved all nine of their children equally, but as in most families, the naughty child commands the most attention.

Several times, Dan ran away from home and on being found and returned home, he was given whatever it was that he wanted. I do remember one time that he ran away; he ended up in Ohio. When upon being returned home he was asked why he ran away, he replied that he wanted a new pair of shoes, which he promptly got although some of us needed shoes much more than he did.

Dan hated school and constantly played hooky. A truant officer usually brought him back to school or home. Holy Name Catholic School could no longer handle him; therefore, he was sent to Masbaum Public School. Dad would take Dan to school and see that he went into the building. Dan would promptly exit the rear door of the school. On one occasion, he was found by the police, drunk and sick in Juaniata Park. He was returned home in a police patrol car. He still refused to attend school. Finally, he had to appear with Dad before Magistrate Holland who questioned Dan about his truancy. The judge sentenced him to serve time in a reformatory for incorrigible boys, where upon he was placed in handcuffs and a prison uniform and taken out to a "paddy wagon." At the last minute, while being placed in the van, a policeman came out and informed Dad and Dan that the magistrate had changed his mind and had decided to give Dan another chance. He was, however, sent to attend the Daniel Boone School. This was a school for incorrigibles who could sleep at home but had to report to school every morning. Once in school, there was no way of slipping out. This did nothing for Dan except give him the opportunity to associate with some of the worst young men in our society. Dan only spent about a year at Daniel Boone, until at the age of fourteen, he was permitted to get a job and quit school. Many years later, as adults, I told Dan that the episode in the court had been a setup arranged by Dad and his good friend, Magistrate Holland.

"Dan, will you please get up."

I can still hear Mom's usually quiet tone begin to show signs of exasperation as she raised her voice. The rest of us were downstairs and getting ready for school, but Dan was still in bed. Mom had made numerous trips up and down the two flights of stairs to get him out of bed. Finally tiring, she would sit down on the top step and call out again, "Danny, get up." As we got older, Mom was too shy to go into our bedroom to get us out of bed. This was a daily routine during the school year. I wonder just how many times she climbed those stairs.

Dan did not like getting up to go to work anymore than going to school. He had very few jobs and rarely held them for any length of time. He usually found a girlfriend who worked and supplied him with funds that would enable him to frequent his favorite bars or haunts. When he was dating Marie, he would go to her house or a movie after supper and stay with her until perhaps eleven o'clock and leave because she had to get up to go to work. From there he would go to "Elwood's Bar." The bar would close at two in the morning, where upon Elwood would pull the curtains and lock up. He, Dan, and their cronies would play cards until seven or eight in the morning. More than once, I met Dan coming in when I was going out to work. He would then sleep for most of the day, to get his rest before going out again that night.

After the attack on Pearl Harbor on December 7, 1941, Phil was the first member of the family to be drafted into the service. Dan was next, then Frank. I volunteered to go in with Frank. I did this in the hope that we could stay together. John was the last to go because he was married and had two children. Even that did not keep him out very long. The McLaughlins now had five sons in the service; a fact that Dad was proud of but was reluctant to admit. Dad took offense whenever someone would tell him that he should be glad to have five sons in the service. He took no joy in having his sons serve in a war because it brought him and Mom much more worry than pleasure.

Dan was stationed at some nice bases. While the rest of us went into the Army, Dan went into the Army Air Corp, at that time a part of the Army. He found himself stationed in Lincoln, Nebraska; New York City; Washington D.C; and Miami, Florida.

Among other assignments, Dan was the Headquarters Gardener in Miami and a general's driver in Washington and New York. Dan made extra money in Florida by pressing uniforms for other airmen. He would press military pleats in the shirts, three in the back and two in the front. He was voted the "Best Dressed Airman" on the base. He always was fastidious about his appearance and could look neater in work clothing or denim jeans than others could in dress pants or suits.

Did Dan have good duty and enjoy life in the service? Not really. Just as he had been a truant in school, he found life in the Army much too confining and demanding of his free time, ergo, he would frequently go A.W.O.L, (absent without leave). This of course meant time in the stockade. Even among the hard cases in the Army prison, he managed to come out on top. He was selected to be a judge on the "Kangaroo Court," where he sat in judgment of other inmates who broke the prisoner's code of conduct.

Military Police came to our house on one occasion and asked my parents where Dan could be located. They thought that he was home on leave. Dad told the MP's that Dan was out and that he would be back later. After Dan came home and had gone to bed, the MP's returned and with drawn guns, they went into his bedroom, aroused Dan and took him away. I can only imagine what this scene did to Mom. Another time, he was A.W.O.L. for a couple of months. He was staying in an apartment a few blocks away from home and all of this time, Mom and Dad thought he was at camp.

He was neat and meticulous at all times. I have already mentioned how a pair of jeans on Dan looked as though they had just come off of the rack. Everyone talked about what a sharp dresser Dan McLaughlin was. Of course he was, he had Phil's shoes, John's shirt, Frank's pants, and the only thing of mine that would fit him, my tie. Dan always looked as if he were going to a party, which he probably was.

Still in spite of his shortcomings, everyone seemed to like Danny. He was fun, personable, and always ready to give anyone a helping hand. Upon meeting Dan for the first time, people would be captured by his charm and personality. I came to love him more in later years than I did when we were young. We became very close and at one point he confided in me as to why he behaved the way that he did when we were kids. He felt that the scars on his body were not only physical but also psychological. All of his life, he felt different than other kids and would never go without a shirt, even while swimming. This of course did not mask the scars on his neck which were quite obvious, Many of his misdeeds were done just to gain attention while at other times he felt driven by inner demons. He believed that he was different; therefore, he would act differently. It really seemed like a waste of a good life and mind. With the right guidance, Dan could have been anything that he wanted to be.

CHAPTER EIGHT
CALIFORNIA BOUND

CHAPTER EIGHT

CALIFORNIA BOUND

Joe Schum and Margaret Dwyer had made preparations for their coming wedding, Bill Molter and I were invited to be in the wedding party along with Marge's brothers. The plans were for a double ceremony because Joe's youngest sister, Dot, was going to marry Conrad "Connie" Fields. Connie was a member of the Fields family who lived just two doors from us on Arizona Street. The Fields and their ten children were good friends of my parents. Everyone was jovial and happy during the week preceding the double wedding. During that week, Dot discovered that Connie was somewhat less than trustworthy and loyal. Even though he had plans to get married, he was still dating someone else. Dot, of course, called off her part of the wedding. She was devastated but managed to compose herself and joined the wedding party for Joe and Marge. The ceremony went on without any problems and also without Connie Fields. A good time was had by all at the American Legion Hall that evening. Sometime after their marriage, Joe and Marge, playing matchmaker, tried to make a couple of myself and Jane Herron. Jane, Marge's best friend, was also in the bridal group. She was a sister of "Fish" Herron, a classmate of mine at Holy Name. She was an exceptionally nice girl; however, our first and only date was really emotionally cold and distant, ending with both of us knowing that there would not be a second date. Jane, much later in life, became the loving mother of thirteen children. Apparently, the fire was there, lying dormant, waiting for the right person to light the flame and share her life.

Shortly after the wedding, Dot and Marie went out to San Diego to visit their Aunt Marge and Uncle Lou. Uncle Lou was a retired Navy man who loved San Diego and decided to make his home there. San Diego, at that time, was a small beautiful Navy town with ideal weather. It had grown during the war and contributed that growth to the Navy Yard and nearby Camp Callen. It was still a good place to retire. The girls were to stay out there for a few weeks, however they never did return to Philadelphia. Both girls had made a decision to stay and make their home in California.

Joe and Marge began their married life in a small apartment nearby. They were both working and trying to save some money. Life was starting out good for them. Within the year, Joe's father retired from the Philadelphia Fire Department. He had spent many years steering the rear wheels of a long ladder fire truck. I never could understand how he could maneuver around those narrow city streets. After retiring, Mr. and Mrs. Schum sold their house and all of their furniture and moved out to San Diego to be with the girls. I am sure that Joe was hurt by this sudden and rapid move. Some months later, Marge had become pregnant and they were happily looking forward to the birth of their first born. This brought on thoughts of a possible move for them to California. It was during this time that a cousin of Bill Molter was getting married. I did not know her very well; however, it was through Bill that I was invited to attend the wedding and reception. The party was held in a hall above the "Giant Market" on Front Street. The hall was filled with gayety and laughter. Friends and relatives were having a wonderful time as most people were still experiencing a period of relief and enjoyment after years of worry and heartache that accompanies a time of war. I noticed an attractive young lady who, I was to learn later, was a cousin of Bill's. I hesitantly approached her and asked her for a dance. She accepted and we headed for the dance floor. Before we even reached the dance floor we were stopped by someone who claimed to be her boyfriend. He objected to my interest in the girl and became rather loud and obnoxious. Was this the peace that I had come home to? Bill had to step in before the situation could get worse and smoothed things over. I certainly did not need this so I decided to leave. I descended the flight of stairs and stepped out into a deserted Front Street. I slowly walked along the sidewalk heading for home. The "EL" was screeching along the overhead tracks toward the curve onto Kensington Avenue, where the screech would turn into a loud scream. I began to think to myself once again, "What the hell am I doing here?" "What is it all about?" Not very long ago, I was in Europe where I witnessed suffering and death on a large scale and now I come home and almost get into a fight over a dance. It just doesn't make any sense. I stopped at the corner and looked around me. Nothing had changed. The same stores still lined both sides of Front Street. The corner where Clyde and I had sold colored sawdust, at Christmas time, was still the same as was the Dauphin Street entrance to the "EL." What had changed? Perhaps it was only me. What did I really expect? I was having a difficult time assimilating into the lives of friends and family. Small problems that affected others now seemed picayune and unimportant to me. The overhead elevated bridge had a tendency to make the night darkened street even darker. The sidewalks, illuminated by a few garish lights, coming from some of the closed shops, were littered with paper trash and cigarette butts and garbage from half-eaten food that was wantonly discarded by people in their haste to get home. Another train was passing overhead. I shook as the train rumbled past. Looking down, I very carefully walked forward trying to avoid stepping into waste deposited by untethered dogs. How could I stay here? At that moment, I decided that I couldn't.

When I returned to our house, Phil was sitting, in the dark, on the marble front step, the steps that Mom scrubbed to absolute whiteness every Saturday morning. This was a ritual performed by every mother on the block. I joined my brother on the step and informed him of my plans to leave. I made an attempt to enlighten him to the reasoning behind my decision. He came back with every reason that he could think of to dissuade me. We talked for hours. Even after going to bed, Phil continued to harangue me far into the night. This discussion went on for many nights. Some nights, he kept me up until three o'clock in the morning. He did not have to get up for work, but I did. Finally, I told Dan and Dad about my plans. They knew, as I did, that it was going to upset Mom, but they both supported me in whatever decision I would reach. Dad talked to me at great lengths. He hated to see me leave home again but he encouraged me to follow my heart and mind and that if I felt strong enough in my decision, then by all means I should do it. He also told me that I would always be welcome to come home. He realized that in many ways I had always been different than my older brothers. I was forever questioning and had more desire and drive than the others. Whether I succeeded or failed was secondary to my push to at least try. Dad was far more knowing and intelligent than his education indicated. Once again, the most difficult part was going to be, telling Mom. She was such a loving and caring person that any action that caused her grief or worry was like tearing her heart out. Her family was her whole life and she just naturally wanted all of her children near her, especially so soon after our separation during the war. I would be saying goodbye to her for the second time in four years.

When Joe and Marge heard my plans, they both suggested that I might join them in their move to California. I had been stationed at Camp Callen near San Diego so I was fairly familiar with parts of Southern California. I accepted their offer and we began to make plans for our move. I quit my job at Sears Roebuck and the Schums turned in their resignations. Joe bought a 1941 two-door maroon Pontiac. I withdrew all of my savings from the bank to pay for my share of the trip. When Joe withdrew their savings, he came back to their apartment and threw the money in the air and bills came gently floating down onto the bed. Hopefully, we would have enough to see us through the coming trip.

On the day of our departure, early in the morning, I bid farewell to my family and made a hasty exit to avoid a tearful goodbye. I realized that some members of my family were against my leaving and did not bother to come out to see me off. The Schums picked me up at the house. The trunk and the entire back seat of the Pontiac were jammed with bags, boxes, and suitcases. Every available space was filled with some small article. What little that I had did not add to the problem. There was no room in the back seat; therefore, the three of us had to sit in the front with Marge in between Joe and me. Marge, at this time was about seven months pregnant. We started off on our long journey across the country. When I say across, I don't mean that literally because Joe wanted to show Marge some of the places that we were stationed while in the service. We began the trip by heading south on old Route 17 with stops at Camp Davis, North Carolina and Camp Stewart, Georgia. We did not turn west until we reached Jacksonville, Florida. The journey south was rather pleasant and enjoyable. At night, we stayed at small motels. In those days there were no large and comfortable motels such as Holiday Inn, Hilton, or even Howard Johnson to cater to the comfort of weary travelers. Most motel or roadhouse rooms were rented by the hour to couples desiring a place for a secret or illicit tryst; thus, forcing one to examine the bedding before accepting the room. Heading west, we traveled through the Florida panhandle and then onto Mobile, Alabama, along the Gulf of Mexico to New Orleans, where we spent the night. The most difficult leg of the trip was yet to come. We had to traverse the width of Texas in scorching hot weather. Poor Marge had to be sweltering from the oppressive heat. This was before the advent of air-conditioning in cars, and we still had to cross New Mexico and Arizona. When we finally crossed the desert and came to Yuma, Arizona, we were stopped at an inspection station before entering the state of California. When the troopers saw that we were eating oranges, they confiscated the bag of fruit that we had in the car. They ordered us to unload the car so that they could make a thorough inspection. We stood in the hot Arizona sun and removed every piece of our belongings while they searched for fruit. No fruit or vegetables were permitted to cross the border into California. It was then that we noticed that we had a flat tire. That was the only problem that we encountered during the entire trip. At least we did not have the weight of the loaded car when we changed the tire. When the police were satisfied and we had a new tire, we repacked the car and were on our way. To this day, I do not know how Marge survived the ordeal of standing beside that car in the blazing hot sun, patiently waiting for the troopers to complete their search and for Joe and I to change that tire. I was surprised that she did not pass out.

Finally, we reached San Diego and made our way to Nile Street. Pop and Mom Schum, Marie and Dot were waiting on the front lawn for us. Without unloading the car, the three of us collapsed in the living room. At last, we had reached our final destination. Joe and I could not waste time before finding work. Pop Schum, Marie and Dot were working at a Venetian blind factory. Pop had retired from the Philadelphia Fire Department after having served twenty-five years. He later applied for a job as a gardener at the San Diego Horticulture Garden. He told the interviewer that he had some experience at gardening back in Philly and was hired immediately. He worked there for another twenty years, retired and collected another pension. Joe found work at an electronic and radio repair shop. This was before the advent of television. Joe did become an expert television technician.

After being turned down at several companies, I made my way to the Consolidated Aircraft factory on the Pacific Highway. Consolidated Aircraft manufactured large air liners and military aircraft. The company was still in the process of transition from war material to civilian passenger planes. After a battery of written and oral tests, I was hired as an inspector in the finishing paint department. My duties were to check all painted and finished parts and subassemblies and see that all aluminum sheets were properly anodized, and finally to inspect the interior of the finished aircraft to see that the color scheme for each airline was properly coordinated. Sounds like a good job which in truth it was; however, the pay was no greater than any other job.

On November 2, 1947, Howard Hughes attempted to fly his all wood "Spruce Goose," the largest airplane in the world at that time. Unfortunately, he only flew it about a mile, after which he packed it away in storage in a warehouse never to see the light of day again. His eight engine craft was not the only large airplane in production during that period. Consolidated also had built a gigantic plane. It was an eight engine military cargo plane. The tail was ten stories high and a B-17 could park under its wing without any trouble. It was capable of transporting hundreds of men and equipment any where in the world; quite a feat at that time. Unlike Hughes plane, this one could and did fly long distance. I saw it take off the day that it was to fly from San Diego to Fort Worth, Texas. That was the last that I ever heard anything about it. Probably because that seemed to be the end of propeller driven planes....

There was also another innovative idea in commuter aviation that was being perfected at Consolidated. It had already been proven feasible. The aeronautical engineers had already built a small four-seater fiberglass automobile that could be driven to an airport where an assembly of wings and a motorized propeller would be attached to the roof of the car. The pilot and passengers could then fly to their destination, land at a nearby airport, have the wing and propeller assembly removed, and then drive into the city to conduct their business. The same procedure would be repeated for the return trip. Unfortunately, the engineers, on a trial run ran out of gas and crashed. The end of a good idea that was far ahead of its time.

When I became settled in my job at the aircraft factory, after paying Mom Schum for board, which was very little, buying some new clothes, and spending some on my new social life, I managed to put some money away. Joe and Marge Schum following the birth of their son, Joe Jr, settled down into married life. I was now somewhat on my own socially. I don't mean to infer that I was no longer included in the family activities because that would be far from the truth. Initially, I had spent a lot of time with the family on picnics and beach parties. When the newness of being in Southern California eventually wore off, every day life became the same as anywhere else. At the first beach party, on the first weekend after arriving in San Diego and not realizing the intensity of the California sun, I stayed out in the sunlight far too long and suffered the worst sunburn that I had ever experienced at that time or since. Mom Schum had warned me to get out of the sun but I was still too young to heed such sage advice. I spent several days lying in bed, itching, and writhing in abject discomfort. The Schum Girls, having been in California for some time, were busy with their own lives. As attractive young ladies, Dot and Marie had no trouble acquiring dates. Both girls worked, during the day, at a local Venetian blind factory and taught dancing, a few nights a week, at a studio in downtown San Diego. Dot, at that time, was dating an aspiring young comedian named Eddie Lyle. Eddie was an outgoing glib character in the early stages of polishing his act. He and I became friends and he introduced me to the private lives of singers, musicians, and entertainers. I was asked to design music stands for one of the up and coming local bands. Needless to say, Ed was always on stage and would go into his act anytime or anyplace, even without pay. We could be waiting in a restaurant, a crowded lobby of a theatre, or even on a bus when he would unexpectantly go into his routine, to the enjoyment and pleasure of his captive audience. The hoped for and expected applause was music to his ears. Traveling in these circles always ended up by frequenting several night spots after the musicians had finished their own gigs. Entertainers from clubs all over town would meet, after hours, and join in impromptu jam sessions that would go on into the early morning hours. I got caught up in the excitement and began to spend more and more time in night clubs and dance halls, coming home at all hours of the night. These people were night people but I had to get up in the morning and go to work. This night life, of course, led to more drinking than I really desired. At one point, I told Mom Schum that I thought perhaps it would be best if I found another place to stay. She began to cry and told me that she would not hear of any talk of my leaving so naturally I remained with the Schums. I dated several girls from work, but none that would lead to any kind of relationship. I wanted to improve on my dancing ability which was in much need of improvement, so I enrolled in a course at "Arthur Murray's" dance studio. Although Dot and Marie were giving dance instructions, I was just uncomfortable in having them teach me. It was probably the best thing to do because it enabled me to meet more people. I bought a new beige suit, the first new suit since being discharged, a shirt and tie and then had a picture taken by a professional photographer. He must have touched up the picture because, I must admit, I didn't took too bad. I bought several large color photos, sent one home to my mother and also gave one to Mom Schum. I did not realize it at the time, but that picture caused some dissension within the family. Marie McCorrison, my brother Dan's girlfriend told me that when the picture arrived, the family was sitting at the kitchen table. It was then being passed from one family member to another. When Marie got to look at it she studied it seriously and remarked in jest, "You know, Joe always was the best looking one of the McLaughlin boys." That said,

Phil picked up his cup and saucer, raised them in the air and threw both across the table at Marie. His face was flushed in anger as he rose from the table and indignantly left the room.

On several weekends, I traveled with my show business friends to Del Mar, La Jolla, and Hollywood. On one trip to Hollywood, I happened to meet Walter Hartinstine, an Army buddy of mine, who was now known by the stage name, Walter Marsh. He was the same Private Hartinstine who had put on a show for the troops at Camp Davis, N.C. Walt was in town to attend an instructional dance seminar under the guidance to Jack Cole, a choreographer at the leading movie studios. At dinner, Walt and I discussed the possibility of he and I working together sometime in the future. Although the possibility of that happening was very remote, I did promise that I would give it some thought. I had no idea where the path of my life would ultimately take me because I really did not have any direction.

Scenes of the California coastline passed before my eyes as the train moved north. As I sat by the window, I saw the beaches, now crowded with sunbathers, where we had practiced beach landing in anticipation of island hopping in the Pacific Campaign, some of the same beaches where I accompanied the Schum family on weekend beach parties. The train rolled past La Jolla and the hills that I, along with Sergeant Webb, had surveyed in instrument and Survey Training. I reflected on my time in San Diego. I had said goodbye to the Schums that morning as the family stood on the front lawn. When I left, Marge was crying, not because I was leaving, but I suspect because she was so homesick, homesick for her family and her friends back in Philly. If I had made any lasting relationships, perhaps I would have remained in San Diego, but I had a destiny far more different from the one that I had recently been pursuing. Fortunately, I came to the realization that my future was not in the lifestyle that I had been living. What was I seeking? I didn't even know myself.

After spending a weekend visiting acquaintances in Los Angeles and Hollywood, I once again boarded a train, this one heading east. It was to be a rather uneventful trip and I kept to myself and my thoughts, I spent most of my time reading books, stopping only to go to the dining car for meals. This was the fourth time that I had traversed the width of the country. Perhaps this would be the last time that I would be arriving in Philly by train. As the train approached Philadelphia, I began to see some familiar areas, one that I had previously seen when coming home on leave. When we got to the city, I hailed a cab. This time I could afford to use a taxi for the trip home from the station. All too familiar neighborhoods passed by; crowded streets, kids running and yelling down the pavements as I had done, paper blowing along the streets, traffic was fairly heavy because horse and wagons were now a thing of the past. For several blocks, we drove under the Frankford "El" until we came to Jasper Street. The scene was as it had always been; kids were bouncing a ball against the side wall of the building where I had a corner store, people were sitting on the white marble steps engrossed in conversation stopping only momentarily to glance at the passing taxi cab. Yellow cabs were a rare sight in this neighborhood. When the cabbie stopped the car at the curb in front of my parent's house, Mrs. McCash and Mrs. Grassberger were sitting on a stoop across the street engaged in gossip. It seemed they had been doing that ever since I left. Some things never change. I paid the fare, got my suitcase and entered the house. Upon seeing me, there were screams and greetings from Dad, Dan, and Marie who were sitting in the dining room. Mom came out from the kitchen and stood in the doorway. I was met with many hugs and kisses finally making my way to Mom. She held me so tightly, not wanting to let me go. Even as a grown man, it was nice to be in Mom's arms once again. I could smell the familiar aroma of her cooking. While we stood there, my older brother Phil came into the house. It was obvious that he had started drinking early that day. When Phil saw me, he began to make some rather nasty remarks directed at me.

CHAPTER NINE
A LOVE WORTH SEEKING

CHAPTER NINE

A LOVE WORTH SEEKING

"Oh Oh! The prodigal son has returned."

"How long are you going to stay this time?"

Mom called out to him to be quiet because I might leave again. How right she was because I was ready to grab my suitcase and make a run for the door. Dad and Dan made an attempt to intervene, to no avail. Phil continued to harangue me until I told him to shut up or I would knock him on his ass. Trying to avoid him and alleviate the situation, I walked into the living room with Phil following me making cutting remarks. I could hear Mom crying in the background. I turned and surprising him, I sent a wide, fast swing at my older and bigger brother sending him sprawling on the sofa. He remained there in total shock and began to laugh.

"You did it, Joe." He yelled, "You, did it."

"I don't believe it. You did it."

I don't really know if I hit him hard enough to knock him down or perhaps in his staggering walk he lost his balance but, never the less, that did end the confrontation and I knew that I would not be staying home very long. The next couple of weeks were pleasant visiting with Mom, Dad, Dan and Marie, going to see Frank and Jean, John and Marge, and their families. I stopped by to see Jim Kelly and, of course, my old buddy, Bill Molter. They were all now married and had familial responsibilities. A couple of times I spent a few hours going for a solitary horse ride in the park. Ida was happily married. I spent some time in the art museum and strolling around Boat House Row thinking about Oscar and the Saturdays in the Malta Boat House. This reminded me that I should go to see Mrs. Glenn. I stopped by to see how Johnnie Roberts and his wife were doing. I had the honor of being best man at their wedding before I left for California.

I stood on the step of the house on Norris Street where Oscar had lived. I rang the doorbell expecting to surprise Mrs. Glenn. It had been a number of years since last I had seen her. No doubt she had changed. The door opened and I was met by an attractive young lady accompanied by a teenage girl. I asked if I could see Mrs. Glenn. She invited me into the house and I followed her into the living room, which was basically as I had remembered it. We sat down in the same area, if not the same chairs, that I had sat in while conversing with Mrs. Glenn while waiting for Oscar. The woman began by telling me that Mrs. Glenn had passed away during the time that I was away. She was married to Mr. Mercer, Stella Glenn's brother, and that they had taken over the house after her death. Nothing more had to be said. I left the house with a dull, hollow feeling in my heart. So much for that part of my life, a part of my life that was gone forever but cherished in my memories always.

A few weeks after I returned to Philly, I once again became restless. Going back never seems to live up to one's expectations. Some of my old haunts and neighborhoods remained physically the same, but the people had changed as I had changed. I made the rounds of places of the past: Holy Name Church and School, movie theatres such as the Kent and Broadway, some bar rooms, the Philadelphia Art museum, and Boat House Row, where specters of Oscar and his friends clouded my memories forcing me to shake my head to return to the present and reality. Of course I had to visit "Reds" Molter, Jimmy Kelly, and Johnny Roberts. They all welcomed me warmly; however, they were all now married and settled into married life with other priorities. These were all old and dear friends, still I felt like the proverbial fifth and unnecessary wheel. One Saturday morning, I went to visit Jim and Helene Kelly. They were living in a third floor apartment on Kensington Avenue. Their front windows were only a few feet from the tracks of the Frankford-Market Street elevated tracks. Every few minutes a train would come rumbling by, heading either north or south, making conversation difficult if not impossible. Helene wanted to go to the food market, so I walked along with them. It was decided that while she was marketing, Jim and I would spend some time in a bar across the street. While having a cold beer, we amused ourselves in a game of shuffleboard. I cannot even pretend that I was proficient at this fairly new bar room game. We both played miserably, missing most relatively easy shots. A couple of young guys sitting at the bar, watching Jim and I struggle at the game, challenged us to a game. From the very first shot, neither Jim nor I could miss a shot. We played like pros, winning three straight games. Naturally they and others in the room thought that we had suckered them into playing. Fortunately we were only playing for beers and not money; therefore, we were lucky to get out of there with our lives never again to enter that establishment.

Former girlfriends were also married and unavailable. Their husbands, understandably, were not very happy to see me; therefore, I stayed away. I could not and would not go back to any of my old jobs. Time moves on, I suppose.

I found myself on the Market Street "El" going to the end of the line at the 69th Street Station in Upper Darby where I could catch the Liberty Bell Express, a rapid transit trolley connecting Philadelphia to Allentown and the Lehigh Valley. It was a fast but pleasant non-stop ride through the countryside and farmlands of rural Pennsylvania. I looked out the window and watched the beautiful scenery rapidly pass by sometimes in a haze rather like a movie projector running amok and out of control. Soon the farms made a definite change. After crossing over a mountain range, we descended into the Lehigh Valley, an area only about sixty miles from Philly, we always referred to as "Up State." The trolley traveled past well-kept farms that were obviously "Pennsylvania Dutch" or "Amish." The properties were clean and neat, the main farmhouses were freshly painted or whitewashed. Apparently, it was a wash day. A clothes line stretching from an upstairs window to a nearby tree was sagging from the weight of washed, mostly black, clothing. The wash was hung in an orderly fashion with the largest sizes hanging at the far end of the line gradually going down the line until reaching the smallest size nearest the house. The huge red barns had intricately designed signs displayed above the doors; signs that I later found out were

"Pennsylvania Dutch" hex signs. Some of the bright red side walls were emblazoned with advertising in large bold letters, "MAIL POUCH TOBACCO." It was obvious that we were now traveling through Pennsylvania Dutch country. As we descended into the Lehigh Valley, the headquarters building of the Pennsylvania Power and Light Company stood out above all other buildings in Allentown. It was the tallest structure in the entire Valley. After crossing the Eighth Street Bridge, the trolley arrived at its destination at Hamilton Street in Allentown. I got off into a seemingly busy intersection. I made an attempt to get my bearings; however, not being familiar with the area, I saw nothing that would guide me. I did know that Walter Hartenstine was located on Fifth Street. Allentown, although located in a farming area, was the home of several well-known and respected businesses: Mack Trucks, the world renowned maker of strong, reliable vehicles and the often used term, "Built like a Mack Truck," Hess Brothers department store known nationally for its upscale merchandise; and, of course, Max Hess the flamboyant owner who attracted stars of the political and theatrical worlds to his unique establishment where the menus, meals, and strawberry pies were oversized; where priceless works of art were prominently displayed throughout the store for all to see and enjoy; where children's meals were served in a toy stove; where you could relax and enjoy a leisurely lunch as lovely young models in couture designed gowns and bathing suits strolled around the room presenting store fashions from the "FRENCH ROOM." Every year, Hess's held an in-store flower show that could rival any show in Philadelphia or New York. A sale at Hess's often drew hundreds of shoppers gathered at the store entrances. When the store opened, the doors were literally torn off. Woe be it to anyone who had the misfortune to stand in the way of this rushing horde.

Walking east on Hamilton Street, Allentown's main street, brought me to Seventh Street and the town square. In the center of the square prominently stood a large monument to the soldiers and sailors of the First World War; thus, forcing motorists to drive around the monument to continue driving on Hamilton Street or Seventh Street. Unlike other small town squares, this one sported an underground public restroom where strangers or travelers could get a shoeshine, clean up with a shave, and use all of the other facilities. After freshening up, I continued walking east. At Fifth Street there was the palace like "Colonial Theatre" that was similar to the large movie houses in Philly. Next to the Colonial was and is the old stone County Court House. I then turned south on Fifth, heading one block to Walnut Street. Nearing the end of the block, I could hear the distinct rhythmic sound of a drum that led me to a building bearing large letters proclaiming the "WAL-MAR DANCE STUDIOS." Upon entering the large studio, my old Army buddy, Walter Hartenstine also known in the dancing profession as Walter Marsh, was beating out rhythm for several young girls dancing in front of a long row of mirrors. Walter was well known as a dance instructor and choreographer. Mrs. Claire Jacoby was sitting at the piano accompanying the dancers. One wall of the studio had large mirrors from the floor almost to the ceiling with a ballet barre running the entire length of the wall. Above the mirrors and continuing around the room were framed 8 x 10 glossy professional photographs of dancers, entertainers, and beauty pageant winners. The floor gave the appearance of constant use and was marked from the tapping of many feet. A mixture of sweet perfume and sweat of hundreds of young aspiring dancers filled the air. There definitely was a feel of fun, entertainment, and hard work throughout the room.

When the lesson was over, Walter and I went to a local restaurant for lunch where we talked about the possibility of working together. After much discussion, we agreed upon the idea of opening an entertainment bureau along with Walter's dance studio. He would run the studio and I would manage the agency. Using talent from the studio, including "The Dancing Wal-Marettes," a chorus line of beautiful young girls, we could book shows in nightclubs, theatres, and private parties. We could run bus trips to Radio City Music Hall in New York City, and shows in Philadelphia and Atlantic City.

One of our first ventures was a private party for Theodoredis Banana Company at the Colonade Night Club in Bethlehem. The Colonade was located in an old bank building. As was appropriate for a business dealing in bananas, the entire stage was decorated with a backdrop of bunches of the bright yellow fruit. There where hundreds of them. The complete show was banana oriented with the chorus line dressed in tropical costumes trimmed in, of course, bananas. The show was a hit with the "by invitation only" audience. When the party came to a close, we approached Mr. Theodoredis to inquire about the distribution of the edible set. He told us to do as we pleased and take all of the fruit. We shared the bananas with the cast and still we had enough to keep Stella Marsh, Walter's mother, busy in her kitchen making banana cream pies, banana pudding, and many other ways to make use of all of the tropical fruit.

About that time, we were involved in staging a vaudeville show at the LYRIC THEATRE in Allentown. It appeared to be the swan song or ending of the fabulous vaudeville era. Gigs were getting few and far between for migrating actors, hoofers, and variety acts. Movie theatres started to discontinue offering stage shows. Television was entering the field of entertainment and, like it or not, it would make a big impact on the way that the American public would spend their money on amusement and entertainment. Friday, Saturday, and Sunday nights, the traditional time for the working public and their families to seek rest and enjoyment after a long, hard and sometimes difficult week, became, as more TV sets were available and affordable, the time for families and friends to gather in the living rooms across America. They sat there with their eyes transfixed on that little screen watching Jack Benny, Bob Hope, Uncle Miltie, and Ed Wynn. Entertainment would never be the same.

Staging shows often necessitated trips to New York City seeking costumes, material, and scenery. We usually made our way to Kate Shea's. Kate was a silver-haired lady, probably not as old as I thought. She operated a costume shop devoted to filling the needs of Broadway and off-Broadway shows. One could get lost in the array of costumes, beads, bangles, and sequins gathered together in one place. All of it meant to dazzle and amaze theatre goers.

During one of these trips, we heard that Pete DiFalco was in New York studying dance at the Ethnological Dance Center. I did not even know what ethnological meant. Pete was an Army buddy of ours from the 490th. The last time that I had seen Pete we were pulling guard duty in Georgia. This was before he was shipped out to go to Europe as an interpreter during the invasion of Italy. Pete had told me of his aspirations of becoming a dancer. We arrived at the dance center and made our way into the lobby where we inquired about Pete. Someone paged him and a short time later an unfamiliar figure came prancing down the hallway. He was bare-chested and barefooted sporting earrings and bracelets on both his ankles and wrists. This was certainly not the Pete that I had remembered. We greeted each other cordially but not with an abundance of warmth. I must admit that I was taken aback by this rather strange behavior. We waited for Pete to finish his dance session. He changed into street clothes and we all went out for lunch. We got reacquainted talking about our days in Camp Stewart, Georgia, I am sure that the man that we pulled out of the water went on to achieve his lifelong dream.

A few years earlier, a new company had located between Allentown and Bethlehem. Western Electric, a producer of telephone equipment had just completed a vacuum tube facility on Union Boulevard which was, at that time, a part of Route 22, the main road going to Bethlehem and Easton into New Jersey and then on to New York City. The tube shop had been located in New York until an accidental explosion blew out its walls. The company, the manufacturing branch of AT&T, the American Telephone & Telegraph Co., began to look for a building in a less populated area. A representative of Western Electric happened to be in Allentown where he was apprised of a parcel of land conveniently located between Allentown and Bethlehem on Union Boulevard. Today, of course, the two cities have expanded so that they meet at Club Avenue, where a nine hole golf course once stood. The Allentown Club, an employee group, planned to have an all employee musical revue with an all employee cast. Mr. Don Grant of the personnel department asked Walter to stage the show and choreograph a dance routine. The final production was a huge hit because many in the group were really talented. My acquaintance with Mr. Grant would serve me well in the near future.

At the end of the school year, it was time for a spring revue. Actually, Walter had been working on it throughout the year. Class routines and solo dances had to be choreographed and practiced. Costumes had to be designed and made, mostly by Mrs. Marsh and her group of reliable friends. I was busy designing and building several stage sets including a set for "Slaughter On Fifth Avenue." It was also my responsibility to design a thirty-eight page program book. The revue would require three nights to include all of the students at the WAL-MAR Studio. When it came close, to opening night, the hustle and bustle was unbelievable.

On Saturday, I drove down to Philly to bring Mom, Dad, Frank, and Jean back to Allentown to see the show. I do believe that it was the first time that my mother had been outside of the city. I took them into the theatre, gave each of them a program with my artwork and credits and my photograph displayed on several pages. Mom was delighted. My family was enthralled at the display of talent by these young people. Once again Walter had produced, staged, and directed a show to be remembered and talked about for a long time. He truly was a dance master and instilled desire and achievement in young aspiring dancers. Some of these neophytes would go on to become professionals in the entertainment business, some would join the famous "Dancing Rockettes" at the Radio City Music Hall in New York City, several became beauty pageant winners, and one is a famous drummer in Las Vegas. I was singled out and spotlighted when Walt thanked me for my contribution and work in getting this show to the stage. My parents, sitting in the audience, must have felt a little twinge of pride.

After the show, I took my family to a rooming house where I had reserved lodging for them. What was my Dad's response to all of this? "What kind of town is this? There is a church on every corner and I had to walk ten blocks to find a bar to get a glass of beer." Oh well!

We received a call from Tony Grant, a dance instructor from Margate, New Jersey. Tony was taking over the production of the Children's Theatre, "The Stars of Tomorrow," on Steel Pier in Atlantic City. He wanted Walter and I, through the WAL-MAR Dance Studio, to locate and supply young talented boys and girls to sing, dance, and entertain on the Pier. There was an abundance of talent at the WAL-MAR Studios. Walter was one of the best instructors in the business. For the entire summer, we rented a part of an apartment building and then sublet rooms to the children and their families, for a week or two, while they performed at the Pier. I helped to stage the shows and designed some of the sets. Off stage, these kids were just like all other kids on the beach, enjoying the water and just having a great time. When the curtain rose on the stage of the little theatre, they were pure professional, putting on a great show and performing like stars in the aptly titled "Stars of Tomorrow." Many of them did become stars in their own right, dancing at Radio City and on Broadway. One lovely lady became "Miss Pennsylvania of 1949." I have always had a special rapport with children. A relationship with kids takes complete honesty and an ability to deal with them on their own level. Treating them with love, understanding, and respect is always returned tenfold. I recall that on my birthday that year, all of the kids at the dance studio pooled their nickels and dimes together and presented me with a wristwatch. That gift was held dear and precious to me for many years and was no less unexpected and appreciated as those that I had received a few years earlier in a prisoner of war camp.

Atlantic City was the greatest tourist and vacation spot in the country. This was before Las Vegas which did not become well known and famous until some years later when Bugsy Segal was sent out by the mob to build the Flamingo Hotel and Casino. Poor Bugsy overextended himself and through fast living spent more money than his backers allowed. Bugsy was repaid by a shotgun blast to the head, through a window, while he sat on a sofa in his living room.

This was the Atlantic City of glitz and glamour, tourist traps, bums, hookers, gangsters, chic socialites, the Steel Pier where a lady on horseback dove into a tank of water, and top stars of the day appeared in person on stage. The boardwalk where vendors hawked their wares day and night and visitors crowded the boards in shorts and casual attire; but as night fell, the night people came out in their finest, the men in white linen suits and the women in gowns and beautiful hats. This was the city of Hackney's Sea Food, speak-easys, and night clubs such as Skinny D'Amato's "500" Club. I was in the audience of the "500" at one of the first performances of Dean Martin and Jerry Lewis. Lewis, a struggling young comic, had finished his final show a week before and was cleaning out his dressing room. Dean Martin was an amateur boxer now a nightclub singer. Jerry, pretending to be a waiter, came out into the club room and began to heckle Dean. The repartee between them was hilarious and they were an immediate success. Skinny signed them up for a long-term engagement. Word of their comedy act spread and started them off on a long and profitable career.

One of my responsibilities was to approach the star performer or main attraction in the big theatre and endeavor to have the "star" come back stage in the Children's Theatre and talk to the Stars of Tomorrow" and to offer them a few words of encouragement. The group of celebrities included such names as Jane Russell, young Frank Sinatra, Jerry Colona, Henny Youngman, and many others. Most of these people were delighted and even attended the kid's show, sitting in the front row and applauding as vigorously and loudly as anyone else in the audience. After the show, they would go back stage, talk to the kids, and sign autographs. The most friendly and affable, by far, was "Professor" Colona, the sidekick and second banana to Bob Hope. The majority of the headliners were courteous and delightful, but a few permitted their ego to get in the way and flatly refused to talk to the budding entertainers.

All of these kids and their parents had a wonderful time during these summer performances. Between shows, everyone went swimming in the surf and frolicked on the beach next to the Steel Pier. I feel sure that these kids, now grown up, look back on those days with pleasure and delight, as do I.

The night sky was clear and full of stars, a typical summer night at the shore. Except for our few voices, there was no other sound to interrupt the steady beat of the ocean waves rushing toward the sandy shore before retreating back into the waiting sea. A short time earlier, we had exited the stage door of the Steel Pier and were now walking down the famous boardwalk to our rooming house on Montpelier. To my knowledge, my Mom and Dad had never been to Atlantic City. It is possible that Dad had gone to the shore on a fishing trip with some of his bar room cronies, but even that is only a guess. Mom, I am sure, except for the trip to Allentown, had never been out of Philadelphia. This was the perfect opportunity. I arranged to stop at the house to pick up my parents and Dan and Marie. They were packed and ready to go when I pulled up outside of the house. Philly is perhaps halfway between Allentown and Atlantic City; therefore, the trip was only slightly over an hours drive. Thank goodness, because Dad was nervous and edgy with his younger son behind the wheel even though I had driven trucks, Jeeps, and half-tracks all over Europe. Was he nervous with me or would it have been the same with any of his sons?

The trip was uneventful. I was thankful that I had chosen a fair weather weekend because it gave everyone a chance to enjoy the scenery and fresh air of the New Jersey countryside. The fresh air that was occasionally interrupted by the pungent odor of fresh cow manure and fertilizer. One farm after another passed by as we got closer to the shore and could smell the salt air drifting in from the beaches. Each farm had a fruit and vegetable stand with a gaudy painted sign vying for the traveler's attention and money; "Mary's Fruit and Vegetables," "Mike's Fresh Peaches," "Elsie's New Jersey Tomatoes," Not one sign warned tourists of the New Jersey mosquitoes and green flies. Nearing Atlantic City, we could now see the bays surrounding the city. Unlike the skyline of today, the city in the distance appeared to be rather long and flat. The few tall buildings were perhaps eight stories high and the city was about eight blocks wide. Upon reaching Pacific Avenue, I headed north to Montpelier where I had reserved rooms for my family in a large rooming house. Many of the parents of the kids performing at the Steel Pier would stay at this house, therefore, it was a friendly atmosphere. The house was about a mile down the boardwalk from the pier. Transportation was no problem because "Jitneys," small buses carrying maybe fifteen passengers, made frequent trips along the length of Pacific Avenue. After getting settled in their rooms, we walked up to the boardwalk to get something to eat at one of the many stands. This was the very first time that my Mom had seen the ocean, in fact Mom had never worn a bathing suit. She didn't seem to be very excited, but quietly stood there enjoying the view of the vast sea and horizon. We hopped one of the small buses and headed up to the pier near North Carolina Avenue. The boardwalk at that end of the city was, as it is today, crowded with tourists and vacationers. Sales people of all kinds were hawking their wares. There was an air of excitement and frivolity. Everyone was trying to get the most out of a weekend far away from work and home. As usual, there was a long line of people waiting to get into the pier to go on some rides, dance to music of a big band, watch the Girl on the Diving Horse, see a show, and maybe even see a movie star. I guided my family to the stage entrance. We were passed through and went directly to the theatre where I had reserved seats for them. I took them backstage to meet some of the performers. After seeing the "Tony Grant Stars of Tomorrow Show" and the main vaudeville show, everyone was tired and ready to go back to the rooming house. Once again, it was a perfect beautiful summer night, so we decided to walk back to the rooming house. Walking along, engrossed in our conversation and enjoying the night breeze coming from the ocean, we failed to notice that Dad had lagged behind. Turning around, we saw him sitting on a bench some distance away. When we got back to him, he was trying to catch his breath. After letting him rest, we managed to get him to a jitney and rode the rest of the way back. Was this a harbinger of things to come? Perhaps it was. Dad, our own Irish Leprechaun, would be gone in two years, and our beloved Mom would join him the following year.

That's funny, it is so dark. I feel that I am waking up but I don't recall having gone to sleep. It is so quiet. Did I fall asleep or did I, for some reason, pass out? I remember talking to Walter about the arrangements that we had just made regarding a picnic at Bushkill Park. Where the hell is Walter? He was sitting next to me in the car. What is this? It feels like pieces of glass. I know that I have my eyes open but I can't see anything. Everything seems so still, quiet, and peaceful, yet I can hear the sounds of people yelling and screaming, and commotion all around me. I don't seem to feel anything; however, my whole body is sore and aches. As I move my hands, my pants appear to be warm and moist, and in some places, even wet. I feel the same warmth and moisture as I move my hands to my face and head. I sense the unmistakable salty taste of blood in my mouth. I hear someone suddenly yell.

"Hey! Hurry up, this guy is really hurt."

Now I can vaguely see, through the blood covering my eyes, the broken and shattered windshield and shards of glass all over the car. The window on my side is open and someone reaches through. Someone hands me a cloth. It isn't a cloth. It is a white dress shirt. A man had taken it off and was using it to wipe the blood from my face.

"Just take it easy. Someone has called for help."

"They should be here soon."

I sat there in the midst of mounting commotion, feeling no sense of urgency, emotion, or panic. I had often wondered how I would react in an emergency regarding myself. Would I panic? Could I remain calm? Could I move at all? Did I pass out again? Time seemed to be standing still and yet appeared to be flying by. This was a new feeling. Never before had I felt like this. I wonder where Walter is? Was he hurt too? What a weird position to be in. My body wants to move but nothing happens. What in the world am I going to tell Mom? She has enough to worry about.

The door on my side is being forced open. I am floating in air or water as several people lift me from the car.

"Take it easy."

"Watch his legs."

"His legs seem to be ok."

"Someone try to stop the flow of blood."

"I am trying to. Where the hell is it all coming from?"

"Somebody, get these people back."

I am placed on a stretcher, carried to the back of an ambulance, and slid into the back. I hear the door close, the engine start, and the blare of a siren. The ambulance just gets started when it is stopped by a passing train

A man yells out, "Get that train the hell out of here. We have a man dying in here."

"Who is dying? What the hell is he talking about?"

I open my eyes and see Walter sitting on a bench beside the stretcher. I also see two medics one of which is working on me. It can't be them.

"God, they must have been talking about me."

"I can't stop the flow of blood. Where the hell is it all coming from? The nose has stopped bleeding."

We finally arrived at the Sacred Heart Hospital where I am rushed into the Emergency Room. The intern and nurses take over. Their first concern, of course, is to stop the bleeding. They stitch up some cuts on my head and clean the blood from my face. They see that I have had some teeth knocked out, three teeth on the top and one on the bottom. As they open my mouth to halt the blood oozing from my gums, I hear someone say, "Oh my God! Here is where it is coming from. We will have to stitch it back on." Apparently, my tongue had been cut or bitten off and was barely being held on by a thread of flesh.

"You are going to have to hold out your tongue so that I can stitch it."

"Ach Ach" was the only sound that I could make as I attempted to force the stump of my tongue forward.

"That isn't enough. Push it out more."

I tried again in a vain effort.

"That still isn't enough. You are going to have to try much harder. If you can't do it, we will have to put a curved needle through your tongue and pull it out."

"Like hell you will," I am thinking. I use every muscle in my throat and push as hard as I possibly can, gagging in the process. I feel as though I am going to choke to death.

"That's better," says the doctor. "Now I can do it." He proceeds to sew my tongue together with numerous sutures. All of the bleeding has now stopped and the nurses clean me up.

"Boy do I feel lousy. I feel so damned weak. Thank God that is over."

They must have given me another shot. I again feel like I am floating, and drift off into a restful sleep. When I finally wake up, time seems to have been at a stand still. I have no idea of time and space. My body and brain are numb. My eyes slowly open and are greeted by a stark white ceiling rapidly swirling in a timeless orbit. I have a vague feeling of the presence of someone else in the room. I slowly gather my thoughts and realize that I am in a hospital room. I look around and see that Walt is in a bed next to mine. He looked somewhat hazy silhouetted against the shimmering light penetrating the thick film of soot covering the glass panes in the lone window. Soot from a long procession of cars and trucks traveling on the street below. I looked around the room and gazed at the furniture as it is engaged in a seemingly never ending macabre dance. Walter appears to be alright with no outward signs of serious trauma.

"God Joe, you are a mess," he said. "How do you feel? I am really sorry for what happened."

"I feel rotten. What the hell did happen?"

Walt sat up in his bed and proceeded to tell me just what had occurred that morning.

We had gone to Bushkill Park to make arrangements for a picnic for all of the kids at the dance studio. We were going through Bethlehem on our way home. We had been heading west on Hanover Avenue approaching the steel girder bridge across the Lehigh River and then on to Hamilton Street in Allentown. The approach to the bridge had a slight curve to the right immediately before the bridge. Walt was driving and I was sitting relaxed in the front passenger seat. Of course this was before seat belts were required. After making the curve, Walt failed to straighten out and drove right into the third steel girder. I remember the period just before and after, but I did not have then, nor do I have now, any recollection of the actual moment of the accident.

As my vision began to clear, I started to take stock of my surroundings. Why do they always have mirrors in hospital rooms? The room was sparsely furnished but still, a dresser with a large mirror was placed directly in front of my bed. Curiosity got the better of me. With some degree of difficulty, I was able to prop myself up and glance at the strange image staring back at me. Yes, Walter was right, the person that I saw reflected in the mirror was truly a mess. I looked terrible. I had sustained many cuts on my forehead and my right eyelid, two black eyes, a cracked jaw, four teeth were knocked out, bruises on my face and chin, and a sore tongue that caused me to talk with a lisp. Other parts of my body just ached. These things do happen when you try to put your head through a windshield. Within a few days, Walter was released from the hospital. Two days after the accident, Dr. Ziegler, a local dentist, came to my room. My face was still sore, however, he did manage to examine my teeth and make an impression. He realized that appearance meant a lot in our business. With the help of a couple of recent photographs, he was able to fashion a partial plate that looked surprisingly like my natural teeth.

A week after I was released from the hospital, I was expected to attend the wedding of Peggy Stinner, "Miss Allentown of 1947" and John Lush. Immediately after the wedding ceremony, everyone was to attend a reception at a local club. I reluctantly accepted the invitation with no small amount of apprehension since I was still having difficulty in chewing and eating. An affair of this magnitude most certainly would have food to satisfy the taste of every ethnic origin, and lots of it. Foods that I would of necessity not be able to taste or partake of. Truthfully, I was not looking forward to such an evening. The social banquet hall was as I had expected. It was bright and beautiful with white festoons hanging from the ceiling, white candles surrounded by a center piece of white roses at each table. The bridal table was located separately at the far end of the hall. Two tables ran parallel to the bridal table. Several larger tables were placed perpendicular to the other three tables. The bridal party had yet to be seated, but most of the guests had arrived. I was escorted to my place at one of the head tables. There in front of my gold embossed name card, sat prominently on a white dinner plate, three jars of Gerber Baby Food accompanied by a silver spoon with a beautiful white satin bow attached.

Sometime in early November of 1949, Harvey Rinker, a friend of mine and the father of two girls who were taking dance lessons at the studio, and I were standing some distance from the entrance to the studio. Harvey noticed a small group of people at the door to the office.

"My God!" he exclaimed. "Joe, take a look at that young girl."

As I turned and looked in that direction, my eyes became focused on the most beautiful young lady that I had ever seen or even hoped to see. She was about five feet two inches tall, slender, and had light brown hair that was highlighted by a blond streak a couple of inches wide that ran from her forehead to the end of her hair, midway down her back. Her posture was superb, obviously that of a dancer, with a straight back that supported wide shoulders. Her face was a picture of beauty, with features that I had only dreamed of up until that time, was set off by a wide sensuous mouth and two gorgeous green eyes. Eyes that seemed to actually glow with love and kindness. She stood there with one leg slightly bent to the front and her head tilted a little to the back, in an air of pure confidence. This girl exuded poise, charm, grace, and class. I knew at that moment that there was a woman that I just had to meet and know and become a part of my life. I also knew that this had to be the beginning of a new relationship and a new life for me.

"Do you know what, Harve?" I asked.

"I am going to marry that girl." I said before he had a chance to answer.

"Oh yeah! Sure you are," Harvey said. By my expression, he could now see that I was serious.

I introduced myself to Patti Auman and managed to talk to her during the days that followed. She had danced ballet for many years and was now accompanying a young friend to the studio. My desire overcame my fear of rejection, however instead of asking her directly for a date, I decided to take a more circuitous route. One that turned out to be far easier than I could have imagined.

After obtaining Patti's phone number, I called her house and asked to speak to her mother. I introduced myself to Mrs. Auman and requested her permission to ask her daughter for a date. She was very pleasant and courteous and told me that Patti would be delighted and that she was sure that her daughter would accept my invitation.

I breathed a sigh of relief. Boy! That was one hurdle overcome. Mrs. Auman put Patti on the phone whereupon we made arrangements to go out together. It was not of my knowledge at the time, but she had been hoping that I would ask her for a date. In September, I had been at the Lyric Theatre for a rehearsal of a review. I had designed the sets for the dance numbers. This particular scene was a ballet that featured an artist painting several girls as they danced before him. I had drawn a picture of each young lady and the drawings were placed on separate easels. The girls, on cue, would then dance around the easels. This number had been performed on the Steel Pier in Atlantic City.

As the dancers were going through their routine, sitting in the darkness of the nearly empty theatre, was a young lady watching the rehearsal. At that moment, her thoughts began to wander and she was thinking about more than just dancing. She was watching my treatment of these young people and also their reaction to me. As she contemplated this mutual rapport, she quietly said to herself, "Now there is a guy that I would like to marry." This young man and young lady were totally unaware of the destiny that was slowly bringing them together. Was it fate or coincidence that they both had almost the same thought upon seeing each other for the first time?

As I look back on it now, I wonder how she could have had any attraction to me. I was still recovering from the accident with some discoloration remaining on my face and, of course, the persistent but slight lisp. I was in no condition to impress anyone. Oh well, they say that love is blind. Then too, the lights in the theatre were turned down very low.

I was walking on clouds as I contemplated our first date. I couldn't believe that this was really happening. I wanted this evening to go just right. This was to be our first date; therefore, I wanted to make a good impression. After picking Patti up at her house and being scrutinized by both of her parents, we drove to the Anna Maria Restaurant where I had prearranged to have a bottle of wine and a corsage of red roses on the table. As I expected, Patti was radiant, dressed in a lovely blue suit. Could anyone be more beautiful? We both ordered a baked ham dinner, as I recall, but that really didn't matter. We were entirely engrossed in conversation and each other. As luck or fate would have it, as we sat looking at each other across the table, the sound of a favorite song of that period came from a jukebox.

"I want Some Red Roses for a Blue Lady"

That song was to become "our song" from that time forward.

After finishing dinner, we drove over to the Allentown-Bethlehem Airport, which in those days was just a small town airport with very few planes landing or taking off. That didn't bother us in the least because we really did not go there to watch planes.

We left the airport and drove back to Patti's house. Although the hour was late, she invited me in. Her parents and brother had already retired to their bedrooms where, I am sure, Mr. and Mrs. Auman did not close their eyes or ears. Patti and I sat in the darkness of the living room on the sofa in deep conversation interspersed with an occasional long, lingering kiss and some petting. I sensed that someone was at the top of the stairs. Time, of course, seemed to fly by without our noticing. Eventually, we heard some movement from the second floor. Mrs. Auman appeared at the dimly lit landing and called out to us.

"Patricia, it is time for Joe to go home and you better come right to bed."

Patti knew her mother far better than I did, so we reluctantly said "Good Night" and parted with expectations of seeing each other as soon as possible, even the next day, hopefully. We parted with a last but lingering kiss. I drove away with romantic thoughts running through my mind. All that night, visions of Patti ran through my thoughts, interrupting my sleep. The following day, I simply could not keep my mind on my work. I felt like some teenager with a crush on a pretty girt. But she was far more than just a pretty girl. She had entered my life and seemed to hang on. Even if I wanted to, there was no way that I could treat this as just a passing fancy. Everything that I did or tried to do was once again interrupted with anticipation of seeing Patti once again. When the time came for our appointed date, I rushed up to the Auman house which stood in the middle of a block of three-story brick row homes. Their house stood out from the rest of the houses because of a curved porch with a white balustrade. I took the steps up to the porch two at a time floating on air and rang the doorbell. Trying to regain my composure and look cool, I looked forward to my first glimpse of Patti's beautiful face when she answered the doorbell. When the door was finally opened, I was confronted with the stern features of Mrs. Auman's face with Mr. Auman standing in the rear. Patti was nowhere to be seen. Surely this was a bad omen. Then, of course, Mrs. Auman did all of the talking. She gently but none the less firmly told me that I was not permitted to see their daughter again. When I inquired as to the reason behind this rather sudden decision, she told me that she could see very clearly that her daughter was falling in love with me and that they could not allow that to happen. There were, of course, many other reasons that she did not fail to enumerate: I was Catholic, I was Irish, I was in entertainment, I was a veteran of the war and as such, I was a man of the world. I had absolutely no idea of just what had transpired during the course of that day, but there must have been a long serious discussion ending with Patti retiring to her bedroom in tears.

Apparently, I had interfered with Mrs. Auman's plans for her daughter's future. Patti, like most attractive young girls had a high school sweetheart. She had been going steady with a fellow student at Allen High School for a couple of years. He was a very nice young man who played the piano, studied music, and was destined to be a professor of music, an ideal son-in-law for Patti's mother. Mrs. Auman was also a pianist and an opera singer of some local repute. She had set herself up as a matchmaker. Patti's life had been well planned and going along smoothly with an expected wedding until I entered the picture and apparently disrupted everything.

I stood there rather dumfounded. How could they? How could they be so rude and treat me this way? None of their reasons made any sense to me. Never before had I been made to feel inferior to anyone. Never before had I been so rejected. Of course, for many years, Irish-Catholics had been held in low esteem by WASPS (White Anglo-Saxon Protestants). Like my father, Irishmen had a reputation for singing, fighting, and drinking. A reputation not undeserved, I might add, but this was more personal. Dejectedly, I walked off of the porch and headed for the car, more hurt than angry. I drove around for some time trying to sort things out in my own mind and regain my composure.

The next few days were days of depression and angst. I was not able to devote any interest in my work or anything else for that matter. I could not eat properly. All of my thoughts were about Patti. Could I or should I make an attempt to contact her? Should I try, in some way, to see her? I was a total emotional wreck. Patti, in the meantime, was going through the same mental and physical anguish that I was experiencing. She was spending most of her day crying in her bedroom, not eating as she should, therefore, she was losing weight. She was not one to resort to tantrums, so her family knew that this was a serious problem. The situation became so intense that her father wanted to call a doctor. Patti's mother put a halt to any such suggestion. Her reply was, "No, she doesn't need a doctor. We know what is wrong with her." She could sense that her daughter was falling in love. They warned Patti that if she made any attempt to contact me, they would send her to her grandparent's farm up in Seemsville. Had they done so, she would have been out of my reach. I had no idea who her grandparents were or where they lived. To my knowledge, Seemsville could have been in China. All of these events in the Auman household were totally unknown to me. All that I knew was that I had to see Patti and talk to her. If she had no interest in our meeting again, then fine. I would have to accept that, but I wanted to hear it from her.

I began to drive around her neighborhood, hoping to catch a fleeting glimpse of her. Not knowing where she attended church or even her religious affiliation, I parked near various local churches, again, hoping to catch sight of her. In later years, this could be described as stalking and could result in an arrest, but to me, it was simply someone deeply in love or infatuated by a beautiful young lady who had entered my life and just as swiftly disappeared, like a "Will-o-the Wisp." The feeling of utter despair continued for a couple of weeks. One afternoon when I was driving past Fifth and Tilghman Streets, I saw Patti's young brother, Billy, standing on the corner. I stopped the car and beckoned to him. When he came over, I talked to him about Patti and asked if he would please tell her to call me because I had no way of contacting her. This was a dangerous move on my part. He could relay my message or he could tell his parents. Fortunately for me, he decided to do the former. Sitting in the office the following day, I received a call that was sheer happiness and joy for both of us. As for me, I couldn't believe that I was really hearing her voice. Patti expressed gladness and surprise that I, in spite of my rejection, still wanted to continue trying to build some sort of a relationship. She had been struggling, for the past few weeks, to adjust to the realization that we could not be together and yet hoping that I felt strongly enough about her that I would, in some way, contact her. I assured her that my feelings for her were deep rooted and that my resolve to be with her, no matter how short a time, would not waver. I had every intention of seeing her again, at any cost. Hearing the sound of each other's voice was like a gift from heaven. Where do we go from here?

We made arrangements to meet the following afternoon on Church Street, a narrow street next to Leh's Department Store. I parked the car and waited for what seemed to be an eternity. Perhaps she wouldn't come. Maybe she had been found out and her parents had stopped her. I just was not that sure that she could or would be able to get away from the house. Maybe she had second thoughts. Looking in the rearview mirror, I saw someone come around the corner and proceed, poised and self assured with the stride of a ballerina, up the narrow sidewalk. I could not believe my eyes. My God! She is so beautiful.

Nervously, I opened the door and she got into the car. We hastily greeted each other with a kiss and having a fear that someone might see us, we drove away. What now? Where do we go? With a limited knowledge of the area surrounding Allentown, I just headed out of town. Eventually, we settled on Lehigh Parkway, a somewhat remote area with only a few homes along the street. The most time that we could spend together was about an hour because Patti had to get back home before her parents. We continued to meet furtively like this for some time. We would meet at a different place in town and then drive out to the Parkway. Every day our tryst would last a little longer, closer to the time that her folks were due home. Then we would rush back into town in time for her to board a trolley for home. How was she able to get away from the house? It was the pre-Christmas season, so she would make arrangements to go shopping either for herself or for her mother, to purchase Christmas gifts. She would purposely buy the wrong size or color making necessary a return trip into town the following day. This ploy worked just fine up until Christmas. Going into January it became increasingly more difficult for us to meet. Even phone calls were a problem. I, certainly, could not call her home. Patti would call me when her mother and father were at work at the coal yard. In the evening, when her mother was busy downstairs, she would make a quick call to me from the phone upstairs. This was extremely difficult for her because she had never disobeyed or in anyway was she ever deceitful.

In the meantime, at home, Patti's mother was busy making dates for her daughter with Danny hoping to return things to normal. Her efforts only seemed to make matters worse. She did not want to hurt her long time beau, however, she could not avoid treating him rather coldly while on dates. While sitting in the movie theater, as any young man would do, he would try to hold hands. She would, gently but never the less surely, pull her hand away. It was very difficult for Patti too, who now realized that she was not in love with Dan. She pulled away whenever he made an attempt to get affectionate. It was not her intention to hurt him, but her prior feelings for him had vanished and no matter what the outcome of our relationship, she could not return to what had been.

How long could this go on? How much longer could we continue to meet without being discovered? I had hopes that upon learning of our secret liaison, Mrs. Auman would come to realize that we were seriously in love and would relent. Patti assured me that, knowing her own mother, I was dreaming and that no acceptance from her family would be forthcoming. As our secret meetings and telephone calls continued, we became closer and more deeply involved. We then realized that we could not go on without being detected. The thought of not being able to be together was just not acceptable to either of us. We discussed this over and over again without reaching any solution. During one call, I brought up the possibility of our getting married. Pattie seemed to be receptive to the idea, so I asked her if she would marry me. Without any hesitation, she answered, "Yes, of course I will." With that answer, we were now in mutual agreement. Now we had to discuss plans and arrangements. It was not going to be easy by any stretch of the imagination. The road that we had chosen was destined to be filled with many pitfalls and road blocks. It would be extremely difficult for her because she had never disobeyed her parents. This was to be the first time. Oh! What difficult and dangerous paths we are forced to take in the name of love. Patti cautioned me against making any plans without first consulting an attorney. Again, she told me that I did not know her mother. She assured me that her mother would go to any and all lengths to prevent us from seeing each other, much less getting married. I did not fit into her mother's equation of the future. Why then had she encouraged me to date her daughter? I did go to talk to a lawyer to make sure that any action on my part could not be construed as being illegal.

The next couple of weeks were filled with days of stressful anticipation. On the days that we could manage to meet, Patti would leave the house carrying clothing and a hat box that contained some of her possessions. In this manner, she was able to get some of her clothing out of the house and give them to me to keep. She knew that there was no way that she could get back into the house. How right she was. It would take many months before she could enter the house even on a temporary basis. After seeing a lawyer, I went to a jeweler to have a wedding ring formed. It was fashioned extra wide, in fact, it was so wide, that Patti could not bend her finger, therefore, I later had to have it narrowed. Still, I have never seen a band quite so wide.

On the 23rd of January, I drove down to Washington D.C. alone because, according to my lawyer's instructions and trying to avoid any legal entanglements, I could not take Patti across the Pennsylvania state line. She was to fly down by herself and meet me there. I stopped in the Washington area to find out where we could wed and to acquire lodging. The nearest town that we could get married was Rockville, Maryland. I managed to reserve a room at the Fairfax Cabins on U.S. Highway No. 1. Fairfax Cabins was a new unfinished complex of small cabins. My cabin had concrete blocks in place of steps leading up to the door. Keep in mind that during that time, not many people traveled great distances. Motels, as we know them, were virtually nonexistent. There simply were no Holiday Inns, Howard Johnsons, or Hilton Hotels with their large suites and king and queen-size beds. This room was just barely large enough to hold a small dresser, one night table, and a bed. Yes, it did have an indoor bathroom, a rather tight one-person bathroom.

On the 24th, Patti was hurriedly albeit anxiously preparing to leave the house after her parents had left. Walter Marsh was parked on Green Street waiting to pick her up and drive her to the Philadelphia Airport. She left the house by the back door with an armful of clothing, hoping not to be seen. As she was walking down the backyard path, a next door neighbor spotted her and he asked in a loud voice.

"Patti, where are you going with all of those clothes?"

She continued to walk down the path and without missing a step, she answered.

"Oh! I have to take them to the dry cleaners."

Appearing satisfied, he turned and re-entered his own home. She hurried down the back alley and got into the waiting car. There was still ample time for her to change her mind.

Standing in the airport terminal, looking out the large plate-glass window, my mind traveled over the past few weeks. All of my thoughts had been of Patti Auman. I tried to work, I thought of her. I tried to read, I thought of Patti, Walter's mother tried to get me to eat her good cooking, I thought of Patti Auman. Others tried to get me into conversations, t thought of Patti. My God, she is so beautiful. We should have had more time to really get to know each other and to date openly. We could have waited for months to think about getting married. We both knew that we were taking a drastic move. I knew the ETA of her flight and riveted my eyes on the distant winter sky. Again, I harbored some very strong doubts. Did she change her mind? Would she be on board the plane? Maybe, at the last moment she had been found out. Eventually, a small dot appeared in the distant sky. I kept my eyes focused on it as it became increasingly larger until I could distinguish it as an oncoming plane, a four-engine aircraft with twin tails that I immediately recognized as a Constellation. The silvery airplane seemed to glisten in the afternoon sunlight as its wheels finally touched the ground. It rapidly used up the length of the runway, turned and taxied toward the terminal, coming to a stop in front of the window affording me a perfect view as the passengers deplaned. Of course, I had eyes for no one until I saw Patti get off of the plane and walk across the tarmac. What a relief and what a beautiful sight. She wore a beige suit and a long red coat to ward off the wintry chill. With her long hair gently blowing in the wind, she walked along with her head held high and with the poise, grace, and stride of a trained ballerina. Upon seeing her, one would think that she was an experienced traveler, which of course, she was not. I lost sight of her as she entered the terminal building but shortly, she came up the stairs to the upper level. The rest of the passengers and their waiting relatives were just a blur until I spotted that red coat. When she saw me, her face seemed to light up and break into a wide beautiful smile, a friendly smile that could forever light up a room and assure people, upon meeting her, that here was a lady who was just as nice as she was pretty. We saw each other at the same time and rushed to meet. We embraced one another with relief and our kiss lasted for some time. When we finally parted, Patti looked at me and said in feigned anger, "Where were you? I expected you to be at the plane. When I didn't see you, I thought Oh, no, Joe wouldn't do this to me." I assured her that I had my eye on her every second. I told her how self-confident she looked when getting off the plane. Then she remarked, "I made up my mind that I was not going to look like a hick or some country bumpkin." She most assuredly did not.

Once again, my life seemed to have taken a varied and somewhat circuitous route, however this time, my travels culminated in my meeting Patti Auman, my future life, my future wife. How could I be so fortunate?

Patti and I left the airport terminal and walked to the waiting car, a 1949 Kaiser built by the same Henry Kaiser who built the Liberty and Victory ships during the recent war. We were both aware that our actions would cause an uproar at home and a frantic search to locate us; however, we were determined to be together in spite of all the odds. As we drove along Pennsylvania Avenue, I had some difficulty keeping my eyes on the road. Not only was my beautiful Patti sitting next to me in a car heading to Rockville, Maryland where we would be united in matrimony, but she was busy changing into a dress for our marriage. She had brought along a cocoa brown dress with a form fitting bodice with a scoop neck and a flaring skirt. The dress was accentuated with a brown brocaded wrap-around overskirt. Naturally, I attempted to take a peek with a sidelong glance. She was really quite beautiful despite the loss of several pounds during the last couple of months. When we reached Rockville, I drove to the home of William B. Adams, a Baptist minister. The house was a typical small town home with a front lawn and a backyard surrounded with a low, white picket fence. When the reverend assured himself that we both desired to be married, he agreed to perform the marriage rites. His wife was to be a witness as, I am sure, that she had done many times before. When he was reciting the vows, Mrs. Adams stood beside him momentarily interrupted from cooking their evening meal. We could smell the appetizing aroma wafting in from the kitchen. Their teenage son was sprawled out upon the sofa loudly munching on potato chips. Certainly not the most auspicious of occasions. Certainly not the wedding that neither Patti nor I envisioned for her. Most assuredly, she deserved much, much more. Like most young girls,

I am sure, she had looked forward to a church wedding with all the trappings: a beautiful gown, bridesmaids, ushers, and a fabulous reception. I regret that I spoiled all of this for her; however, I am writing these thoughts and memories during the 60th year of our marriage. A marriage that by all accounts should never have lasted as was predicted by many of our acquaintances. A marriage admired by many and envied by some. A marriage where never a voice was raised in anger but was filled with mutual love and respect. I sincerely hope that I have made it up to her. I have been blessed with a wife, life-long friend, and mother of our children far better than I ever deserved or in my wildest dreams ever expected. During all of these many years, my dear wife has grown from a beautiful girl to a beautiful woman and always a gracious lady beautiful physically and spiritually. This is not the end but truly,

THE BEGINNING

ACKNOWLEDGMENTS

First and foremost I must thank Pat, my wife, my companion, my friend, my love and my life. I thank her for her patience during the years of putting this book together. I thank her for her understanding when I would wake her in the middle of the night after I would get a thought or memory that just had to be written down.

Of course, I must thank all of the people who were a part of my life without whom this story would not have been possible.

I thank my mother and father who suffered and struggled many years during the "Great Depression."

I thank Stanton (Oscar) Haines, my friend and mentor who entered my young life at the right time to guide and educate me, but sadly had to leave me so early and abruptly.

My thanks to the United States Army for taking a young city kid and turning him into a man.

I thank God for protecting and bringing five brothers home safely from the war.

I must also thank all of the students at the Wal-Mar dance studio who through their dedication and hard work at their own art form inspired me to continue and pursue my own.

My gratitude and love to the Sisters of Holy Name Catholic School who provided me with an elementary and moral education that has no equal.

I also thank Rachel Thompson of the Greater Lehigh Valley Writers Group for her critique and help in finally getting my story "THE DIE IS CAST" published.

My thanks also to Michael Troisi For his wonderful photographic enhancement.

Special thank you to Kathy Holotyak for her invaluable help typing the manuscript and entering it into a computer.

A big thank you to Cheryl McLaughlin for her contribution of our family history and geneology.

I want to deeply thank Representative Charles Dent and his staff, for his assistance in obtaining a copyright and registration in the Library of Congress.